Communications
in Computer and Information Science 50

T0237899

Tai-hoon Kim   Wai Chi Fang
Changhoon Lee   Kirk P. Arnett (Eds.)

# Advances in Software Engineering

International Conference
ASEA 2008, and Its Special Sessions
Sanya, Hainan Island, China, December 13-15, 2008
Revised Selected Papers

 Springer

Volume Editors

Tai-hoon Kim
Hannam University
Daejeon, South Korea
E-mail: taihoonn@empal.com

Wai Chi Fang
National Chiao Tung University
Hsinchu, Taiwan
E-mail: wfang@mail.nctu.edu.tw

Changhoon Lee
Korea University
Seoul, South Korea
E-mail: crypto77@cist.korea.ac.kr

Kirk P. Arnett
Mississippi State University
Mississippi State, MS, USA
E-mail: kpa1@msstate.edu

Library of Congress Control Number: Applied for

CR Subject Classification (1998): D.2, D.3, D.4, H.5, I.7, C.2

ISSN        1865-0929

ISBN 978-3-642-10241-7 Springer Berlin Heidelberg New York

springer.com

© Springer-Verlag Berlin Heidelberg 2009

Typesetting: Camera-ready by author, data conversion by Scientific Publishing Services, Chennai, India
Printed on acid-free paper      SPIN: 12792887        06/3180       5 4 3 2 1 0

# Preface

As software engineering (SE) becomes specialized and fragmented, it is easy to lose sight that many topics in SE have common threads and because of this, advances in one sub-discipline may transmit to another. The presentation of results between different sub-disciplines of SE encourages this interchange for the advancement of SE as a whole. Of particular interest is the hybrid approach of combining ideas from one discipline with those of another to achieve a result that is more significant than the sum of the individual parts. Through this hybrid philosophy, a new or common principle can be discovered which has the propensity to propagate throughout this multifaceted discipline.

This volume comprises the selection of extended versions of papers that were presented in their shortened form at the 2008 International Conference on Advanced Software Engineering and Its Applications (http://www.sersc.org/ASEA2008/) and 2009 Advanced Science and Technology (http://www.sersc.org/AST2009/).

We would like to acknowledge the great effort of all in the ASEA 2008 and AST 2009 International Advisory Board and members of the International Program Committee, as well as all the organizations and individuals who supported the idea of publishing these advances in software engineering, including SERSC (http://www.sersc.org/) and Springer.

We would like to give special thanks to Rosslin John Robles, Maricel O. Balitanas, Farkhod Alisherov Alisherovish, Feruza Sattarova Yusfovna. These graduate school students of Hannam University attended to the editing process of this volume with great passion.

We strongly believe in the need for continuing this undertaking in the future, in the form of a conference, journal, or book series. In this respect we welcome any feedback.

April 2009

Tai-hoon Kim
Wai Chi Fang
Changhoon Lee
Kirk P. Arnett

# Organization

## General Chair

Haeng-kon Kim      Catholic University of Daegu, Korea

## Program Co-chairs

Tai-hoon Kim      Hannam University, Korea
Akingbehin Kiumi      University of Michigan-Dearborn, USA

## Publicity Co-chairs

Guojun Wang      Central South University, China
Tao Jiang      Huazhong University of Science and Technology, China
Jongmoon Baik      Information and Communications University, Korea
June Verner      University of New South Wales, Australia
Silvia Abrahao      Camino de Vera, Spain

## Publication Chair

Yong-ik Yoon      Sookmyung Women's University, Korea

## System Management Chair

Sang-Soo Yeo      Hannam University, Korea

## International Advisory Board

Tien N. Nguyen      Iowa State University, USA
Jose Luis Arciniegas Herrera      Universidad del Cauca, Colombia
Byeong-Ho KANG      University of Tasmania, Australia

## Program Committee

Aditya K Ghose      University of Wollongong, Australia
Ajay Kumar      Indian Institute of Technology Delhi, India
Aliaa Youssif      Helwan University, Egypt
Ami Marowka      Shenkar College of Engineering and Design, Israel
Chengcui Zhang      University of Alabama at Birmingham, USA
Chia-Chu Chiang      University of Arkansas at Little Rock, USA

# Table of Contents

# An Enhanced Content Distribution Method Using Metadata Annotation in CDN*

Jung-Eun Lim[1], O-Hoon Choi[1], Hong-Seok Na[2], and Doo-Kwon Baik[1,**]

[1] Dept. of Computer Science & Engineering, Korea University, Seoul, Korea
[2] Dept. of Computer & Information Science, Korea Digital University, Seoul, Korea
{jelim,ohchoi,hsna99,baikdookwon}@gmail.com

**Abstract.** A user who uses a multimedia files demands a high capacity file via internet. However, it is difficult to guarantee QoS about providing high capacity files by internet because that has an inconstant bandwidth. For guaranteeing the QoS, CDN (Content Delivery Network) is generally used as a method of contents delivery service. Based on CDN, we propose Content Distribution and Management (CDM) using Metadata system which can provide advanced transmission and searching method. For enhancing a transmission rate, CDM system supports segment unit based transmission method that can be possible parallel transmission. Also, we propose a distribution method through substance based search. CDM system can primarily distribute the files which includes content that user wants. Information about substance of file is stored in metadata through contents metadata management interface, and then the information is inserted to the high capacity file itself. When user requests a high capacity file that user wants, CDM system doesn't transmit all of applicable contents but firstly transmits a particular part of applicable files. Also when contents distribute with substance search of CDM based on metadata, its transmission speed is 4.8 times faster than existing CDN. Therefore a proposed CDM system can guarantee QoS for user.

**Keywords:** CDN, QoS, Metadata, Content Distribution, Searching.

## 1 Introduction

Internet provides a relatively low quality streaming service than contents transmission method via existing broadcasting and storage, because internet has inconstant bandwidth. Now, CDN is used to satisfying a request about high quality streaming service of user contents use. CDN solved network bandwidth problem as decentralization contents distribution server [1-4]. CDN transmits contents as decentralizing multi servers in close location to user that internet bandwidth is guaranteed. But since CDN transmits high capacity contents file as file unit, it can't support firstly transmission via substance based search [5, 6]. Transmission method using CDN has two problems.

---

* This paper is supported by the second Brain Korea (BK) 21 Project.
** Corresponding author.

T.-h. Kim et al. (Eds.): ASEA 2008, CCIS 30, pp. 1–13, 2009.

- No method of searching based on substance Existing CDN doesn't support searching method based on substance about high capacity contents. Existing CDN uses simple keywords for contents search. The simple keywords are about physical characters of contents file. It is described by contents provider when contents file create. Via only simple keywords searching method, CDN can't catch whole meaning of contents. According to searched result, user may receive high capacity file that user doesn't want. Therefore, CDN may be able to waste of transmission time and network.
- Increasing of file transmission time CDN transmits high capacity file as file unit. After transmission is finishing about one file, transmission about other files is possible. If substance that user wants exists to end part of high capacity file, user can be provided it after all receiving the contents file. Also, if the substance doesn't exist or is different inside received file, user must receive all other files. Because this can cause CDN to transmit unnecessary high capacity file, existing CDN may increase of file transmission time.

To use CDN effectively as solving above problems, we need a method for distributing contents files effectively. For this, this paper proposes Content Distribution and Management (CDM) system using metadata, it can apply in CDN. Roles of CDM system divides into contents distribution using file segment transmission method and management using metadata for substance search of contents [7-11, 17, 18]. The content distribution role means that high capacity content of file unit transmits as segment unit. It can support parallel transmission of content via segment unit transmission. The content management role means that distributed contents file selectively distributes when user requests. For this, this paper defines metadata that it is for dividing high capacity content as low capacity content according to meaning. Since contents provider inserts contents information to the defined metadata, proposed CDM system can selectively distribute when contents transmit according to user request.

In chapter 2, we show basic concept of CDN. Chapter 3 describes about proposed CDM (contents distribution and management) system using metadata. In chapter 4, we implement and evaluate a proposed CDM system. Finally, we conclude in chapter 5.

## 2   Related Works

### 2.1   Basic Concept and Organization of CDN

CDN (contents distribution and management) is network used for providing high quality contents to user in internet with non-regular bandwidth [12-14]. CDN is used to satisfying a request about high quality streaming service of user contents use. CDN transmits contents as decentralizing multi servers in close location to user that internet bandwidth is guaranteed. Like this, CDN consist of multiple servers. Figure 1 shows servers and its terms that CDN consist.

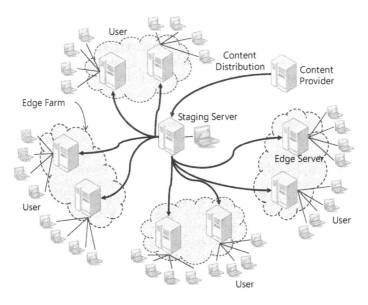

**Fig. 1.** CDN organization servers and its terms

**Staging Server:** It is server for storing contents uploaded from contents provider. The uploaded contents are a target of distribution to other servers. Distribution of all contents starts from staging server. Proposed CDM system executes on staging server and it can be possible selectively distribution of contents using parallel distribution and meaning based search. For meaning based searching, proposed CDM system provides contents metadata management interface that can manage metadata information of contents to staging server. CDN manager can input necessary information for search as inserting metadata about contents.

**Edge Server:** Edge servers that actually deliver customer content to requesting end users. Edge server is distributed to each user region. Since network between edge server and user is constructed with regular bandwidth, user can provide high quality contents from edge server.

**Edge Farm:** Edge farm is logical set that consists of several edge servers is existing close together.

**Map:** Map is path to distribute contents. Distribution path means transmitted path of contents. For this, CDM manager should clearly describe contents flow from staging server to edge server. Contents transmit according to described path.

## 3   Contents Distribution and Management (CDM) System Using Metadata

For an efficient operation and management of CDN, we need an integrated remote management method to distribute and manage contents to several servers. For this, we proposed CDM system (Contents Distribution & Management) [17].

## 3.1  CDM System Architecture

CDM system is installed into CDN staging server. Figure 2 shows architecture of CDM system. CDM consists of 4 modules and 3 interfaces to distributing and managing contents efficiently. Detail descriptions of Modules are below.

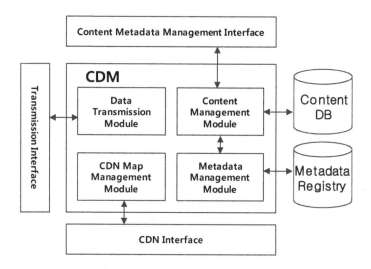

**Fig. 2.** CDM system architecture

**Contents Management Module:** It divides contents into low capacity contents as inserting metadata to contents metadata received by contents provider.

**Data Transmission Module:** It performs transmission error check, redundancy check occurred when file unit transmission and segment unit transmission.

**Metadata Management Module:** It manages metadata stored in metadata registry. It provides proper metadata to contents management module according to contents type.

**CDN Map Management Module:** This module enables CDM system to use map in CDM system. The map is distribution path of contents managed to CDN. CDM system transmits divided low capacity contents file according to distribution path defined in map. The divided low capacity contents file is manufactured via content management module, data transmission module, metadata management module.

**CDN Interface:** It is interface to use CDM system without change about staging server of CDN.

**Content Metadata Management Interface:** It is interface for manager that is used to divide high capacity contents file logically as low capacity contents files.

**Transmission Interface:** It is interface that transmission method can select about high capacity contents file. It supports file unit transmission and segment unit transmission as file transmission method.

**Content DB:** It is database for storing and managing contents provided from contents provider. Metadata inserted by content management module and related information are also stored to Content DB.

**Metadata Registry:** It is registry that provides standard metadata.

## 3.2  Contents Transmission Method Based on Segment

This paper applies segment unit file transmission method to solve the occurred problem when contents of file unit distributes and to re-transmit contents partially when parallel transmission and transmission error occurs. That is a method to transmit high capacity contents as segment unit and to manage transmission information of segment unit. For this, we should get three item of 'file ID' to recognize files according to request, 'Offset' to know start point of file,' File Size' to calculate transmission amount information of file. Figure 3 shows file transmission method of segment unit.

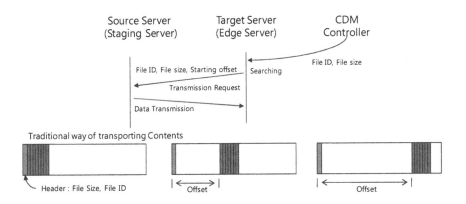

**Fig. 3.** Procedure of contents transmission based on segment

File transmission method of segment unit can prevent re-transmission of whole file that is pointed out as problem of transmission method of file unit. Server, contents receives, has information about contents existing received. Using this, we can extract a transmission start point of contents file (Offset) and file size of contents file. So, we can prevent duplicate transmission of contents file already transmitted. Also, we can transmit some part of received contents file into another edge server even if server don't receive entire of file as managing contents file transmitted with segment unit.

Figure 4 shows that contents parallel transmit using segment based mechanism.

As shown in figure 4, parallel transmission of contents file with segment unit can diminish transmission time of contents. The more edge server exists on distribution path, the more effect of parallel transmission has.

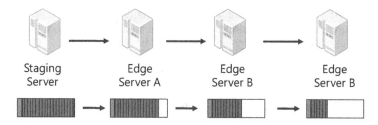

**Fig. 4.** Parallel contents file transmission using segment based mechanism

Also, the parallel transmission enables CDN to do multi source based streaming method. It is method to receive a contents data from several source servers as well as transmission of contents with segment unit transmission method. Figure 5 shows concept and operation process of multi source based streaming method.

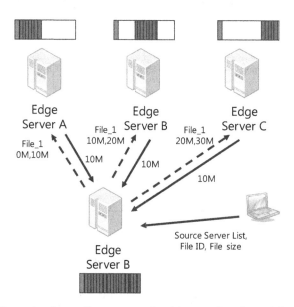

**Fig. 5.** Concept and operation process of multi source based streaming method

As shown figure 5, edge server gains information about contents file will be received from CDM system and information about other servers that contents files have. After Edge server analyzes contents file, it divides the contents file as segment unit. Then edge server requests file transmission to staging server, and it receives divided contents.

Multi source based streaming method can receive contents data concurrently as segment unit from several source servers. Therefore, it can reduce file transmission time. If network problem in a source server occurs, we can receive contents file from other server. Therefore, multi source based streaming method has an advantage to guarantee stability of contents transmission. Also, it can decentralize network load concentrated to one server.

### 3.3 Management of Contents Using Metadata

To efficient distribution and management of high capacity contents, we insert substance into contents file, received from contents provider, using metadata then the contents file divides logically as low capacity contents file. For this, this paper provides content metadata management interface that can use in CDN staging server.

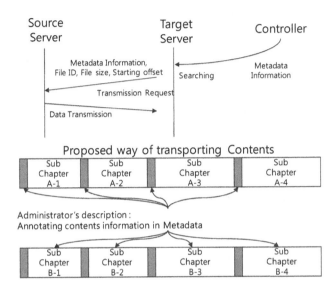

**Fig. 6.** Contents distribution using metadata

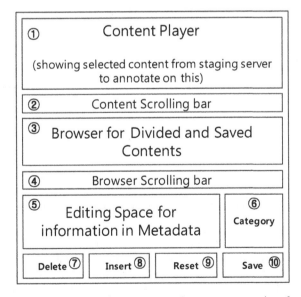

**Fig. 7.** Organization of contents metadata management interface

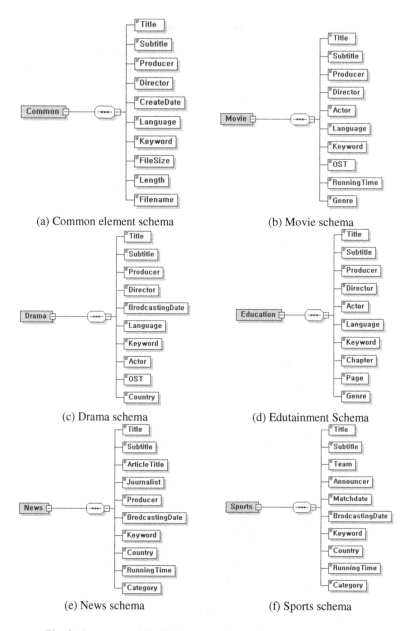

(a) Common element schema          (b) Movie schema

(c) Drama schema                   (d) Edutainment Schema

(e) News schema                    (f) Sports schema

**Fig. 8.** Common and detail element schema of contents metadata

We can insert, delete and store proper additional information about contents substance to metadata via interface. Semantically divided contents file according to substance is transmitted only particular part as segment method when user requests. If user requests contents file with particular substance, proposed method can search it using metadata information. So, user receives low capacity file with necessary substance not a whole of high capacity file. Figure 6 shows that logically divided contents file from high capacity files as classifying with 'Sub Chapter' according to substance using metadata. Also it depicts distribution process via substance based search.

Figure 7 shows organization of contents metadata management interface. Contents metadata management interface provides work space to insert proper information to defined metadata through contents player①. It provides scrolling bar② to seek contents. Also, it provides explorer③ to find easily logically divided contents file according to inserted metadata information. The explorer③ connects with scrolling bar④. ⑤ is space to insert metadata information. Specially, it can insert contents information of screenshot executed to ① using insert button⑧. Inserted time of contents information is logically division time of the contents. Therefore, if a user requests, contents are distributed from the contents of logically divided time. ⑥ is contents classification. According to the six classifications, different metadata is provided to user.

### 3.4 Metadata Definition for Contents Management

Metadata for contents consist of 1 common element set and 5 detail element sets. Common element set includes data element to present physical character of contents, and all data elements of common element are included to all multimedia contents metadata. 5 detail element sets can select one category among "movie, drama, edutainment, news, sports" according to meaning of multimedia content. The selected category includes data element proper to category character.

We defined metadata elements used to contents metadata management interface as XML schemas to figure 8.

## 4 Implementation and Evaluation

### 4.1 Implementation and Simulation Environment

We implemented and evaluated via simulation CDM (Contents distribution and management) system using metadata for enhanced distribution and management of contents. For simulation, we measure contents distribution time from staging server to final edge server. For this, we made virtual servers that has role several edge servers. Also, we set environment variables such as control of artificial delay time, a limited bandwidth and packet loss ratio for simulation.

For simulation, we classify simulation into distribution time via existing CDN, distribution time using CDM with 4 high capacity contents files. In simulation with existing CDN, we did substance search via keyword inserted by service provides. In simulation with existing CDN, we did substance search via added keyword through contents metadata management interface. Figure 9 shows a screen shot is inserting proper information to metadata as well as playing contents file via contents metadata management interface that CDM (contents distribution and management) system provides.

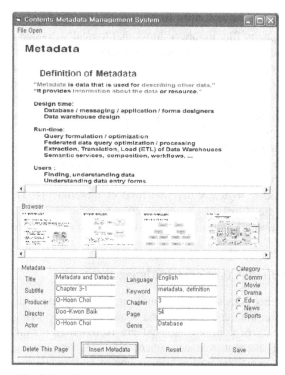

**Fig. 9.** Interface for management of contents metadata

4 high capacity contents files stored into staging server are divided into Sub Chapters according to substance, and then we inserted proper information to divided Sub Chapters. Table 1 depicts file size and some of inserted information about low capacity contents files that substances of total 14 have. Used contents files are physically 4 files but, it can be divided into low capacity files of 14 logically.

Network structure for distribution is composed 2 edge servers with 2 level hierarchies. For performance measurement, we measured distribution time took as distributing same contents file to edge server. Transmission rate are same with 100Mbps. Table 2 shows distribution time according to transmission method. We can recognize that segment unit transmission method is 48% faster than file unit transmission method. Because file unit transmission method that transmits contents file to other edge server after one content file is all transmitting.

For simulation, we first transmitted 4 low capacity contents files of Chapter 1-1, Chapter 1-3, Chapter 3-3, and Chapter 4-4 searched using substance based search. Selected files sizes are 650MB. In case of CDN, file name is chapter 3 that it has metadata keyword and file size is 540MB. We verified via simulation that substance based search method can firstly distribute several low capacity contents files in a fast time that user's request satisfies.

**Table 1.** File divided with contents and inserted keyword

| File name (keyword, file size) | Sub file name of divided file (keyword, file size) |
|---|---|
| Chapter 1 *Introduction* *DB* *320MB* | Chapter 1-1, *(140MB)* *Relational DB, metadata* |
| | Chapter 1-2, *Multimedia Data, Information Integration (180MB)* |
| Chapter 2 *ER model* *690MB* | Chapter 2-1, *Entity Set (180MB)* |
| | Chapter 2-2, *Attribute (150MB)* |
| | Chapter 2-3, *Relationship (210MB)* |
| | Chapter 2-4, *ER Diagram (150MB)* |
| Chapter 3 *Introduction* *Metadata* *540MB* | Chapter 3-1, *Metadata, definition (230MB)* |
| | Chapter 3-2, *Metamodel (90MB)* |
| | Chapter 3-3, *Metadata Registry, MDR (120MB)* |
| | Chapter 3-4, *Interoperability (100MB)* |
| Chapter 4 *SQL* *560MB* | Chapter 4-1, *Projection (180MB)* |
| | Chapter 4-2, *Selection (140MB)* |
| | Chapter 4-3, *Comparison (180MB)* |
| | Chapter 4-4, *Schema, metadata (160MB)* |

**Table 2.** Kinds and results of measurement test about contents distribution time

| Contents size | Distribution time of file unit (sec) | Distribution time of segment unit (sec) |
|---|---|---|
| 320MB | 6.6 | 3.4 |
| 690MB | 14.3 | 7.2 |
| 540MB | 11.2 | 5.6 |
| 570MB | 11.9 | 5.8 |

**Table 3.** Distribution simulation results of low capacity contents via search based on contents substance

| Transmission type | Contents size | Total distribution time (sec) | Related file number |
|---|---|---|---|
| File unit | 540MB | 11.2 | 1 |
| Segment unit | 650MB | 6.6 | 4 |

To distribute information metadata includes, if all high capacity contents files of Chapter 1, Chapter 2, Chapter 3, Chapter 4 transmit, CDN should transmit files of total 1420MB size. This means that it spends time of 4.8 times than CDM system. Table 4 shows distribution simulation results of high capacity contents that include substance that user want.

**Table 4.** Distribution simulation results of high capacity contents via search based on contents substance

| Transmission type | Contents size | Total distribution time (sec) | Related file number |
|---|---|---|---|
| File unit | 1420MB | 319.2 | 3 |
| Segment unit | 650MB | 6.6 | 4 |

## 5  Conclusion

CDN (contents distribution and management) is network used for providing high quality contents to user in internet with non-regular bandwidth. This paper proposed CDM (contents distribution and management) system and applied file transmission method of segment unit for solving increase problem of transmission time that existing CDN has. Also, we proposed contents management method using metadata and implemented it as contents metadata management interface for enhancing efficiency of contents distribution and enlarging convenience of contents management. When proposed CDM system applied to CDN, we verified that CDM system can distribute high capacity file with same size 48% faster than existing CDN. Also when contents distribute using distribution method with substance search based on metadata, its transmission speed is 4.8 times faster than CDN. CDM system can enhance QoS of user as firstly providing divided low capacity contents file with substance that user wants.

## References

1. Hofmann, M., Beaumont, L.R.: Content Networking: Architecture, Protocols, and Practice. Morgan Kaufmann Publisher, San Francisco (2005)
2. Buyya, R., Pathan, M., Vakali, A.: Content Delivery Networks. Springer, Germany (2008)

3. Pathan, A.-M.K., Buyya, R.: A Taxonomy and Survey of Content Delivery Networks. University of Melbourne Working Paper (2007)
4. Buyya, R., Pathan, M., Vakali, A.: Content Delivery Networks. Springer, Heidelberg (2008)
5. Choi, O.-H., Lim, J.-E., Lee, D.-H., Na, H.-S., Baik, D.-K.: A multimedia contents management system based on a metadata-net in home network. IEEE Transactions on Consumer Electronics 54(2), 468–473 (2008)
6. Choi, O.-H., Lim, J.-E., Baik, D.-K.: MDR-based framework for sharing metadata in ubiquitous computing environment. In: Yang, L.T., Amamiya, M., Liu, Z., Guo, M., Rammig, F.J. (eds.) EUC 2005. LNCS, vol. 3824, pp. 858–866. Springer, Heidelberg (2005)
7. ISO/IEC JTC 1/SC 32, ISO/IEC 11179: Information technology- Specification and standardization of data elements, Part 1~6 (2003)
8. Kusmierek, E., Du, D.H.C.: A Network-Aware Approach for Video and Metadata StreamingRaghuveer. IEEE Transactions on Circuits and Systems for Video Technology 17, 1028–1040 (2007)
9. Smith, J.R., Schirling, P.: Metadata standards roundup. Multimedia, IEEE 13(2), 84–88 (2006)
10. Missier, P., Alper, P., Corcho, O., Dunlop, I., Goble, C.: Requirements and Services for Metadata Management. Internet Computing, IEEE 11(5), 17–25 (2007)
11. Nishimoto, Y., Baba, A., Kimura, T., Imaizumi, H., Fujita, Y.: Advanced Conditional Access System for Digital Broadcasting Receivers Using Metadata. IEEE Transactions on Broadcasting 53, 697–702 (2007)
12. Ng., T.S.E., Chu, Y.H., Rao, S.G., Sripandkulchai, K., Zhang, H.: Measurement-based optimization techniques for bandwidth-demanding peer-to-peer systems. In: Proceedings of IEEE INFOCOM 2003, SF (April 2003)
13. Massoulie, L., Vojnovic, M.: Coupon Replication Systems. Sigmetrics (2005)
14. Felber, P.A., Biersack, E.W.: Self-scaling Networks for Content Distribution In Self-Star. In: International Workshop on Self Properties in Complex Information Systems (2003)
15. File Transfer Protocol (FTP), http://tools.ietf.org/html/rfc959
16. HTTP - Hypertext Transfer Protocol, http://www.w3.org/Protocols/
17. Lim, J.-E., Choi, O.-H., Na, H.-S., Baik, D.-K.: An efficient content distribution method using segment metadata annotation in CDN. International Journal of Advanced Science and Technology(IJAST) 1(1), 85–90 (2008)
18. Choi, O.-H., Lim, J.-E., Na, H.-S., Seong, K.-J., Baik, D.-K.: A method for enhancing contents management using additional metadata in CDN. In: The 8th Application and Principles of Information Science, Okinawa, Japan, January 11-12 (2009)

# Feature Tracking in Long Video Sequences Using Point Trajectories

Jong-Seung Park, Jong-Hyun Yoon, and Chungkyue Kim

Department of Computer Science & Engineering, University of Incheon,
177 Dohwa-dong, Nam-gu, Incheon, 402-749, Republic of Korea
{jong,jhyoon,ckkim}@incheon.ac.kr

**Abstract.** This article proposes a robust method for tracking sparse point features that is stable to long video sequences. To improve the stability of feature tracking in a long sequence, we use feature trajectories of tracked points. We predict feature states in the current image frame and compute rough estimates of feature locations. A search window is positioned at each estimated location and a similarity measure is computed within the window. Through the refinement using the similarity measure, an accurate feature position is determined. To reduce false matches, an outlier rejection stage is also introduced. Experimental results from several real video sequences showed that the proposed method stably tracks point features for long frame sequences.

## 1 Introduction

During the last several decades, video tracking technology has been advanced for the practical uses on the surveillance, analysis and representation of video footage[1]. Tracking of feature points is one of the most important issues in the fields of image analysis and computer vision. Feature tracking is a major source of errors in an application and hence a stable feature tracking is necessary to build a practical application. When an image sequence is given as an input, two sets of feature points are extracted from each pair of two neighborhood frames. Then, a matching algorithm evaluates the feature correspondences between the two sets of feature points. Feature tracking is a very important field in various computer vision applications since it provides the fundamental data for further analysis. They can also be used to estimate object shape toward the object reconstruction and recognition. However, the development of related applications has suffered from the instability of tracking methods. Feature tracking is unstable in nature and false correspondences can be occurred at any unexpected time.

In this paper, we propose a robust feature tracking method for long video sequences. Extraction of good features is also an important issue for the robust feature tracking. Feature points should be extracted in stable locations that are invariant with respect to image translation, rotation and scaling[2]. We detect features from scale-space extrema of differences of Gaussians. We first build a Gaussian image pyramid from an image frame. We then compute difference of Gaussians and select the extrema of the difference of Gaussians as feature locations.

T.-h. Kim et al. (Eds.): ASEA 2008, CCIS 30, pp. 14–28, 2009.

When a set of feature points are extracted at the current frame, we compute state variables using the trajectories of the tracked features from the first frame up to the immediate previous frame. Then, we predict feature positions in the current frame. Each predicted position is used as the initial position in searching a more accurate feature position in the current frame. We estimate more accurate feature position by minimizing the matching error between two successive frames.

In our method, we allow the camera to move freely in the physical space. However, if a target object also moves together with the camera, it is very difficult to solve the problem due to the occurrence of occlusion and the motion ambiguity even at the short camera movement[3]. In such cases, the moving objects must be detected in advance and should be handled separately. To avoid such an ill-posed problem, we assume that all objects in the physical space are static.

## 2    Related Work

In this section, we describe two popular tracking methods, the Kanade-Lucas-Tomasi (KLT) method and the Scale Invariant Feature Transform (SIFT) method. Many of the previous two-dimensional tracking methods are based on these two methods or slight improvements of these methods. We overview the two methods and discuss the properties and limitations of the methods.

### 2.1    KLT-Based Feature Tracking

In the KLT tracking method[4], the extraction of good feature points is more important than the establishment of a good searching window. Let $I(\mathbf{x}, t)$ be a set of sequential images, where $\mathbf{x} = [x, y]^T$ denotes an image coordinate and $t$ denotes a time variable. If the frame rate is sufficiently high, successive frames would have sufficiently small displacements and intensity variations. Eq. (1) describes the intensity function with respect to time where $\delta(\mathbf{x})$ is a motion field that means the movement of the point $\mathbf{x}$:

$$I(\mathbf{x}, t) = I(\delta(\mathbf{x}), t + \tau) \ . \tag{1}$$

If the input frame rate is sufficiently high, the movement can be described only by a translation. The movement can be represented by Eq. (2) where $\mathbf{d}$ is the displacement vector of $\mathbf{x}$:

$$\delta(\mathbf{x}) = \mathbf{x} + \mathbf{d} \ . \tag{2}$$

The main problem of feature tracking is to estimate the displacement vector $\mathbf{d}$ for each feature point[2].

However, it is difficult to obtain an accurate displacement vector of the motion model $\mathbf{d}$ due to the variety of the physical environment, the lighting condition, and the noises in images. The KLT method defines an error criterion and iteratively increases the accuracy by minimizing the error. The matching problem can be solved by finding the location of the minimum error[5][6]. The feature matching error is described in Eq. (3) which means the sum of squared differences (SSD):

$$\epsilon = \Sigma_w \left[ I(\mathbf{x} + \mathbf{d}, t + \tau) - I(\mathbf{x}, t) \right]^2 \ . \tag{3}$$

In Eq. (3), $w$ denotes the set of pixel positions in the search window and $\mathbf{d}$ denotes the displacement vector of the feature position. The first order Taylor expansion is applied to $(\mathbf{x} + \mathbf{d}, t + \tau)$ and we obtain a linear equation which is described in Eq. (4) where $I_x$, $I_y$, and $I_t$ are partial derivatives of $I(x, y, t)$ with respect to $x$, $y$, and $t$, respectively:

$$\mathbf{Gd} = \mathbf{e} \tag{4}$$

$$\mathbf{G} = \Sigma_w \begin{bmatrix} I_x^2 & I_x I_y \\ I_x I_y & I_y^2 \end{bmatrix}, \ \mathbf{e} = -\tau \Sigma_w I_t \begin{bmatrix} I_x \\ I_y \end{bmatrix} \ .$$

KLT feature tracking is based on the linear system described in Eq. (4). Given two input images, we get the solution $\hat{\mathbf{d}}$ by solving $\hat{\mathbf{d}} = \mathbf{G}^{-1}\mathbf{e}$ and find the pose of a feature point in the new input frame. This process is iterated using the Newton-Raphson schema until the estimated displacement is converged to an equilibrium solution.

For the feature extraction, the eigenvalues $\lambda_1$ and $\lambda_2$ of $\mathbf{G}$ are computed. According to the magnitude of two eigenvalues, we classify the structure of the pixel into one of three types. If both of the two eigenvalues are approximately zero, there is no structure. If only one eigenvalue is approximately zero and the other is far from zero, the structure is classified as an edge. Finally, if two eigenvalues are largely different and far from zero, the structure is classified as a corner point. We are only interested in corner pixels. Hence, we accept a pixel as a feature point if $\lambda_1$ and $\lambda_2$ satisfy the condition $\min(\lambda_1, \lambda_1) > \lambda$ where $\lambda$ is a predetermined threshold.

## 2.2   SIFT-Based Feature Tracking

The feature extraction employed by the SIFT method[8] is advantageous over the KLT method when the camera is allowed to move freely. For the feature extraction, a Gaussian image pyramid is produced from an input image. The feature locations are determined by computing the differences of Gaussian at each level and choosing the locations of extrema. More stable feature points are selected by removing the points of low contrast. Feature points on edges are not appropriate and such points should be excluded. Harris corner detector is used to remove the feature points along the edges[7]. By removing unstable feature points, SIFT becomes robust to noise.

Followings are the major steps of the SIFT feature tracking method. The first step initializes the set of local feature vectors at the first frame. Detected feature vectors are invariant to scale, rotation, and translation[8]. The second step is to select stable feature locations. In this step, unstable feature points are removed from the set of extracted local feature vectors. The unstable features of low contrast are rejected from the feature set. The features that are poorly localized along the edges are rejected by the Harris edge detector. In the third step, the feature orientations are computed. One or more orientations are assigned to each feature point location based on local image gradient directions. The orientation histogram is formed from the gradient orientations of extracted feature points. The orientations are quantized to 36 levels and accumulated to corresponding histogram bins. Then a dominant direction is selected by detecting the highest peak in the histogram, and any other local peaks that are within 80% of the highest peak in the histogram are also selected as dominant directions. In the fourth step, the feature vectors are created. The eight dominant directions are used to create the 4×4 orientation histogram. Therefore, one feature point has a 4×4×8 dimensional feature vector. Finally, the feature vector is modified to reduce the effects of the illumination change. Each feature vector is normalized to a unit length. Then, all values larger than 0.2 are bounded to 0.2 and feature vectors are normalized again to a unit length.

## 3   Improving the Feature Tracking Accuracy

To improve the stability of feature tracking in a long sequence, we use trajectory information of two-dimensional feature points. We predict the feature states in the current frame using the trajectories of feature states from the first frame up to the immediate previous frame. We define state variables to represent feature states and, using the state variables, we compute rough estimates of the feature locations on the current frame. A search window is positioned at each estimated location and a similarity measure is computed within the search window. An accurate feature position is determined through the refinement using the similarity measure. Once the feature position is determined from the similarity measures, the current feature states are updated and kept in the trajectory buffer. To reduce false matches, the outlier rejection stage is also introduced.

For the stable and robust feature tracking, each step of the tracking should be processed as accurate as possible. The three main steps are the extraction of stable feature points, the prediction of feature states, and the computation of feature correspondences. In this section, we describe each step in detail explaining how to improve the accuracy of feature tracking.

### 3.1   Feature Extraction

The reliable feature extraction is the first fundamental step for the robust feature tracking. It is desirable to extract feature points that are unique and distinguishable from other feature points. Feature points are commonly chosen from the corners on the image. Extraction of good features directly drives the improvement of the robustness of feature tracking. Good features would be tracked well even in case of translation, rotation, and scaling of local image patches over a sequence of frames.

Our feature extraction method is similar to the method of scale-space extrema[8][9]. In the first stage, we determine the locations of feature points that are computed by the difference of the Gaussian function[9]. The scale space is computed using the input image $I(x, y)$ and the scale Gaussian $G(x, y, \sigma)$. The scale space is defined by Eq. (5), which is the convolution of $G$ with $I$:

$$L(x, y, \sigma) = G(x, y, \sigma) * I(x, y) .$$
(5)

In the scale space, the difference of Gaussian (DOG) is used for the computation of keypoint locations[9]. The DOG filter corresponds to $G(x, y, k\sigma) - G(x, y, \sigma)$. The difference of two Gaussian images separated by a factor $k$ are represented by:

$$D(x, y, \sigma) = L(x, y, k\sigma) - L(x, y, \sigma) .$$

The DOG function estimates an approximate value using the scale-normalized Laplacian of Gaussian. If the computed difference is the maximum or the minimum, the location is considered as a feature point location. Such feature points are more stable than feature points from other extraction methods.

## 3.2   State Modeling for Feature Tracking

We assume that target objects are static but the camera is allowed to move freely in space. Let $\mathbf{x}_n = (x_n, y_n)$ be a feature point in the $n$'th image. Then the movement from $\mathbf{x}_n$ to $\mathbf{x}_{n+1}$ is described by:

$$\mathbf{x}_{n+1} = f(\mathbf{x}_n, \mathbf{p}_n) .$$
(6)

In Eq. (6), $\mathbf{p}_n = (p_{n,1}, \ldots, p_{n,m})$ is the vector of state variables that describes the state transition from the previous frame to the current frame. Hence, the problem of tracking is to estimate the state vector $\mathbf{p}_n$. A simple form of the state vector is induced when $m = 2$, which means $\mathbf{p}_n = (p_{n,1}, p_{n,2})$ where $(p_{n,1}, p_{n,2})$ is the translation vector from $\mathbf{x}_n$ to $\mathbf{x}_{n+1}$:

$$x_{n+1} = x_n + p_{n,1}, \ y_{n+1} = y_n + p_{n,2} .$$

Let $\mathbf{p}_n$ be the state vector at the $n$'th frame. Each state vector is kept in an array called the state trajectory buffer. The state trajectory buffer is used to predict new feature locations. When processing the $n$'th frame, the trajectory buffer would contain $(n$-1$)$ state vectors $\mathbf{p}_1, \mathbf{p}_2, \ldots, \mathbf{p}_{n-1}$ . To estimate a feature location at the current frame, we utilize the trajectory of state variables from the first frame up to the $(n$-1$)$'th frame.

   Since the frame rate is high in a real-time video stream, we can roughly estimate the new feature location using the velocity of the feature movement at the immediate previous frame. We simply approximate the velocity of the state vector by:

$$\mathbf{v}_{n-1} = \mathbf{p}_{n-1} - \mathbf{p}_{n-2} .$$

Then, the state vector at the $n$'th frame is updated using the previous feature position and the current state vector:

$$\mathbf{p}_n = \mathbf{p}_{n-1} + \mathbf{v}_{n-1} .$$
(7)

Finally, using $\mathbf{p}_n$ from Eq. (7), the new feature location is predicted by Eq. (6).

Once the predicted location is determined, we put a search window on the predicted location. Then we find the correspondence using an intensity-based similarity measure. We compute and compare the similarity measures by moving the window around the predicted location. The location of the highest similarity measure or, equivalently, the lowest dissimilarity measure is chosen as the corresponding location. The size of the search window is adaptively determined according to the residual error.

### 3.3  Rejection of Outliers

We use the Random Sample Consensus (RANSAC) algorithm[10] to reject outliers among tracked feature points. The RANSAC is a robust algorithm to identify wrong tracked features[11]. The basic idea is as following. We make a data model consisting of the minimum number of data from the collected data set. The randomly selected data set is used to estimate the model coefficients which are computed using a least squares optimization method. After making the model, we apply the model to the unselected data. The evaluated value is compared with the observation. Then we compute the minimum number of features where the difference from the observation is smaller than a predefined threshold. The threshold value is used to determine whether a feature is an inlier or an outlier[12]. An inlier is the feature whose difference between the computed value and the observed value is smaller than the threshold. This computation is iterated until reaching the predefined number of repeats. We select the final model to have the maximum number of inliers. The feature set is the set of the inlier features in the final model.

### 3.4  Tracking Feature Points

In the following, the overall steps of our feature tracking method are described. At the initialization step, we extract a sufficient number of feature points in the first frame. Then the set of extracted feature points are tracked over the sequence. For each successive captured frame, we predict the feature locations using the state vectors in the trajectory buffer. Since a real-time video stream has a sufficiently high frame rate, we assume that the current feature position can be predicted from the previous feature location using the state vector. We predict each new feature location by finding the location of the smallest error.

The predicted feature position is used to initialize the location of the search window. Each predicted feature position is refined further using the measurement data. For the refinement, we compute the similarity of the image patches centered at the feature locations. The final refined feature location corresponds to the location of the maximum similarity. If the maximum similarity is too low then the feature point is considered to be failed in matching and is excluded from the feature set. Once the final feature locations are determined from the refinement, we update the state vectors and push them into the trajectory buffer.

After all the feature correspondences are computed, we choose outliers. Outliers are caused by the occlusion due to some camera movements. Rejection of outliers is a necessary step to improve the feature tracking accuracy. If a tracked feature point is revealed as an outlier, it is excluded from the feature set. If the number of feature points in the current set becomes smaller than a predefined number of features, new feature points are extracted on the current frame and added into the feature set.

The overall algorithm of our feature tracking method is described below.

Step 1 (Initializing features):

    1.1 Capture and load the first frame. Set $n \leftarrow 1$.

    1.2 Extract $N$ feature points from the first frame and add them to the feature set.

Step 2 (Predicting feature locations):

    2.1 Capture and load the next frame. Set $n \leftarrow n + 1$.

    2.2 Repeat steps 2.3–2.5 for each $i$'th point in the feature set.

    2.3 Predict the feature state vector $\mathbf{p}_n^i$ using the state trajectory.

    2.4 Predict the feature location using Eq. (7).

    2.5 Set the search window $w_i$ based on the predicted feature location.

Step 3 (Finding correspondences):

    3.1 Repeat steps 3.2–3.3 for each $i$'th point in the feature set.

    3.2 Compute the similarity measure at the search window $w_i$.

    3.3 Refine and determine the final feature location.

Step 4 (Rejecting outliers):

    4.1 Choose outliers using the RANSAC algorithm and exclude them from the feature set.

    4.2 Update the feature state vectors using the new feature set and push them into the trajectory buffer.

Step 5 (Adding new features):

    5.1 Check the number of the feature points in the new set. If the number is less than the given threshold then extract new feature points and add them to the set.

    5.2 Go to Step 2.

## 4   Experimental Results

We implemented our tracking method and applied it to several long video sequences. Each sequence contains at least 100 frames. The video frames were grabbed at general indoor and outdoor environments. The camera was moved arbitrary in the physical environment. However, all the captured objects are assumed to be static.

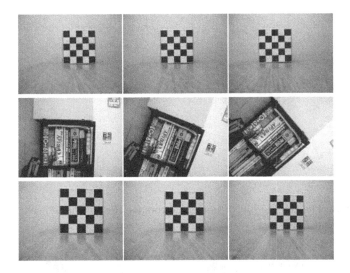

**Fig. 1.** Input frames acquired during camera translation (top), rotation (middle), and scaling (bottom)

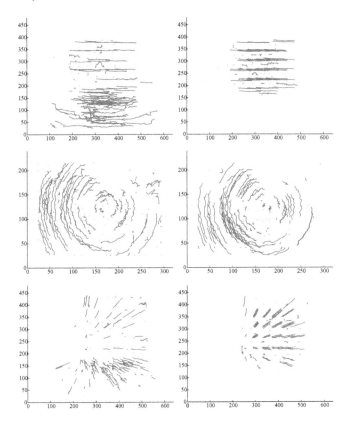

**Fig. 2.** Trajectories of feature points for the three sequences shown in Fig. 1

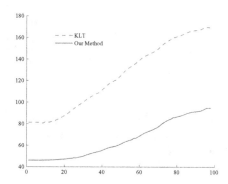

**Fig. 3.** The comparison of tracking errors for the translation sequence

**Fig. 4.** Input teddy bear frames acquired while the camera translating horizontally

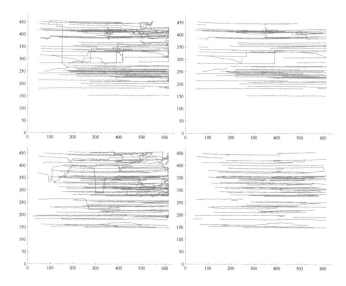

**Fig. 5.** The comparison of feature trajectories for the sequence shown in Fig. 4

## 4.1   Feature Tracking in Short Simple Camera Movement

Fig. 1 shows three sample images taken from each of three image sequences of 100 frames. The figures contain camera motions of translation, rotation, and scaling. For each sequence, we initially extract 300 feature points and track them over 100 frames. We compared our tracking method with the KLT tracking method and the results are shown in Fig. 2. In the figure, the left side shows the result of the KLT tracking method and the right side shows the result of our method. The comparison indicates that our method provides better results mainly due to the outlier rejection.

Fig. 3 shows the tracking error measured along the 100 frames of the translation sequence shown in Fig. 2. Because the camera was moved in a parallel direction with respect to the target object, the $x$-coordinates of all feature points are nearly the same. The errors were computed by subtracting each $x$-coordinate value from the average value and adding all the differences. As shown in the two error graphs, our method gives better results than the KLT tracking method.

Fig. 4 shows three sample images from the teddy bear sequence. When grabbing the sequence, the camera was translated to the horizontal direction. Fig. 5 shows the feature trajectories: the top row shows the feature trajectories from the KLT tracking method and the bottom row shows the trajectories from our tracking method. The tracking results before and after the outlier rejection are shown in the left side and right side, respectively. Though some outliers are still remained in the KLT tracking, most of the outliers are removed in our method.

## 4.2   Feature Tracking in General Camera Movement

Fig. 6(a) shows four sample images of an outdoor sequence. The camera was moved with rotational and translational components around a flower bed. The arrows connecting sample images indicate the path of the camera movement. The tracking result is shown in Fig. 6(b). Upper figures are from the KLT method and lower figures are from our method. The tracking results before and after the outlier rejection are shown in the left side and right side, respectively.

Fig. 7(a) shows three sample images from an indoor keyboard image sequence. The camera was moved with rotational and translational components. Fig. 7(b) shows the extracted features in the first frame using two different feature extraction methods. Fig. 7(c) shows the feature trajectories. Upper figures are from the KLT method and lower figures are from our proposed method. The tracking results before and after the outlier rejection are shown in the left side and right side, respectively. Most of the outliers are removed in our method, whereas some outliers are still remained in the result of the KLT method.

## 4.3   Error Analysis Using Epipolar Distance

We evaluated the tracking errors to verify the accuracy of the proposed method. The ground truth of the feature movement is unknown and, hence, we use the epipolar distance as an error criterion[13]. The epipolar distance is based on the

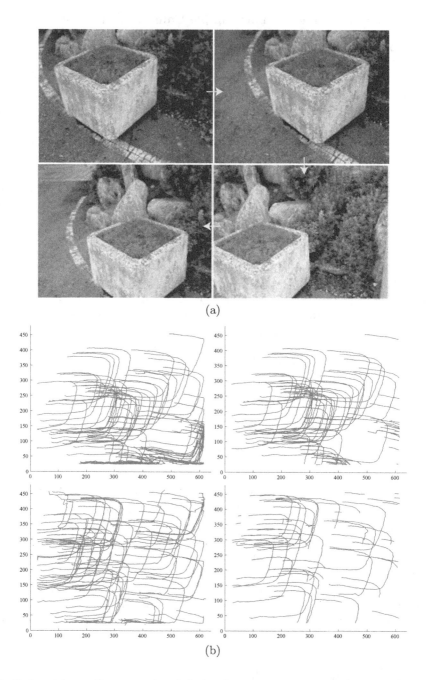

Fig. 6. Input image frames captured during free camera movement in an outdoor environment (a) and feature trajectories before and after removing outliers (b)

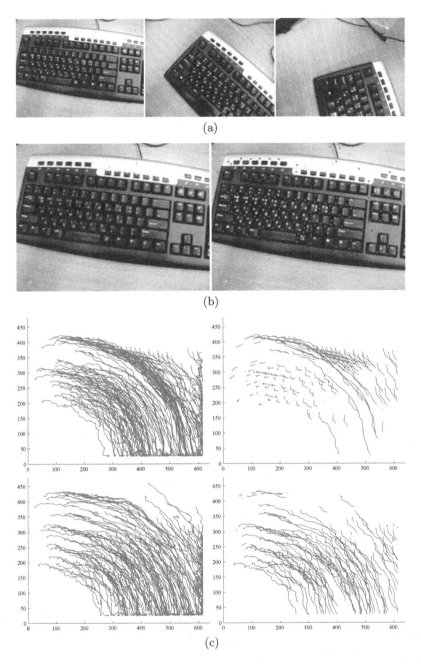

**Fig. 7.** Input image frames captured during general camera movement in an indoor environment (a), extracted features for the first keyboard image using two different methods (b), and feature trajectories before and after removing outliers (c)

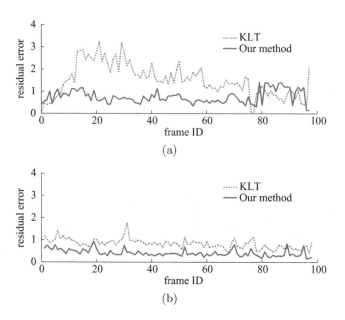

**Fig. 8.** The comparison of residual errors for the tracked feature points

epipolar geometry and measures the accuracy in image matching problems. The epipolar geometry represents the geometric relation between two images[14].

The geometric relation between two frames is described by a fundamental matrix[15]. The relation between the correspondence between $\mathbf{x}_i$ and $\mathbf{x}'_i$ is represented by a fundamental matrix $\mathbf{F}$. The point corresponding to $\mathbf{x}_i$ lies on the epipolar line $\mathbf{F}\mathbf{x}_i$ on the opposite image and, similarly, the point corresponding to $\mathbf{x}'_i$ should be on the epipolar line $\mathbf{F}^T\mathbf{x}'_i$. We evaluate the residual error by computing the distance between the epipolar line and the corresponding feature point. The residual error $\epsilon$ is described by the following equation:

$$\epsilon = \frac{1}{N} \sum_{i=1}^{N} \left[ d(\mathbf{x}'_i, \mathbf{F}\mathbf{x}_i)^2 + d(\mathbf{x}_i, \mathbf{F}^T\mathbf{x}'_i)^2 \right] . \tag{8}$$

In Eq. (8), $\mathbf{x}_i$ is a feature point in the current frame and $\mathbf{x}'_i$ is the corresponding point in the set of features.

Fig. 8 shows the residual errors for the above two experiments. Fig. 8(a) is the residual error graph for the translation experiment and Fig. 8(b) is for the scaling experiment. The residual error is represented by pixel unit. The error is within a single pixel in most cases and the proposed method shows better accuracy in terms of the epipolar distance.

## 5   Conclusion

This paper presented a feature tracking method that tracks point features robustly over long image sequences. Our approach is different from previous works in the sense that the proposed method uses the trajectories of previous feature movements. First, we extract feature points that are invariant to two-dimensional transformations. Using the feature state vectors, we predict the next feature positions and refine the locations by computing similarity measures. For each frame, outliers are detected and they are excluded from the feature set. During the feature tracking, new features can be consistently added to persist robust tracking on a long sequence.

Our tracking method will be useful for the implementation of various augmented reality applications and three-dimensional reconstruction applications. Furthermore, if reliable feature trajectories are provided, accurate estimation of a three-dimensional structure is also possible. The proposed method is also useful to improve the accuracy of the model-based three-dimensional object tracking.

However, good tracking results are not always guaranteed due to the irregularity and diversity of the real environment. A set of feature points possibly contains unexpected outliers and, hence, more accurate outlier rejection scheme is required to reduce the possibility of false matching. Our future research includes improving the robustness of feature tracking further to ensure there are no outliers in the feature set. Our future work also includes inferring the camera poses and the structures of three-dimensional objects from the tracked feature points.

**Acknowledgements.** This work was supported by grant No. RTI05-03-01 from the Regional Technology Innovation Program of the Ministry of Knowledge Economy.

# References

1. Hartley, R., Zisserman, A.: Multiple view geometry in computer vision. Cambridge University Press, Cambridge (2000)
2. Shi, J., Tomasi, C.: Good features to track. In: IEEE Conference on Computer Vision and Pattern Recognition, pp. 593–600 (1994)
3. Zinßer, T., Gräßl, C., Niemann, H.: Efficient feature tracking for long video sequences. In: Proceedings of the 26th DAGM Symposium, pp. 326–333 (2004)
4. Tomasi, C., Kanade, T.: Detection and tracking of point features. Tech. Rep. CMU-CS-91132 (1991)
5. Tommasini, T., Fusiello, A., Trucco, E., Roberto, V.: Making good features track better. In: IEEE Conference on Computer Vision and Pattern Recognition, pp. 178–183 (1998)
6. Sinha, S., Frahm, J., Pollefeys, M.: GPU-based video feature tracking and matching. In: Workshop on Edge Computing Using New Commodity Architectures (2006)
7. Harris, C., Stephens, M.: A combined corner and edge detector. In: Proceedings of the fourth Alvey Vision Conference, pp. 147–151 (1998)
8. Lowe, D.: Object recognition from local scale-invariant features. In: International Conference on Computer Vision, pp. 1150–1157 (1999)
9. Lowe, D.: Distinctive image features from scale-invariant keypoints. International Journal of Computer Vision 60(2), 91–110 (2004)

10. Fischler, M., Bolles, R.: Random sample consensus: a paradigm for model fitting with applications to image analysis and automated cartography. Comm. of the ACM 24, 381–395 (1981)
11. Tommasini, T., Fusiello, A., Roberto, V., Trucco, E.: Robust feature tracking. In: Proceeding of the Joint Workshop of AI*IA and IAPR-IC, pp. 93–98 (1998)
12. Matas, J., Chum, O.: Randomized RANSAC with sequential probability ratio test. In: IEEE International Conference on Computer Vision, vol. 2, pp. 1727–1732 (2005)
13. Bourel, F., Chibelushi, C., Low, A.: Robust facial feature tracking. In: 11th British Machine Vision Conference, pp. 232–241 (2000)
14. Yinan, S., Weijun, L., Zhuang, M., Yuechao, W.: A high-accuracy algorithm for computing fundamental matrix. In: IEEE International Conference on Robotics and Biomimetics, pp. 733–736 (2004)
15. Zhang, Z., Loop, C.: Estimating the fundamental matrix by transforming image points in projective space. Computer Vision and Image Understanding 82, 174–180 (2001)

# A Model-Driven Framework for Dynamic Web Application Development

Ronnie Cheung

Hong Kong Polytechnic University,
Hong Kong SAR,
China
csronnie@gmail.com

**Abstract.** Developing web-based applications is a time-consuming task. Because of the diversity and complexity of web applications, it is difficult to develop web applications in an object-oriented manner. In terms of the Model-View-Control framework (MVC), the control layer has two responsibilities, one is to retrieve the data for the view layer, and the other is to control the navigational structure of the view layer. This makes the boundary between the control layer and view layer unclear. To address these issues, we have developed a web application design framework called XFlash for generating reusable web-based components. In the XFlash framework, we have applied the object-oriented hypermedia design methodology to model web application structures, and provide a model-driven approach for the view layer design. By using this approach, it is possible to develop web user-interfaces in a model-driven manner.

**Keywords:** Object-oriented hypermedia design methodology, Web application design framework.

## 1 Introduction

Developing a web-based application is a time-consuming task. Because of the diversity and complexity of web applications, it is difficult to develop a web application in an object-oriented manner. Web engineering differs from the traditional software engineering approaches for software development. The design of web applications must be flexible enough to support adaptive changes. Components provide maximum flexibility to increase their reusability in different applications and to work under changing environments [5]. However, traditional component-based software engineering approaches are not suitable for web-based application development. The developer of web applications needs to implement the system with several languages, such as HTML, JavaScript, and Java. It is difficult for the developer to extract the web user-interface component models for reuse.

In the XFlash framework, we provide a model-driven approach for web user-interface development. The object-oriented hypermedia design methodology (OOHDM) [2] is used to model the web application structure. By providing enhancements to the OOHDM approach, we design the navigational structure of a web

T.-h. Kim et al. (Eds.): ASEA 2008, CCIS 30, pp. 29–42, 2009.

application using the abstract user-interfaces model rather than the navigational model. In terms of the abstract user-interfaces model, we applied the component-based model driven approach [4] to designing the web user-interfaces.

In order to validate our approach, we implemented a model driven-framework - XFlash. The XFlash framework is based on the OOHDM approach. It helps developers to design the user-interfaces model with a visual graphical editor. For traditional web applications, web user-interface components are built out of several language, such as HTML, JavaScript and Java. It is difficult for developers to implement web user-interface components in an object-oriented manner. In the XFlash framework, web user-interfaces components are implemented with a single language - Action-Script. Furthermore, the XFlash framework generates flash movies to build the web user-interface components. Because of the hierarchical structure of the XFlash framework, we can implement web user-interfaces in a component-based manner. This approach contributes to developing reusable web user-interfaces component for different web applications.

The model-driven framework has following characteristics:

- Model-driven—the designer provides the outline model of a special application. The model is the conceptual model of the OOHDM approach, which is used to describe the business model of the web application. Based on the conceptual model, the navigational model is deduced, which is used to describe the data retrieve structure of web applications. Finally, the developers can design the web user-interfaces model. Different from traditional user interface design and development, we focus on the model-driven approach rather than concentrating on the layout of individual user-interface components.

- Reusability—our target is to improve the web user-interface component reusability. In terms of traditional web application development, the web user-interfaces are implemented in several languages, such as HTML, JavaScript etc. As a result, the developer has difficulty in implementing the web user-interfaces in an object-oriented manner. In the XFlash framework, we implement the web user-interfaces in a single language, namely "ActionScript". This contributes to developing the web user-interfaces in an object-oriented manner. Furthermore, in terms of web user-interface modeling, we also implement the web user-interface models in a component-based manner.

## 2 Related Work

Schwabe [2] toke forward a methodology which is used to design the web based application, namely object oriented hypermedia design methodology (OOHDM). The Object-Oriented Hypermedia Design Method is a model-based approach for building large hypermedia applications. It has been used to design different kinds of applications such as: web sites and information systems, interactive kiosks, multimedia presentations, etc. They proposed a series of steps to implement web applications. For each phase of development, an object-oriented approach is used to model the desired result. They proposed three models to describe the web application structure, namely the conceptual model, the navigational model and the abstract user-interface model. From the perspective of OOHDM, the whole development process for web-based applications is divided into four steps: conceptual model design, navigational model design, abstract interview design and implementation. Güell [6] describes the phases in the design and implementation of Hypermedia Applications as following diagram.

**Fig. 1.** Phases in the design and implantation of hypermedia applications

Treating conceptual, navigational and interface design as separate activities allow us to concentrate on different concerns one at a time. As a consequence we get more modular and reusable designs, and we obtain a framework to reason on the design process, encapsulating design experience specific to that activity. Besides, the inter-face design primitives can be easily mapped to non object-oriented implementation languages or environments (such as HTML or Toolbox) and thus OOHDM can be used regardless of whether the target system is a pure object-oriented environment one or a hybrid one (as those we usually find in the Internet).

Currently, most of the prevalent web frameworks are based on the Model-View-Control (MVC) framework. A special web application structure is organized as a tri-layer structure with the MVC framework. In terms of the OOHDM approach, the conceptual model is mapped onto the model layer, the navigational model is mapped onto the control layer [3], and the abstract user-interfaces model is mapped onto the view layer. However, both the OOHDM approach and the MVC framework do not give a clear boundary between the view layer and the control layer. Because of the limited capability web user-interfaces, the behavior of the view layer is implemented in the control layer. In this way, the object-oriented structure of the model is not fully represented in the MVC framework.

The XFlash framework incorporates both the layer structure of MVC model and the model-driven approach of the OOHDM approach. We design the navigational structure in the abstract user-interfaces model rather than the navigational model, and the navigation behavior of a web application is implemented by the web user-interfaces rather than the control layer component.

There are many systems implementations of the model-driven approaches. A typi-cal example is the MODEL-BUILD-DEPLOY platform. The primary objective of the system is to organize and visualize the structure and components of software intensive systems. The models visually represent the requirements, subsystems, logical and physical elements, the structural and the behavioral patterns. However, it is not appli-cable to web application development. In the XFlash framework, we propose an ap-proach for developers to design web user-interfaces models in a component-driven manner. This contributes to web user-interface components reusability for different web applications.

# 3 Systems Architecture

The model driven framework is implemented using the Eclipse plug-in system, which can be integrated with the Eclipse Java program development platform seamlessly. The developers need not switch between different kinds of development environment [1]. The model-driven framework provides a visible graphical editor to help the developer design the web user-interfaces model and the corresponding XML descriptor files for the web user-interface components. In addition, the model-driven framework is able to generate the SQL statements based on the navigation model, for data retrieval using the view layer components. The following figure is the architecture of the model-driven framework - XFlash.

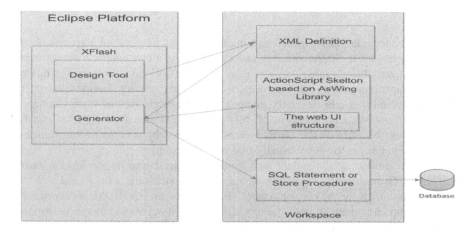

**Fig. 2.** The XFlash architecture

According to the XML definition file, XFlash generates the web user-interfaces component source code automatically. Furthermore, the ActionScript file is parsed by XFlash to generate the executable web user-interfaces.

## 3.1 The XML Schema of the Web User-Interface Components

In terms of the web user-interfaces component, we define four basic component schemas.

1)   The JFrame Component
     The following table is the schema of the JFrame component:

```
<complexType name="JFramae">
    <attribute name="id" type="string"></attribute>
    <attribute name="height" type="int"></attribute>
    <attribute name="width" type="int"></attribute>
    <attribute name="title" type="string"></attribute>
</complexType>
```

2)    The JPanel Component

In addition to the JFrame component, we provide the Panel component, which can be inserted into the other container components, such as the JFrame component, or the other Panel components. The following is an XML schema for the JPanel component:

```
<complexType name="JPanel">
    <attribute name="id" type="string"></attribute>
    <attribute name="tag" type="string"></attribute>
    <attribute name="location" type="string"></attribute>
</complexType>
```

The "id" attribute is the identifier of the Panel. According to the identifier, a package which contains the panel will be created. For example, "example.person.PersonPanel" means that the "PersonPanel" is contained in the directory "example/person". The "location" attribute is used to describe the panel component location relative to the parent component which contains the panel component.

3)    The JMenu Component

We define the Menu component, which appends a menu bar to the main frame. Figure 3 is the Ecore model of the Menu component, which is similar to the JMenu component of Java Swing. The figure below shows the source code example of Menu component, and the screen painter is the final result generated from the examples.

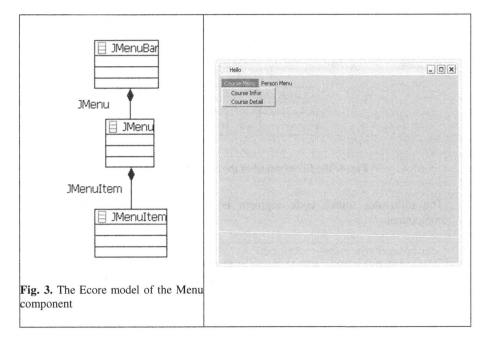

**Fig. 3.** The Ecore model of the Menu component

```
<JFrame id="example.mainframe.MyFrame" title="Hello">
  <JPanel id="example.course.MenuPanel" location="North"
              tag="menuPanel">
    <JMenuBar tag="menuBar" id="JMenuBar" location="Center">
      <JMenu tag="menu" title="Course Menu" id="JMenu">
        <JMenuItem id="JMenuItem" tag="courseItem"
                    title="Course Infor">
        </JMenuItem>
        <JMenuItem id="JMenuItem" tag="courseInforItem"
                    title="Course Detail">
        </JMenuItem>
      </JMenu>
      <JMenu tag="menu2" title="Person Menu" id="JMenu">
      </JMenu>
    </JMenuBar>
  </JPanel>
</JFrame>
```

4) The primary component

The primary component is the basic component, such as Button etc, which cannot contain other components.

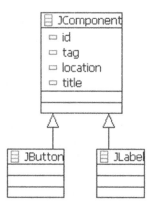

**Fig. 4.** The Ecore model of the primary component

The following source code segment is the XML schema of the JButton component:

```
<complexType name="JButton">
  <attribute name="id" type="string"></attribute>
  <attribute name="tag" type="string"></attribute>
  <attribute name="location" type="string"></attribute>
  <attribute name="title" type="string"></attribute>
</complexType>
```

The "id" attribute is used to identify the JButton component, the "title" attribute is the caption displayed on the component. The "location" attribute is used to locate the component the parent component, which contains the JButton.

## 3.2 The Navigational Model XML Description File

In OOHDM, an application can be seen as a navigational view over the conceptual model. This view is built during navigational design taking, into account the types of intended users, and the set of tasks performed by the application [3]. Usually, the navigational model describes the navigational structure and the data retrieval structure of the navigational space. However, the navigational model complicates application development in terms of the followings:

1)  In terms of Model-View-Control (MVC) framework, the boundary between the view layer and the Control layer is unclear.
2)  The Control layer takes charge the behavior of View layer, this breaks the major aspects of MVC framework for separating the view and control layer.

In the XFlash framework, we modify the navigational model of the OOHDM approach. The navigational model just describes the data retrieval structure. For the navigational structure, we describe the details in the abstract user interface model. We model the navigational model using the following procedures:

- The business domain class is mapped onto the Ecore class
- The retrieval structure is mapped onto the association relationship.

Figure 5 is the link model of the XFlash framework:

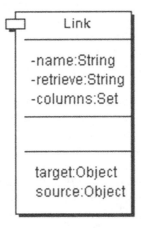

**Fig. 5.** The link model of XFlash

Figure 6 is an example of navigational model structure. In this context, the relationship between professor and course is one-to-many. We present this relationship with a link class. XFlash stores this link class as an XML descriptor file.

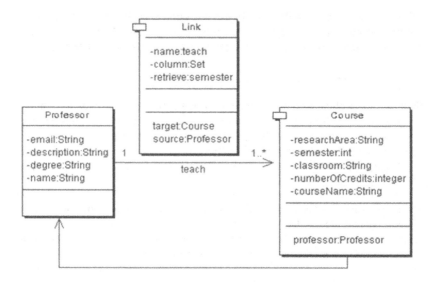

**Fig. 6.** An example of navigational model

The sample XML descriptor file for the navigational model is shown in the following example (Here we assume that the database has been built according to the conceptual model). Furthermore, based on the XML file, XFlash generates the SQL statements used by the data engine for data retrieval : select course.name, course.semester, course.classroom from course join professor where professor.name = @parameter/.

```
<Link name='teach'>
    <target name='Course'>
        <column id='name'>
        <column id='semester'>
        <column id='classroom'>
    </target>
    <source name='Professor' retrieve='name'/>
</Link>
```

### 3.3 The Visible Graphical Editor

By using the Eclipse Modeling Framework and Eclipse Graphical Framework, we develop a Visible Graphical Editor, which helps the developer to design the abstract web user-interfaces model. Using the web user-interface model, the XFlash framework generates the XML descriptor files, which are used for generating the web user-interface components.

For traditional web applications, a web page is the basic element of the whole web application. Here, the web page is generated as a Flash movie rather than a traditional web page. Because of the hierarchical structure of Flash movie, our web user-interface component structure is organized as a tree structure, which uses the Ecore model to represent the web-interface model.

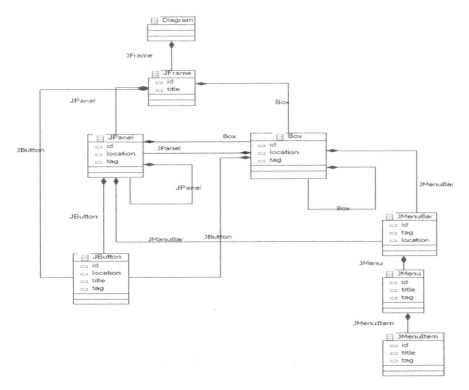

**Fig. 7.** The Ecore model of the Visual Graphical Editor

In the Ecore model, the aggregation relationship describes the inclusion relation among the classes. In terms of the web application development, we also provide an inclusion relation among the web nodes. For example, for an academic web application, the "MainMenu" represents the entry point of the web application; it consists of "LaboratoriesMenu", "CourseMenu", "PersonalCategoryMenu", and "Research-Menu". Figure 8 is the aggregation relation structure of the web application. In the XFlash framework, developers can design the model using a visual graph editor. Figure 9 shows the web interface components generated using the XFlash framework.

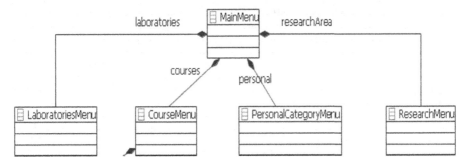

**Fig. 8.** The aggregation relation among web node class

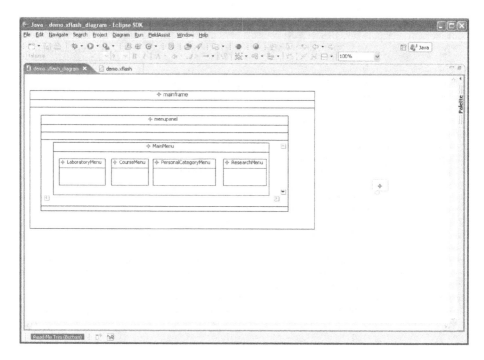

**Fig. 9.** The Menu Structure Layout designed by XFlash

According to the layout structure shown in Figure 9, XFlash generates the XML descriptor file (as shown in Figure 10).

```
<?xml version="1.0" encoding="UTF-8"?>
<null:Diagram xmi:version="2.0" xmlns:xmi=http://www.omg.org/
      XMI xmlns:null="null">
  <JFrame id="mainframe">
   <JPanel id="menupanel">
     <JManuBar id="MainMenu" tag="menuBar" location="CENTER">
       <JMenu id="LaboratoryMenu" title="Laboratory"
                    tag="lMenu"/>
       <JMenu id="CourseMenu" title="Course" tag="couseMenu"/>
       <JMenu id="PersonalCategoryMenu" title="Personal"
                    tag="personalMenu"/>
       <JMenu id="ResearchMenu" title="Research"
                    tag="researchMenu"/>
     </JManuBar>
   </JPanel>
  </JFrame>
</null:Diagram>
```

**Fig. 10.** The XML descriptor file

### 3.4 Application Code Generator

The Application Code generator is the engine used to generate ActionScript source code for the Flash movie. The Eclipse JET framework is used to implement this module. The application code generator consists of three modules, which are shown in Figure 11:

1) Template module: this module defines the basic syntax of ActionScript.
2) The code generator : this module is the executer of code generation. The main task of the code generator is to parse the XML file, and combine the template with the data.
3) The compiler: the task of the compiler is to compile the ActionScript source code into a Flash movie file.

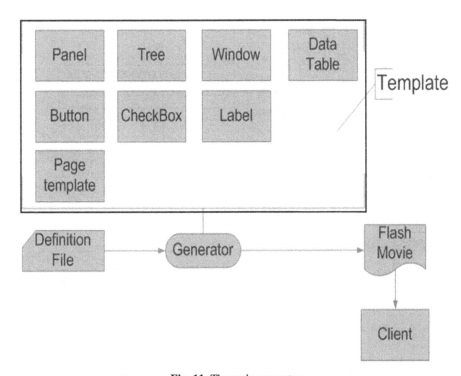

**Fig. 11.** The code generator

The generator takes a single definition file, the web user-interface model, as the input file. In order to generate the output file, the generator uses a set of nested templates, and binds the template with XML data by inserting data into the hot spot of the template file.

In the XFlash framework, we design a special component called the container component. It contains the other component to be included as its child component. In order to improve the component reusability, we implement every container component model as an independent component, which not only contains other components but also contains the other container components as well.

For example, consider a web user-interface model as shown in Figure 12. The "MainFrame" contains two sub-panels, "Panel2" and "Panel3", and the sub-panels derive from the same type panel, "example.components.Panel2". At the same time, in every sub-panel, there is a panel, "Panel3", contained in every sub-panel; both panels are derived from the same type panel, "example.components.Panel3".

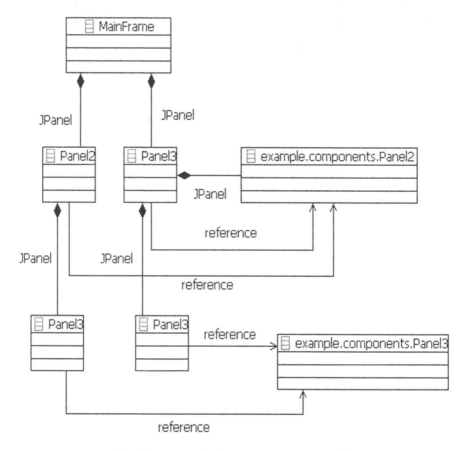

**Fig. 12.** An example showing component reusability

According to the user-interface model, the model descriptor file is generated (as shown in Figure 13):

Although the web user-interfaces model file contain four JPanel XML tag, only two JPanel components are generated, because that the panel① and the panel③ have the same id value, which means they refer to the same panel component, "example.components.Panel2". Similarily, panel② and panel④ refers to the same panel component. As a result, the code generator module generates two independent

```
<JFrame id="example.componentreuse.MainFrame" title="XFlash
Demo">

    ①<JPanel id="example.components.Panel2" location="EAST"
                  tag="panel2">

        ②<JPanel id="example.components.Panel3" location="EAST"
                    tag="panel3">
        </JPanel>
    </JPanel>

    ③<JPanel id="example.components.Panel2" location="NORTH"
                    tag="panel3">

        ④<JPanel id="example.components.Panel3" location="EAST"
                    tag="panel3">
        </JPanel>
    </JPanel>
</JFrame>
```

**Fig. 13.** The model descriptor file

ActionScript files for every panel. This approach contributes to the reusability of the container components for different web applications.

## 4  Conclusions

In this project, we have developed a model-driven methodology for web application development. In terms of web user-interfaces development, we have implemented a generator for generating the user-interfaces components from the XFlash framework. Different from traditional web user-interface development using different computer languages, we implement the web user-interfaces using a single computer language - the ActionScript, and organize the structure of web interfaces using design patterns. Our approach contributes to the reusability of web user-interface components in different applications. Finally, our approach generates flash components to implement the web user-interface elements.

## Acknowledgment

This project is supported by RGC CERG grant no. PolyU 5200E/04 of the HKSAR.

## References

1. Cheung, R.: A Design Automation Framework for Web-based Applications. In: Proceedings of the 3rd International Conference on Computer and Information, USA, pp. 11–18 (2004)
2. Schwabe, D., Rossi, G.: An Object Oriented Approach to Web-based Application Design. Theory and Practice of Object Systems 4, 207–225 (1998)

3. Diaz, A., Gordillo, S., Rossi, G.: Specifying Navigational Structures by Querying Hypermedia Design Models. In: Proceedings of the 3rd Basque International Workshop on Information Technology, France, pp. 125–130 (1997)
4. Gamma, E., Helm, R., Johnson, R., Vlissides, J.: Design Patterns—Elements of Reusable Object-Oriented Software. Addison-Wesley Professional Computing Series (1995)
5. Göbel, S.: An MDA Approach for Adaptable Components. In: First European Conference on Model-Driven Architecture – Foundations and Applications, Germany, pp. 74–87 (2005)
6. Güell, N., Schewabe, D., Vilain, P.: Modeling Interactions and Navigation in Web Applications. In: Mayr, H.C., Liddle, S.W., Thalheim, B. (eds.) ER Workshops 2000. LNCS, vol. 1921, pp. 115–127. Springer, Heidelberg (2000)

# Experience with MOF-Based Meta-modeling of Component-Based Systems

Petr Hnetynka[1] and Frantisek Plasil[1,2]

[1] Department of Software Engineering
Faculty of Mathematics and Physics
Charles University in Prague
Malostranske namesti 25, Prague 1,
118 00, Czech Republic
{hnetynka,plasil}@dsrg.mff.cuni.cz
[2] Institute of Computer Science
Academy of Sciences of the Czech Republic
Pod Vodarenskou vezi 2, Prague 8
182 07, Czech Republic
plasil@cz.cas.cz

**Abstract.** Component-based development has become a widely used technique for developing not only large enterprise applications, but in fact for any type of applications, including embedded ones. To allow comfortable and easy development, component systems have to provide a rather a big set of development supporting tools including at least a tool for composition and repository for storing and retrieving components. In this paper, we evaluate and present advantages of using MOF and meta-modeling during definition of component system and also during development of the supporting tools. Most of the presented arguments are based on a broad practical experience with designing the component systems SOFA and SOFA 2; the former designed in the classical ad hoc "manual" way, while the latter via meta-modeling.

**Keywords:** Component-based development, model-driven development, meta-models.

## 1 Introduction

Component-based development (CBD) has become a well-understood and widely used technique for developing not only large enterprise applications, but in fact for any type of applications, including embedded ones. Using this technique, applications are built by composing already developed components. Every component system (i.e. a system and/or framework allowing to develop and compose components) uses a different view as to what a software component is, but a generally agreed consensus is that "component" means a black-box entity with well-defined interface and behavior. The interface of a component comprises the services provided by it and the services required from other cooperating components and/or an environment (container). To specify its particular view on

T.-h. Kim et al. (Eds.): ASEA 2008, CCIS 30, pp. 43–54, 2009.

components, a component system defines its component model, i.e. a set of abstractions, which together define components, their composition, etc. Thus, the term component has to be always interpreted in the scope of a given component model.

In order to allow really fast and comfortable development and management of component-based applications, component systems should provide rather a big set of development supporting tools and infrastructure. These tools and infrastructure usually comprise of at least a tool for developing and composing components and a repository storing and serving already developed components.

However, creating such an infrastructure is rather tedious and time-and-other-resources-consuming task. This is probably why especially academia-based component systems provided sophisticated component models with plenty of advanced features, but with no or very limited support for real development of components at a large scale. In order to overcome this problem, modern component systems try to heavily employ modeling and meta-modeling approaches that allow automatic generation of many supporting tools.

The component models of classical ("old") component systems were usually defined by an ADL (Architecture Definition Language). Since these ADL languages were proprietary, the development tools were developed completely manually from scratch. Another related problem was that the semantics of a component model had to be typically defined in a natural language. Finally, as the cores of component models had been very similar (in many case in fact the same), a straightforward idea was to allow interoperability between models and use component from one model in another. This issue is not only making components exchangeable between the systems but also it requires interoperable tools to allow developing and managing such heterogeneous applications. But with hand-made tools and infrastructure, the interoperability was quite difficult.

As stated above, the modern component systems usually use meta-modeling approaches to define their component models and, more interestingly, to automatically generate repositories, tools for development, editors for designing and composing components, etc.

Additionally, meta-models provide means for defining semantics in a formal way (at least partially), and also there are approaches supporting easy interoperability and transformations between different models.

All these advantages of the meta-modeling approaches bring faster development and maintenance of the component systems themselves and therefore faster adoption of the systems to the production.

## 1.1  Goal and Structure of the Paper

In this paper, based on our experience with designing and developing component systems (SOFA in particular) and analysis of several existing component systems, such as Fractal and Koala, we present the advantages of meta-modeling approach in component systems. Also we evaluate and compare the meta-modeling approach with the classical one by comparing the SOFA [22] (based on ADL) and SOFA 2 [7] (based on meta-model) component models. To achieve the goal, the paper is structured as follows. Section 2 presents an overview of meta-modeling principles and contemporary component models. In Section 3, we articulate advantages of using meta-models for component systems specification, design, and implementation, while Section 4 compares SOFA and SOFA 2 definitions and also presents related work. Section 5 concludes the paper.

## 2    Background

### 2.1    Models and Meta-models

Models and meta-model are the main concept in MDD (model-driven development), which is one of the most popular development paradigms nowadays. In MDD, a system is developed as set of models. A typical approach starts with modeling the system on a platform independent level, i.e. capturing only the business logic of the system, leaving out any implementation details. In a series of transformation, this platform independent model is then altered into a platform specific model, i.e. a model reflecting also the details specific for the platform chosen for implementation (such as Java and .NET).

The abstractions featuring in a model M, i.e. the elements to be used for modeling, are described by a meta-model, i.e. a model of M. Many times, the meta-model is referred to as a domain specific language, since it defines a means for modeling system in a specific domain.

An important standard employing the idea of MDD is the OMG's Model Driven Architecture (MDA) [16] specification. For describing meta-models, OMG has defined the Meta-Object Facilities (MOF) [17] standard. It defines a language and framework for specifying and constructing meta-models and for implementing repositories holding instances of models. To enable interchange of these instances among repositories, MOF defines an XML based format denoted XMI (an abbreviation of "XML Meta-data Interchange").

MOF idea is based on the four layer modeling hierarchy shown on Figure 1. A meta-model definition is on the layer M2. On the layer M1, there are models defined using a particular meta-model while on the layer M0, there are instances of the models. The meta-models are defined in the MOF language, which resides on the layer M3. This highest layer is where the hierarchy has its "fix-point" because the MOF language is defined in this language as well.

Since the MOF language does not have any specific visual representation, for specifying meta-models, a subset of UML class diagrams is used. As an aside, since the versions 2.x of both UML and MOF were introduced, there is a common core of the MOF and UML meta-models.

In the rest of the paper, by "meta-model" we always mean a MOF-based meta-model.

The primary meta-model elements are the class (defining abstractions), and association[1] (defining relations among classes). For illustration, Figure 2 shows

---

[1] To be precise, they should be named meta-classes and meta-associations (as they express meta-model) but for the sake of simplicity, we use only terms classes and associations in the paper.

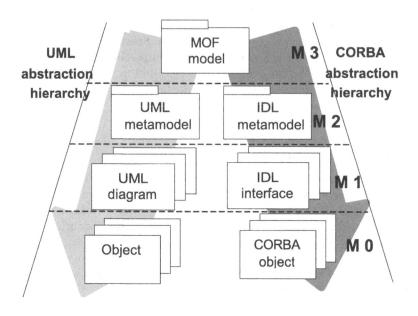

**Fig. 1.** MOF hierarchy examples

a tiny subset of the core of the SOFA 2 meta-model (details are explained in Section 3.1).

## 2.2 Component Models

As mentioned in Section 1, to allow really fast and efficient application development via component composition, a component system has to provide a rather large set of development and management tools. These tools should provide at least a functionality for component composition (defining the architecture of an application composed of components) and a repository to store the already available components (both those designed ad hoc to fulfill a very specific task, and generic ones intended for reuse).

Classical component systems like Darwin [14], Wright [1], and others are defined around their ADL. In fact, an ADL determined the corresponding component model via the syntactical constructs corresponding to particular abstractions and their relation. The semantics was described in plain English. These systems did not provide any repository and thus they were intended for capturing the architecture and component composition, not providing means for component reuse. ACME [9] was an attempt to create a common ADL (de-facto standard) but it was not widely adopted. Tools for all these ADLs were developed manually ad hoc and usually allowed to reason about correctness of behavior composition.

Contemporary component systems usually provide more complex infrastructure since they are not ADL centered. In the following overview we focus on several component systems which deal with the whole component lifecycle (from design to run-time).

An industry-based system is the CORBA Component Model (CCM) [15]; it is based on a flat component model, i.e. components cannot be composed hierarchically. Components are described in CORBA IDL v.3 and composition is done at run-time (i.e. there are no IDL constructs for that). The run-time infrastructure is defined by the OMG deployment and configuration specification and offers a repository, deployment environment, etc. — all of them described by meta-models.

The Koala component model [19] is the based of another industrial system and allows creation of hierarchical component-based embedded applications. It uses its own ADL (heavily inspired by Darwin) and the developed components are stored in a repository for further reuse. Also, there are tools for visualization of architectures. The whole infrastructure, including an ADL compiler and repository were designed ad hoc and written manually.

Fractal [4] is an abstract component model, which has multiple implementations (in Java, C, ...). Components are primarily built at run-time using API calls (defined in the Fractal specification). An ADL also exists, but it can be viewed as a "shortcut" for creation components and architectures — all definitions of components are transformed into the API calls. The specification of Fractal does not prescribe existence of any repository but there are attempts to do so.

The SOFA component model [22] and, especially, its new version SOFA 2 [7] furnishes a general purpose component system. The original version of SOFA was defined by ADL and the repository and all tools were written by hand while SOFA 2, has been redesigned using a meta-model and most of its supporting tools and the repository have been generated from the meta-model. In a more detail, the comparison between these versions is discussed in Section 4.

The list of component system above definitely is not complete (especially the list of those designed in academia is not a shore one) but it provides a base for comparing SOFA with those designed at least partially for industrial applications. There are also other contemporary component systems defined by a meta-model, for example Palladio [3], PRISMA [21], and others, but most of them do not support the whole component lifecycle (usually they focus on design only). For more details see Section 4.

# 3   Applying MOF in Component Model Design and Implementation

As mentioned in Section 1 and Section 2.2, many contemporary component systems are converting to or have been defined from the beginning by a meta-model. From these component systems, most of them use for their meta-model definition and repository generation the Eclipse Modeling Framework (EMF) [8], which is an implementation of the MOF standard (even though EMF does not rigorously comply with the MOF standard the differences are very subtle, not visible to

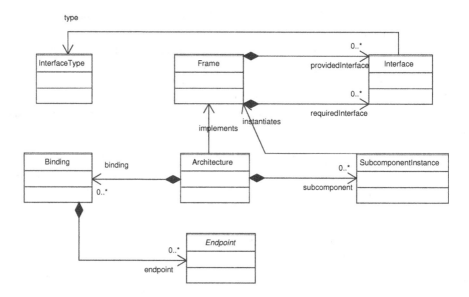

**Fig. 2.** A core of the SOFA 2 meta-model

the developer using EMF). In addition to being a mature tool well supported an maintained, EMF is popular since it is available freely as an open source plugin for Eclipse, and also since a framework for generating model editors from a meta-model definition (called GMF — Graphical Modeling Framework [10]) is available.

In summary, based on experience with SOFA 2, the three most important benefits of using meta-models are (i) the definition of the component model syntax but also its semantics, (ii) the relatively fast and semi-automated creation of the development supporting tools, and (iii) the semi-automated creation of runtime management tools. In the rest of this section, we go through these topics in more details.

### 3.1  Defining Semantics of a Component Model

In a component model specification, the meta-model defines the elements and abstractions (and also the associations among them) forming the component model. Importantly, by the associations, it explicitly defines the relations among these abstractions.

Figure 2 shows an example of a meta-model, which is a core subset of the meta-model of the SOFA 2 component system. It defines there basic abstractions of SOFA 2: component type (called Frame), component implementation (called Architecture), and interface type. A frame provides black-box view of a component instance by defining its provided and required interfaces, which are defined using interface type. The frame is implemented by an architecture, which can contain subcomponents instances (defined again by frames) and bindings among these subcomponents. If the architecture does not have subcomponents, any component instance defined by the frame is a primitive component the implementation of which is to be provided in an underlying programming language.

Via associations, the meta-model in an easy-to-comprehend way determines (at least partially) the semantics of the component model; obviously, there is a part of the semantics that has to be defined informally in plain English, e.g. "Frame is a component type". In addition to the classes and associations, relations can be more precisely defined by constraints added to the classes and associations. These constraints are typically expressed by OCL (Object Constraint Language). A particular constraint in the SOFA 2 core might be, for example: `self.subcomponent->forAll(s1,s2 | s1.name<>s2.name)`, meaning that the names of subcomponents in the architecture determined by self have to be distinct.

To summarize, meta-model and constraints provide a complex, but simple to use and understand, standard means for expressing both the abstractions of a component model and also their semantics in a formal way. On the contrary, a component system defined by ADL requires its semantics to be defined mostly in plain English and is thus more likely ambiguity and error prone.

## 3.2   Infrastructure Creation

Second, and even more important advantage of meta-modeling approach is the simple creation of the infrastructure (tools) for component development. As we already noted, the tools are crucial for a successful adoption of a component system (below we assume that is base on a component model CM).

Once the meta-model CMM of CM has been defined, it is very easy to create the following development infrastructure tools. First, the repository storing designed components (i.e. instance of CM) can be generated completely automatically. This is one of the main functionalities provided by MOF. Another "for-free" obtained functionality is the option to interchange data among such repositories in the XMI format.

Furthermore EMF can automatically generate a semi-visual editor for CM. The editor is very simple but it enforces maintaining the relations among abstraction by allowing to create and connect only correct elements in the way compliant with the meta-model of CM.

Moreover, an EMF extension GMF can generate a more sophisticated visual editor for CM. In addition to CMM, the developer specifies the style of visual representation of each abstraction (element), and then the most of the editor is automatically generated as an Eclipse plugin (the plugin can be launched as a part of the Eclipse IDE, or configured to run as standalone application built over the core of Eclipse). There are still functionalities that have to be designed and developed by hand (like connections to the repositories), but the visual part of the editor is fully generated.

Another contribution to development infrastructure creation is the potentially easy interoperability between component systems. As the component definitions are stored in the generated repositories and a repository can export these definitions in XMI, a transformation between component models CM1 and CM2 can be done very easily, assuming they are based on similar abstractions. This way, e.g., a component designed for CM1 can be transformed and reused in CM2. Moreover, OMG already provides a standardized language called QVT (Query-View-Transform) [18] for performing queries in and transformations on models. QVT by itself does not automatically transform component definitions, but it provides means for an easy and standardized definition of a transformation.

### 3.3    Creation of Runtime Management Tools

In a similar way as the tools for component development, tools for runtime management can be generated. This is particularly important for a component system which allows creating distributed application, where it is necessary to deploy component instances into particular run-time nodes.

Again, to define deployment environment model EM (based on abstractions for e.g. set of hardware nodes, their interconnections, their properties like current load and memory usage), a meta-model EMM has to be defined. Then a repository can be generated from it and for instance used by (i) an environment monitoring tool which feeds the repository with the current status of the environment (current instance of EM), by (ii) a deployment tool which based on the requirements of the deployed application and the current environment status (current instance of EM) creates deployment plan, and by (iii) a GMF visualization tool helping to observe the current status of the environment. Moreover, EMM can include a meta-model of deployment descriptor to allow an automated generation of an EMF/GMF editor.

And again as in the case of development tools, having EMM yields the benefit of achieving relatively easily deployment interoperability among the component systems based on similar abstractions.

## 4    Evaluation and Related Work

*Evaluation.* In essence, we have so far argued that with the MOF-based meta-models the designers and developers of a component system can focus mainly on the definition of a component model, its abstractions, relations, etc., and the "boring" parts of the implementation can be automatically generated. To justify our claims about the advantages of MOF-based meta-models, we present a brief comparison of two version of the SOFA component system: the original one (further "old SOFA") defined by ADL, and the new one (SOFA 2) defined by a meta-model. Basically, this section is a substantial extension of the comparison we published in [13], where we focus only on the process of implementing repositories.

As described in Section 2.2, old SOFA was specified by a definition of its ADL, which had a CORBA IDL — like structure, with constructs added for describing component types and implementations (architectures). The other necessary descriptors (like deployment descriptor) had also a proprietary structure. The repository for storing all the old SOFA model elements was developed completely by hand. As mentioned in [13], the development of the repository took approximately four person-months. A significant amount of additional time was spent on debugging the implementation. The semantics of the component model was defined only by description in plain English. As SOFA evolved and new features were added, each of such additions and/or changes (e.g. the introduction of software connectors for communication among components) required hand-made changes in the implementation of the repository and also of all related tools, and again took rather nontrivial amount of time for debugging.

On the contrary in the case of SOFA 2 — based on experience gained during development and usage of old SOFA — the ADL-based definition of the component model has been replaced by an EMF-based meta-model. Currently, all the SOFA 2 semantics which could not be expressed via EMF is specified in plain English. Applying OCL constraints is left as a near-future work.

With the aim to emphasize the positive experience with semi-automated generations of the SOFA 2 development and deployment supporting tools from the EMF-based meta-model, we provide below a brief overview of the gained benefits:

(1) Component repository — its development took only one person-month and most of the time was spent on designing and tuning the meta-model and the actual repository was generated within few seconds (only the layer providing remote access to the repository was written by hand).

(2) For developing SOFA 2 components, a GMF-based visual tool proved to be essential. Naturally, the core part of the tool is generated from the meta-model. The components developed by the tool are directly stored into the repository. As an aside, developing components via ADL is still possible, but this is intended as a supplementary option (it was employed during the initial stages of the SOFA 2 development when the visual tool was not ready). Nevertheless, since ADL can be interpreted as another SOFA2 meta-model, particular frame and architecture specification in ADL (model instances) are transformed via XSLT and then directly fed into the repository. An intention is to apply QVT (Sect. 3.2) for this purpose in the future.

(3) As to runtime management tools, an EMF-based meta-model of the deployment plan was designed and via GMF a corresponding visual editor was generated. Even though additional tools featuring the functionality mentioned in Section 3.3 will be subject to future work, the flexibility gained by the existence of the meta-model in terms of generating these tools is incomparable with the ad hoc formed, hard-to-maintain deployment supporting tools of old SOFA.

In addition to automated generation of the supporting tools mentioned above, we identified the following improvements of the meta-modeling approach in SOFA 2 over the "classical way" the old SOFA was designed.

(i) The key advantage we very much appreciate has been the lucidity of the meta-model allowing to immediately see the context and consequences of a proposed modification; this very much helps with achieving and maintaining the component model consistency.

(ii) Most of the changes to the SOFA 2 component model mean only updating the meta-model and then a regeneration of the repository (and other tools).

(iii) The definition of the meta-model significantly reduces the time required to understand the SOFA 2 component model; usually it is sufficient only to show the meta-model to a person familiar with commonly CBD used concepts and, because SOFA 2 uses those as well, he/she immediately understands details of the SOFA 2 component model. This proved to be quite important and beneficial during our participation in a joint project [23] while sharing details on SOFA 2 with our partners

(iv) As to transformation between component models, we have done a simple Fractal ADL to SOFA2 ADL transformation based on the XSLT format. This way, we achieved relatively easily the reuse of several Fractal components, developed for the CoCoME contest application [5], in the SOFA 2 version of the contest application [6]. Once a Fractal meta-model is available (see below), a QVT-based transformation could be created for this purpose.

As the only potential disadvantage we see the fact that the repository interface is generic and, therefore, less intuitive than a single purpose, hand-written one [13]. On the other hand, the generic interface following standards can be seen as an advantage, since the generic clients for the repository available elsewhere can be reused.

Overall, compared to old SOFA, the definition of the SOFA 2 meta-model in EMF was a big step forward, in terms of the component model design and specification, implementation of supporting development tools, and deployment environment design.

*Related work.* To our knowledge, few contemporary component systems have been defined by a MOF-based meta-model.

One of them is the Palladio component model [3]. It is a design tool, allowing to compose component at the architecture design level (no run time features, nor implementation of primitive components is taken into account). Palladio primarily focuses on quality-of-service (QoS) description and validation, simulation and even prediction of QoS. The model is completely defined in an EMF-based meta-model. Also all the tools for defining and composing components at the architecture level and also the simulation tools are generated with the help of GMF.

Another one is the PRISMA component system [21], which core is also described using EMF and development tools are again generated. PRISMA describes software architectures, heavily employing concepts of aspect-oriented development (again, however, no runtime features, nor implementation of primitive components is taken into account). The core of the system is also described using EMF and development tools are again generated.

The component model of Fractal [4] is primarily defined by Java API with semantics description in plain English (Section 2.2). All the tools for developing and managing components were designed and implemented ad hoc (even the development visual tool). Recently, initiatives to design a meta-model of Fractal were announced with the aim to exploit potential benefits (an initial version of the meta-model and tools can be already found in the Fractal SVN [12]).

Also outside the software components community, strong tendencies to move to the meta-model-based definition can be currently witnessed. First, there is a bunch of MDA-based frameworks for developing applications. An example of such a framework is AndroMDA [1]. It is a generator framework which transforms models (primarily UML ones) into an implementation. It supports transformations into technologies like Spring, JB, .NET, Hibernate and Struts; moreover, thanks to the modular design of AndroMDA, it is possible to add new transformations to support other models and target platforms.

Another approach of employing meta-models is used in Software Factories (SF) [11]. For specifying meta-models and DSLs, SF do not use specifically MOF, but the overall approach is similar. A software factory is based on three main concepts — software product line, model-driven development, and component-based development. In short, a software factory is a model-driven product line, which, based on models and domain specific languages (DSL), produces specific types of products (from a single product family). The developer of a particular software factory designs a software template (containing definitions of meta-models, transformation, DSLs, etc.) and this software template is loaded as a plugin into an IDE. Consequently, the IDE becomes the software factory. For specifying meta-models and DSLs, SF do not use specifically MOF, but the overall approach is similar.

A similar functionality is provided by openArchitectureWare [20]. It is a modular MDA/MDD framework built with help of EMF. While SF are only an generic approach, openArchitectureWare is specific framework with more general goals, i.e. to support definition of any kinds of models, their transformations and validation. It is built using EMF and also the Eclipse platform.

## 5   Conclusion

In this paper, based on our experience gained while designing and developing the component systems SOFA and SOFA 2 and also participating in the Q-ImPrESS international project, we discussed and presented the power of MOF-based models and meta-models applied in designing component systems. We argued that its usage significantly reduces the time necessary to develop supporting tools. Advantageously, since the interfaces of these tools follow standards, it is much more easy to provide interoperability among different component systems and their tools. The key advantage we experienced and appreciated was the lucidity of the meta-model, allowing to immediately see the context and consequences of any proposed modification; this very much helps with achieving and maintaining the component model consistency. This is mostly because the meta-model formally in an easy-to-read and comprehend way defines the semantic relations among the component model abstractions — in many cases no additional description in plain English is required.

## Acknowledgments

This work was partially supported by the Czech Academy of Sciences project 1ET400300504.

## References

1. Allen, R.: A Formal Approach to Software Architecture, PhD thesis, School of Computer Science, Carnegie Mellon University (1997)

2. AndroMDA, `http://galaxy.andromda.org/`
3. Becker, S., Koziolek, H., Reussner, R.: Model-Based Performance Prediction with the Palladio Component Model. In: Proceedings of WASP 2007, Buenos Aires, Argentina (February 2007)
4. Brunneton, E., Coupaye, T., Stefani, J.B.: Recursive and Dynamic Software Composition with Sharing. In: Proceedings of WCOP 2002, Malaga, Spain (June 2002)
5. Bulej, L., Bures, T., Coupaye, T., Decky, M., Jezek, P., Parizek, P., Plasil, F., Poch, T., Rivierre, N., Sery, O., Tuma, P.: CoCoME in fractal. In: Rausch, A., Reussner, R., Mirandola, R., Plášil, F. (eds.) The Common Component Modeling Example. LNCS, vol. 5153, pp. 357–387. Springer, Heidelberg (2008)
6. Bures, T., Decky, M., Hnetynka, P., Kofron, J., Parizek, P., Plasil, F., Poch, T., Sery, O., Tuma, P.: CoCoME in SOFA. In: Rausch, A., Reussner, R., Mirandola, R., Plášil, F. (eds.) The Common Component Modeling Example. LNCS, vol. 5153, pp. 388–417. Springer, Heidelberg (2008)
7. Bures, T., Hnetynka, P., Plasil, F.: SOFA 2.0: Balancing Advanced Features in a Hierarchical Component Model. In: Proceedings of SERA 2006, Seattle, USA. IEEE CS, Los Alamitos (2006)
8. Eclipse Modeling Framework, `http://eclipse.org/emf`
9. Garlan, D., Monroe, R.T., Wile, D.: Acme: Architectural Description of Component-based systems. In: Foundation of Component-based Systems. Cambridge Univ. Press, Cambridge (2000)
10. Graphical Modeling Framework, `http://eclipse.org/gmf`
11. Greenfield, J., Short, K., Cook, S., Kent, S.: Software factories: assembling applications with patterns, models, frameworks and tools. Wiley Publishing, Chichester (2004)
12. Fractal website, `http://fractal.ow2.org/`
13. Hnetynka, P., Pise, M.: Hand-written vs. MOF-based Metadata Repositories: The SOFA Experience. In: Proceedings of ECBS 2004, Brno, Czech Rep. IEEE CS, Los Alamitos (2004)
14. Magee, J., Kramer, J.: Dynamic Structure in Software Architectures. In: Proceedings of FSE'4, San Francisco, USA (October 1996)
15. Object Management Group: CORBA Components, v 3.0, OMG document formal/02-06-65 (Jun 2002)
16. Object Management Group: Model Driven Architecture (MDA), OMG document ormsc/01-07-01 (July 2001)
17. Object Management Group: MOF 2.0 Core, OMG document ptc/03-10-04 (October 2004)
18. Object Management Group: MOF QVT, OMG document ptc/07-07-07 (July 2007)
19. van Ommering, R., van der Linden, F., Kramer, J., Magee, J.: The Koala Component Model for Consumer Electronics Software. IEEE Computer 33(3), 78–85 (2000)
20. OpenArchitectureWare, `http://www.openarchitectureware.org/`
21. Perez, J., Ali, N., Carsi, J.A., Ramos, I.: Designing Software Architectures with an Aspect-Oriented Architecture Description Language. In: Gorton, I., Heineman, G.T., Crnković, I., Schmidt, H.W., Stafford, J.A., Szyperski, C., Wallnau, K. (eds.) CBSE 2006. LNCS, vol. 4063, pp. 123–138. Springer, Heidelberg (2006)
22. Plasil, F., Balek, D., Janecek, R.: SOFA/DCUP: Architecture for Component Trading and Dynamic Updating. In: Proceedings of ICCDS 1998, Annapolis, USA (May 1998)
23. Q-ImPrESS, `http://www.q-impress.eu/`

# Closely Spaced Multipath Channel Estimation in CDMA Networks Using Divided Difference Filter

Zahid Ali, Mohamed A. Deriche, and M. Adnan Landolsi

King Fahd University of Petroleum and Minerals, Dhahran 31261, Saudi Arabia
{zalikhan,mderiche,andalusi}@kfupm.edu.sa
http://www.kfupm.edu.sa

**Abstract.** We investigate time delay and channel gain estimation for multipath fading Code Division Multiple Access (CDMA) signals using the second order Divided Difference Filter (DDF). We consider the case of paths that are a fraction of chip apart, also knwon as closely spaced paths. Given the nonlinear dependency of the channel parameters on the received signals in multiuser/multipath scenarios, we show that the DDF achieves better performance than its linear counterparts. The DDF, which is a derivative-free Kalman filtering approach, avoids the errors associated with linearization in the conventional Extended Kalman Filter (EKF). The Numerical results also show that the proposed DDF is simpler to implement, and more resilient to near-far interference in CDMA networks and is able to track closly spaced paths.

**Keywords:** CDMA Channel Estimation, Non-linear filtering, Kalman filters, closely spaced multipaths, Multiple Access Interference.

## 1 Introduction

Research in time delay estimation has attracted a lot of attraction in the past few years. Time delay estimation techniques are used in numerous applications such a radiolocation, radar, sonar, seismology, geophysics, ultrasonic, to mention a few. In most applications, the estimated parameters are fed into subsequent processing blocks of communication systems to detect, identify, and locate radiating sources.

Direct-sequence code-division multiple-access technology includes higher bandwidth efficiency which translates into capacity increases, speech privacy, immunity to multipath fading and interference, and universal frequency reuse [1,2], over existing and other proposed technologies make it a popular choice. As with all cellular systems, CDMA suffers from multiple-access interference (MAI). In CDMA, however, the effects of the MAI are more considerable since the frequency band is being shared by all the users who are separated by the use of the distinct pseudonoise (PN) spreading codes. These PN codes of the different users are non-orthogonal giving rise to the interference, which is considered to be the main factor limiting the capacity in DS-CDMA systems.

T.-h. Kim et al. (Eds.): ASEA 2008, CCIS 30, pp. 55–65, 2009.

Accurate channel parameter estimation for CDMA signals impaired by multipath fading and multiple access interference (MAI) is an active research field that continues to draw attention in the CDMA literature. In particular, the joint estimation of the arriving multi-path time delays and corresponding channel tap gains for closely-spaced (within a chip interval) delay profiles is quite challenging, and has led the development of several joint multiuser parameter estimators, e.g., [3,4]. These have been extended to the case of multipath channels with constant channel taps and constant or slowly varying time delays [7]. An attempt at extending subspace methods to tracking time delays was given in [6], On the other hand, time delay trackers based on the Delay Lock Loop (DLL) combined with interference cancellation techniques have also been developed for multiuser cases [10]. Near-far resistant time delay estimators are not only critical for accurate multi-user data detection, but also as a supporting technology for time-of-arrival based radiolocation applications in CDMA cellular networks [5,8-10]. The maximum-likelihood-based technique has been employed in [11], and [12] for single-user channel and/or multiuser channel estimation with training symbols or pilots.

The Kalman filter framework based methods were considered in [10, 13-16], where Extended Kalman Filter (EKF) and Unscented Kalman Filter (UKF) has been applied to parameter estimations. Many of the algorithms presented in previous work have focused on single-user and/or single-path propagation models. However, in practice, the arriving signal typically consists of several epochs from different users, and it becomes therefore necessary to consider multi-user/multipath channel models. In this paper, we present a joint estimation algorithm for channel coefficients and time delays in a multipath CDMA environment using a non-linear filtering approach based on the second order Divided Difference Filter (DDF) with a particular emphasis on closely spaced paths in a multipath fading channel.

The rest of the article is organized as follows. In Section 2, the signal and channel models are presented. Section 3 provides a description of the nonlinear filtering method used for multiuser parameter estimation that utilizes Divided Difference Filter. Section 4 describes computer simulation and performance discussion followed by the conclusion.

## 2   Channel and Signal Model

We consider a typical asynchronous CDMA system model where K users transmit over an M-path fading channel. The received baseband signal sampled at $t = lT_s$ is given by

$$r(l) = \sum_{k=1}^{K} \sum_{i=1}^{M} c_{k,i}(l) d_{k,m_l} a_k(l - m_l T_b - \tau_{k,i}(l)) + n(l) \tag{1}$$

where $c_{k,i}(l)$ represents the complex channel coefficients, $d_{k,m_l}$ is the $m$th symbol transmitted by the $k$th user, $m_l = [(l - \tau_k(l)/T_b]$, $T_b$ is the symbol interval,

$a_k(l)$ is the spreading waveform used by the $k$th user, $\tau_{k,i}(l)$ is the time delay associated with the $i$th path of the $k$th user, and $n(l)$ represents Additive White Gaussian Noise (AWGN) assumed to have a zero mean and variance $\sigma^2 = E[|n(l)|^2] = N_0/T_s$ where $T_s$ is the sampling time.

As in [13], in order to use a Kalman filtering approach, we adopt a state-space model representation where the unknown channel parameters (path delays and gains) to be estimated are given by the following $2KM \times 1$ vector,

$$x = [c \, ; \, \tau] \tag{2}$$

with $c = [c_{11}, c_{12}, ..., c_{1M}, c_{21}, ..., c_{2M}, ..., c_{K1}, ..., c_{KM}]^T$
and $\tau = [\tau_{11}, \tau_{12}, ..., \tau_{1M}, \tau_{21}, ..., \tau_{2M}, ..., \tau_{K1}, ..., \tau_{KM}]^T$

The complex-valued channel amplitudes and real-valued time delays of the K users are assumed to obey a Gauss- Markov dynamic channel model, i.e.

$$c(l+1) = F_c c(l) + v_c(l)$$

$$\tau(l+1) = F_\tau \tau(l) + v_\tau(l)$$

where $F_c$ and $F_\tau$ are $KM \times KM$ state transition matrices for the amplitudes and time delays respectively whereas $v_c(l)$ and $v_\tau(l)$ are $K \times 1$ mutually independent Gaussian random vectors with zero mean and covariance given by $E\{v_c(i)v_c^T(j)\} = \delta_{ij}Q_c$, $E\{v_\tau(i)v_\tau^T(j)\} = \delta_{ij}Q_\tau$, $E\{v_c(i)v_\tau^T(j)\} = 0 \, \forall i,j$ with $Q_c = \sigma_c^2 I$ and $Q_\tau = \sigma_\tau^2 I$ are the covariance matrices of the process noise $v_c$ and $v_\tau$ respectively, and $\delta_{ij}$ is the two-dimensional Kronecker delta function equal to 1 for $i = j$ , and 0 otherwise.

Using (2), the state model can be written as

$$x(l+1) = Fx(l) + v(l) \tag{3}$$

where
$F = \begin{bmatrix} F_c & 0 \\ 0 & F_\tau \end{bmatrix}$, $v = [v_c^T \, v_\tau^T]$, $Q = \begin{bmatrix} Q_c & 0 \\ 0 & Q_\tau \end{bmatrix}$ are $2KM \times 2KM$ state transition matrix, $2KM \times 1$ process noise vector with mean of zero and covariance matrix respectively. The scalar measurement model follows from the received signal of (1) by

$$z(l) = h(\mathbf{x}(l)) + \eta(l) \tag{4}$$

where the measurement $z(l) = r(l)$ , and
$h(x(l)) = \sum_{k=1}^{K} \sum_{i=1}^{M} c_{k,i}(l)d_{k,m_l}a_k(l - m_l T_b - \tau_{k,i}(l))$ .
The scalar measurement $z(l)$ is a nonlinear function of the state $x(l)$ . Given the state-space and measurement models, we may find the optimal estimate of $\hat{x}(l)$ denoted as $\hat{x}(l|l) = E\{x(l)|z^l\}$ , with the estimation error covariance

$$P = E\left\{ [x(l) - \hat{x}(l|l)] \, [x(l) - \hat{x}(l|l)]^T \, |z^l\right\}$$

where $z^l$ denotes the set of received samples up to time $l$, $\{z(l), z(l-1), \ldots, z(0)\}$

# 3   Parameter Estimation Using the Divided Difference Filter

For the nonlinear dynamic system model such as above, the conventional Kalman algorithm can be invoked to obtain the parameter estimates [17, 18]. The most well known application of the Kalman filter framework to nonlinear systems is the Extended Kalman filter (EKF). Even though the EKF is one of the most widely used approximate solutions for nonlinear estimation and filtering, it has some limitations [17]. Firstly, the EKF only uses the first order terms of the Taylor series expansion of the nonlinear functions which often introduces large errors in the estimated statistics of the posterior distributions especially when the effects of the higher order terms of the Taylor series expansion becomes significant. Secondly, linearized transformations are only reliable if the error propagation can be well approximated by a linear function. If this condition does not hold, the linearized approximation can be extremely poor. At best, this undermines the performance of the filter. At worst, it causes its estimates to diverge altogether. And also linearization can be applied only if the Jacobian matrix exists. However, this is not always the case. Some systems contain discontinuities, others have singularities. Calculating Jacobian matrices can be very difficult.

DDF, unlike EKF, is a Sigma Point Filter (SPF) where the filter linearizes the nonlinear dynamic and measurement functions by using an interpolation formula through systematically chosen sigma points. The linearization is based on polynomial approximations of the nonlinear transformations that are obtained by Stirling's interpolation formula, rather than the derivative-based Taylor series approximation [18]. Conceptually, the implementation principle resembles that of the EKF, however, it is significantly simpler because uses a finite number of functional evaluations instead of analytical derivatives. It is not necessary to formulate the Jacobian and/or Hessian matrices of partial derivatives of the nonlinear dynamic and measurement equations. Thus, the new nonlinear state filter, Divided Difference Filter (DDF), can also replace the Extended Kalman Filter (EKF) and its higher-order estimators in practical real-time applications that require accurate estimation, but less computational cost. The derivative free, deterministic sampling based DDF outperform the EKF in terms of estimation accuracy, filter robustness and ease of implementation.

## 3.1   Overview of DDF Algorithm

Consider a nonlinear function, $\mathbf{y} = \mathbf{h}(\mathbf{x})$ with mean $\bar{\mathbf{x}}$ and covariance $\mathbf{P_{xx}}$. If the function $\mathbf{h}$ is analytic, then the multi-dimensional Taylor series expansion of a random variable $\mathbf{x}$ about the mean $\bar{\mathbf{x}}$ is given by the following [18]

$$\mathbf{y} \simeq \mathbf{h}(\bar{\mathbf{x}} + \Delta \mathbf{x}) = \mathbf{h}(\mathbf{x}) + D_{\Delta x}\mathbf{h} + \frac{1}{2!}D_{\Delta x}^2\mathbf{h} + \frac{1}{3!}D_{\Delta x}^3\mathbf{h} + \cdots$$

where $D_{\Delta \mathbf{x}}^i \mathbf{h}$ is the total derivative of $\mathbf{h}(\mathbf{x})$ given by

$$D_{\Delta \mathbf{x}}^i \mathbf{h} = \left( \Delta x_1 \frac{\partial}{\partial x_1} + \Delta x_2 \frac{\partial}{\partial x_2} + \ldots + \Delta x_n \frac{\partial}{\partial x_n} \right)^i \mathbf{h}(\mathbf{x}) \Bigg|_{\mathbf{x}=\bar{\mathbf{x}}}$$

The first and second order operators can be written as

$$D_{\Delta \mathbf{x}}h = \left( \sum_{p=1}^{n} \Delta x_p \frac{\partial}{\partial x_p} \right) h(\mathbf{x}) \Bigg|_{\mathbf{x}=\bar{\mathbf{x}}}$$

$$D_{\Delta x}^2 h = \left( \sum_{p=1}^{n} \sum_{q=1}^{n} \Delta x_p \Delta x_q \frac{\partial}{\partial x_p \partial x_q} \right) h(\mathbf{x}) \Bigg|_{\mathbf{x}=\bar{\mathbf{x}}}$$

The second order divided difference approximation of the function is formulated by using the vector form of Stirling's interpolation formula, which is similar to the extension of the Taylor series approximation

$$y \simeq h(\bar{\mathbf{x}}) + \tilde{D}_{\Delta \mathbf{x}}h + \frac{1}{2!}\tilde{D}_{\Delta \mathbf{x}}^2 h$$

where the operators $\tilde{D}_{\Delta \mathbf{x}}$ and $\tilde{D}_{\Delta \mathbf{x}}^2$ are defined as

$$\tilde{D}_{\Delta \mathbf{x}}h = \frac{1}{\gamma} \left( \sum_{p=1}^{n} \Delta x_p \mu_p \delta_p \right) h(\bar{\mathbf{x}})$$

$$\tilde{D}_{\Delta \mathbf{x}}^2 h = \frac{1}{\gamma^2} \left( \sum_{p=1}^{n} \Delta x_p^2 \delta_p^2 + \sum_{p=1}^{n} \sum_{q=1,p\neq q}^{n} \Delta x_p \Delta x_q (\mu_p \delta_p)(\mu_q \delta_q) \right) h(\bar{\mathbf{x}})$$

where $\gamma$ is an interval of length, taken as $\gamma = \sqrt{3}$ for a Gaussian distribution and $\delta_p$ and $\mu_p$ denote the partial difference operator and the partial average operator respectively. The second order DDF algorithm is shown in Table 1.

## 4    Application to Channel Estimation with Multipath/ Multiuser Model

We have simulated a CDMA system with varying number of users and with multipaths using DDF. The delays are assumed to be constant during one

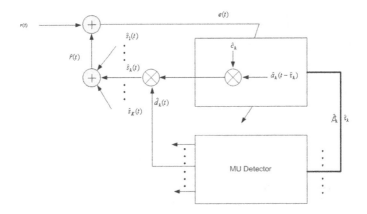

**Fig. 1.** Multiuser parameter estimation receiver

**Table 1.** UKF Algorithm

---

1. Initialization:

$\hat{\mathbf{x}}_k = E[\mathbf{x}_k]$

$\mathbf{P}_k = E\left[(\mathbf{x}_k - \hat{\mathbf{x}}_k)(\mathbf{x}_k - \hat{\mathbf{x}}_k)^T\right]$

2. Square Cholesky factorizations:

$\mathbf{P}_0 = \mathbf{S_x}\mathbf{S_x}^T,$

$\mathbf{Q}_k = \mathbf{S_w}\mathbf{S_w}^T,$

$\mathbf{R} = \mathbf{S_v}\mathbf{S_v}^T$

$\mathbf{S}_{x\hat{x}}^{(2)}(k+1) = \frac{\sqrt{\gamma-1}}{2\gamma}\left\{\mathbf{f}_i(\hat{\mathbf{x}}_k + h\mathbf{s}_{x,j}, \bar{\mathbf{w}}_k) + \mathbf{f}_i(\hat{\mathbf{x}}_k - h\mathbf{s}_{x,j}, \bar{\mathbf{w}}_k) - 2\mathbf{f}_i(\hat{\mathbf{x}}_k, \bar{\mathbf{w}}_k)\right\}$

$\mathbf{S}_{xw}^{(2)}(k+1) = \frac{\sqrt{\gamma-1}}{2\gamma}\left\{\mathbf{f}_i(\hat{\mathbf{x}}_k, \bar{\mathbf{w}}_k + h\mathbf{s}_{w,j}) + \mathbf{f}_i(\hat{\mathbf{x}}_k, \bar{\mathbf{w}}_k - h\mathbf{s}_{w,j}) - 2\mathbf{f}_i(\hat{\mathbf{x}}_k, \bar{\mathbf{w}}_k)\right\}$

3. State and covariance Propagation:

$\hat{\mathbf{x}}_{k+1}^- = \frac{\gamma-(n_x+n_w)}{\gamma}\mathbf{f}(\hat{\mathbf{x}}_k, \bar{\mathbf{w}}_k)$

$\quad + \frac{1}{2\gamma}\sum_{p=1}^{n_x}\left\{\mathbf{f}(\hat{\mathbf{x}}_k + h\mathbf{s}_{s,p}, \bar{\mathbf{w}}_k) + \mathbf{f}_i(\hat{\mathbf{x}}_k - h\mathbf{s}_{s,j}, \bar{\mathbf{w}}_k)\right\}$

$\quad + \frac{1}{2\gamma}\sum_{p=1}^{n_x}\left\{\mathbf{f}(\hat{\mathbf{x}}_k, \bar{\mathbf{w}}_k + h\mathbf{s}_{w,p}) + \mathbf{f}_i(\hat{\mathbf{x}}_k, \bar{\mathbf{w}}_k - h\mathbf{s}_{s,p})\right\}$

$\mathbf{S_x}^-(k+1) = \left[\mathbf{S}_{x\hat{x}}^{(1)}(k+1)\ \ \mathbf{S}_{xw}^{(1)}(k+1)\ \ \mathbf{S}_{x\hat{x}}^{(2)}(k+1)\ \ \mathbf{S}_{xw}^{(2)}(k+1)\right]$

$\mathbf{S_x}^-(k+1) = \left[\mathbf{S}_{x\hat{x}}^{(1)}(k+1)\ \ \mathbf{S}_{xw}^{(1)}(k+1)\ \ \mathbf{S}_{x\hat{x}}^{(2)}(k+1)\ \ \mathbf{S}_{xw}^{(2)}(k+1)\right]^T$

$\mathbf{P}_{k+1}^- = \mathbf{S_x}^-(k+1)(\mathbf{S_x}^-(k+1))^T$

4. Observation and Innovation Covariance Propagation:

$\hat{\mathbf{y}}_{k+1}^- = \frac{\gamma-(n_x+n_v)}{\gamma}\mathbf{h}(\hat{\mathbf{x}}_{k+1}^-, \bar{\mathbf{v}}_{k+1})$

$\quad + \frac{1}{2\gamma}\sum_{p=1}^{n_x}\left\{\mathbf{h}(\hat{\mathbf{x}}_{k+1}^- + h\mathbf{s}_{x,p}^-, \bar{\mathbf{v}}_{k+1}) + \mathbf{h}(\hat{\mathbf{x}}_{k+1}^- - h\mathbf{s}_{x,p}^-, \bar{\mathbf{v}}_{k+1})\right\}$

$\quad + \frac{1}{2\gamma}\sum_{p=1}^{n_x}\left\{\mathbf{h}(\hat{\mathbf{x}}_{k+1}^-, \bar{\mathbf{v}}_{k+1} + h\mathbf{s}_{v,p}) + \mathbf{h}(\hat{\mathbf{x}}_{k+1}^-, \bar{\mathbf{v}}_{k+1} - h\mathbf{s}_{v,p})\right\}$

$\mathbf{P}_{k+1}^{vv} = \mathbf{S}_v(k+1)\mathbf{S}_v^T(k+1)$

$\mathbf{P}_{k+1}^{xy} = \mathbf{S}_{\hat{x}}^{(1)}(k+1)\left(\mathbf{S}_{y\hat{x}}^{(1)}(k+1)\right)^T$

5. Update:

$\mathbf{K}_{k+1} = \mathbf{P}_{k+1}^{xy}(\mathbf{P}_{k+1}^{vv})^{-1}$

$\hat{\mathbf{x}}_{k+1}^+ = \hat{\mathbf{x}}_{k+1}^- + \mathbf{K}_{k+1}\left(\mathbf{y}_{k+1} - \hat{\mathbf{y}}_{k+1}\right)$

$\mathbf{P}_{k+1}^+ = \mathbf{P}_{k+1}^- - \mathbf{K}_{k+1}\mathbf{P}_{k+1}^{vv}\mathbf{K}_{k+1}^T$

---

measurement. For the state space model we assumed $\mathbf{F} = 0.999\mathbf{I}$ and $\mathbf{Q} = 0.001\mathbf{I}$ where $\mathbf{I}$ is the identity matrix. We will be considering fading multipaths and multiuser environment with 2, 5 and 10 user scenario. The SNR at the receiver of the weaker user is taken to be of 10 dB. The near far ratio of 20 dB has been

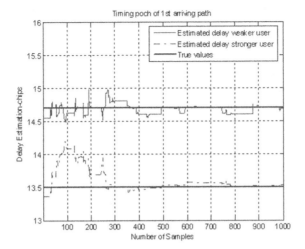

**Fig. 2.** Timing epoch estimation for first arriving path with a five-user/ three-path channel model (with 1/2-chip path separation)

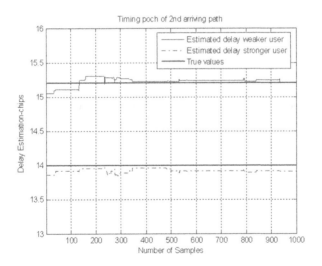

**Fig. 3.** Timing epoch estimation for second arriving path with a five-user/ three-path channel model (with 1/2-chip path separation)

assumed with the power of the strong user is $P_1 = 1$ and that of the weak user is $P_1/10$ . We note that the data bits,$d_{k,m}$ , are not included in the estimation process, but are assumed unknown a priori. In the simulations, we assume that the data bits are available from decision-directed adaptation, where the symbols $d_{k,m}$ are replaced by the $\hat{d}_{k,m}$ decisions shown in Figure 1. We also considered the special case of closely spaced multipaths.

Figures 2, 3 and 4 show the timing epoch in a multiuser scenario with three multipaths with the path separation of 1/2 chip. We have considered the case of the weaker user and have compared it with the stronger user. Proposed estimator converges to the close to the true value approximately in 6-8 symbols even in the presence of MAI and is able to track desired user delay even when the paths are closely spaced. Figures 5, 6 show the mean square error for channel coefficients for the first arriving path and delay estimation in a fifteen user two path scenario. These demonstrate that the estimated values converge to the true values within

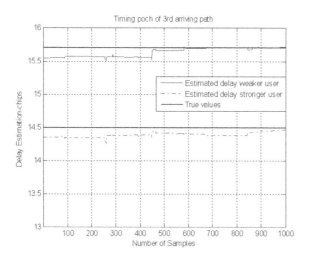

**Fig. 4.** Timing epoch estimation for third arriving path with a five-user/ three-path channel model (with 1/2-chip path separation)

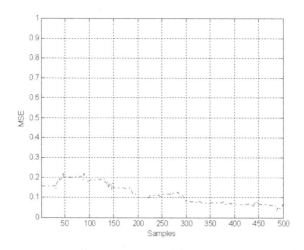

**Fig. 5.** MSE of the channel coefficients for first arriving path with a ten-user/ two-path channel model

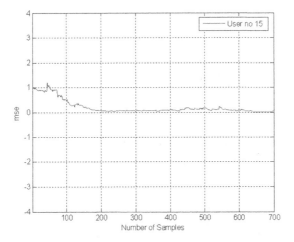

**Fig. 6.** MSE of the first arriving path in a fifteen user/two path

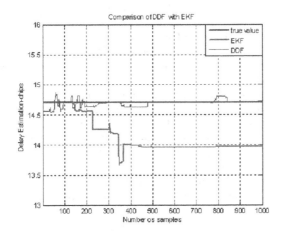

**Fig. 7.** Comparison of the DDF with EKF in terms of timing epoch estimation for first arriving path with a five-user/ three-path channel model (with 1/2-chip path separation

6-8 symbols. Now if we compare the UKF algorithm [10] with the DDF algorithm, we see that the performance of the two is nearly same. This is demonstrated in fig. 7. It is due to the fact that DDF is based on the derivative approximation on Stirling formula whereas UKF is based on Taylor series approximation for the nonlinear function.

## 5   Conclusion

This paper presented a nonlinear filtering approach for CDMA time delay and channel gain estimation over multipath fading based on the DDF. It was shown that the DDF achieves better performance and enjoys moderate complexity compared to the (linearized) EKF algorithm because of the nonlinear dependency of the channel parameters on the received signals in multiuser/multipath scenarios. A general derivation the processing steps was presented, followed by a specialization to the case of time delay and channel gain estimation for multipath CDMA signals, with particular focus on closely-spaced multipath epochs. The numerical results showed that the DDF is quite robust vis-a-vis near-far multiple-access interference, and can also track a given signal epoch even in the presence of other closely-spaced multipaths (within a fraction of a chip).

# References

1. Gilhousen, H.F., et al.: On the capacity of a cellular CDMA system. IEEE Transactions on Vehicular Technology 40(2), 303–312 (1991)
2. Pickholtz, R.L., Milstein, L.B., Schilling, D.L.: Spread spectrum for mobile communications. IEEE Transactions on Vehicular Technology 40(2), 313–322 (1991)
3. Iltis, R.A., Mailaender, L.: An adaptive multiuser detector with joint amplitude and delay estimation. IEEE Journal on Select Areas Communications 12(5), 774–785 (1994)
4. Radovic, A.: An iterative near-far resistant algorithm for joint parameter estimation in asynchronous CDMA systems. In: Proceedings of 5th IEEE Intenational Symposium on Personal, Indoor, Mobile Radio Communications, vol. 1, pp. 199–203 (1994)
5. Strm, E.G., Parkvall, S., Miller, S.L., Ottersten, B.E.: Propagation delay estimation in asynchronous direct-sequence code-division multiple access systems. IEEE Transactions on Communications 44(1), 84–93 (1996)
6. Bensley, S.E., Aazhang, B.: Subspace-based channel estimation for code division multiple access communication systems. IEEE Transactions on Communications 44(8), 1009–1020 (1996)
7. Strm, E.G., Parkvall, S., Miller, S.L., Ottersten, B.E.: DS-CDMA synchronization in time-varying fading channels. IEEE Journal on Select Areas Communications 14(8), 1636–1642 (1996)
8. Latva-aho, M., Lilleberg, J.: Delay trackers for multiuser CDMA receivers. In: Proceedings of IEEE International Conference on Universal Personal Communications, pp. 326–330 (1996)
9. Caffery Jr., J., Stüber, G.: Overview of radiolocation in CDMA cellular systems. IEEE Communication Magazine 36, 38–45 (1998)
10. Caffery Jr., J., Stüber, G.: Nonlinear Multiuser Parameter Estimation and Tracking in CDMA Systems. IEEE Transactions on Communications 48(12), 2053–2063 (2000)
11. Strm, E.G., Malmsten, F.: A maximum likelihood approach for estimating DS-CDMA multipath fading channels. IEEE Journal on Select Areas Communications 18(1), 132–140 (2000)
12. Bhashyam, S., Aazhang, B.: Multiuser channel estimation and tracking for long-code CDMA systems. IEEE Transactions on Communications 50(7), 1081–1090 (2002)
13. Kim, K.J., Iltis, R.A.: Joint detection and channel estimation algorithms for QS-CDMA signals over time-varying channels. IEEE Transactions on Communications 50(5), 845–855 (2002)

14. Lakhzouri, A., Lohan, E.S., Hamila, R., Renfors, M.: Extended Kalman Filter channel estimation for line-of-sight detection in WCDMA mobile positioning. EURASIP Journal on Applied Signal Processing 2003(13), 1268–1278 (2003)
15. Klee, U., Gehrig, T.: Kalman Filters for Time Delay of Arrival-Based Source Localization. EURASIP Journal on Applied Signal Processing 2006(1), 167–167 (2006)
16. Shunlan, L., Yong, M., Haiyun, Z.: Passive location by single observer with the Unscented Kalman Filter. In: IEEE International Symposium on Microwave, Antenna, Propagation and EMC Technology for Wireless Communications, vol. 2, pp. 1186–1189 (2005)
17. Wan, E.A., Merwe, R.: Kalman Filtering and Neural Networks. In: Adaptive and Learning Systems for Signal Processing, Communications, and Control, pp. 221–280. Wiley, Chichester (2001)
18. Alfriend, K.T., Lee, D.-J.: Nonlinear Bayesian Filtering For Orbit Determination and Prediction. In: 6th US Russian Space Surveillance Workshop, St. Petersburg, Russia, pp. 22–26 (2005)

# Building "Bag of Conception" Model Based on DBpedia

Junhua Liao and Rujiang Bai

Shandong University of Technology Library Zibo 255049, China
{ljhbrj,brj}@sdut.edu.cn

**Abstract.** Text classification has been widely used to assist users with the discovery of useful information from the Internet. However, Current text classification systems are based on the "Bag ofWords" (BOW) representation, which only accounts for term frequency in the documents, and ignores important semantic relationships between key terms. To overcome this problem, previous work attempted to enrich text representation by means of manual intervention or automatic document expansion. The achieved improvement is unfortunately very limited, due to the poor coverage capability of the dictionary, and to the ineffectiveness of term expansion. Fortunately, DBpedia appeared recently which contains rich semantic information. In this paper, we proposed a method compiling DBpedia knowledge into document representation to improve text classification. It facilitates the integration of the rich knowledge of DBpedia into text documents, by resolving synonyms and introducing more general and associative concepts. To evaluate the performance of the proposed method, we have performed an empirical evaluation using SVM calssifier on several real data sets. The experimental results show that our proposed framework, which integrates hierarchical relations, synonym and associative relations with traditional text similarity measures based on the BOW model, does improve text classification performance significantly.

**Keywords:** Text classification; DBpedia; Semantic-enriched Representation; SVM.

## 1 Introduction

With the quick increase of information and knowledge, automatically classifying text documents is becoming a hotspot of knowledge management. A critical capability of knowledge management systems is to classify the text documents into different categories, which are meaningful to users. Traditional document classification algorithms are based on the "Bag ofWords" (BOW) approach, which represents a document as a vector of weighted occurrence frequencies of individual terms. However, the BOW representation is limited, as it only accounts for term frequency in the documents, and ignores important semantic relationships between key terms. To break through this limitation, work has been done to exploit ontologies for content-based classification of large document corpora. The authors in [1,2] successfully integrated theWordNet resource for a document categorization task. They evaluated their methods on the Reuters corpus [3], and showed improved classification results with respect to the Rocchio andWidrow-Hoff algorithms. In contrast to our approach, Rodriguez et al. [1] and Urena-Lopez et al. [2] utilized WordNet in a supervised scenario without

T.-h. Kim et al. (Eds.): ASEA 2008, CCIS 30, pp. 66–78, 2009.

employing WordNet relations such as hypernyms and associative relations. Furthermore, they built the term vectors manually. The authors in [4] utilized WordNet synsets as features for document representation, and subsequent clustering. Word sense disambiguation was not performed, and WordNet synsets actually decreased clustering performance. Hotho et al. [5] integrated WordNet knowledge into text clustering, and investigated word sense disambiguation strategies and feature weighting schema by considering the hyponym relations derived from WordNet. Experimental results on the Reuters Corpus have shown improvements in comparison with the best baseline. However, due to the limited coverage of WordNet, the word sense disambiguation effect is quite limited. In addition, WordNet does not provide associative terms as Wikipedia.

Gabrilovich et al. [6,7] proposed and evaluated a method to render text classification systems with encyclopedic knowledge, namely Wikipedia and ODP. They first built an auxiliary text classifier that could match documents with the most relevant articles in Wikipedia. Then, they augmented the conventional BOW representation with new features, corresponding to the concepts (mainly the titles) represented by the relevant Wikipedia articles. Empirical results showed that this representation improved text categorization performance across a diverse collection of data sets. However, the authors did not make full use of the rich relations of Wikipedia, such as hyponyms, synonyms and associated terms. In addition, as pointed out by the authors, the feature generation process can introduce a lot of noise, although the feature selection step can mitigate this problem. In this paper, we tackle these issues.

DBpedia is a community effort to extract structured information from Wikipedia and to make this information available on the Web. It owns a shallow, cross-domain ontology. In our work, we compile DBpedia[8] knowledge into document representation. It facilitates the integration of the rich knowledge of DBpedia into text documents, by resolving synonyms and introducing more general and associative concepts. To evaluate the performance of the proposed method, we have performed an empirical evaluation using SVM[9] on several real data sets. The experimental results show that our proposed framework, which integrates hierarchical relations, synonym and associative relations with traditional text similarity measures based on the BOW model, does improve text classification performance significantly.

The rest of the paper is organized as follows. Section 2 describes DBpedia. In Sect. 3, our methods for compiling DBpedia knowledge into document representation are discussed. The experimental setting and results are discussed in Sect. 4. We conclude our paper in Sect. 5.

## 2   DBpedia

DBpedia is a community effort to extract structured information from Wikipedia and to make this information available on the Web. DBpedia allows you to ask sophisticated queries against Wikipedia, and to link other data sets on the Web to Wikipedia data.

*The DBpedia Knowledge Base*
Knowledge bases are playing an increasingly important role in enhancing the intelligence of Web and enterprise search and in supporting information integration. Today, most knowledge bases cover only specific domains, are created by relatively small groups of knowledge engineers, and are very cost intensive to keep up-to-date as domains change. At the same time, Wikipedia has grown into one of the central knowledge sources of mankind, maintained by thousands of contributors. The

DBpedia project leverages this gigantic source of knowledge by extracting structured information from Wikipedia and by making this information accessible on the Web under GNU Free Documentation License.

The DBpedia knowledge base currently describes more than 2.6 million things, including at least 213,000 persons, 328,000 places, 57,000 music albums, 36,000 films, 20,000 companies. The knowledge base consists of 274 million pieces of information (RDF triples). It features labels and short abstracts for these things in 30 different languages; 609,000 links to images and 3,150,000 links to external web pages; 4,878,100 external links into other RDF datasets, 415,000 Wikipedia categories, and 75,000 YAGO categories.

The DBpedia knowledge base has several advantages over existing knowledge bases: it covers many domains; it represents real community agreement; it automatically evolve as Wikipedia changes, and it is truly multilingual. The DBpedia knowledge base allows you to ask quite surprising queries against Wikipedia, for instance "Give me all cities in New Jersey with more than 10,000 inhabitants" or "Give me all Italian musicians from the 18th century". Altogether, the use cases of the DBpedia knowledge base are widespread and range from enterprise knowledge management, over Web search to revolutionizing Wikipedia search.

*Nucleus for the Web of Data*

Within the W3C Linking Open Data (LOD) community effort, an increasing number of data providers have started to publish and interlink data on the Web according to Tim Berners-Lee's Linked Data principles. The resulting Web of Data currently consists of several billion RDF triples and covers domains such as geographic information, people, companies, online communities, films, music, books and scientific publications. In addition to publishing and interlinking datasets, there is also ongoing work on Linked Data browsers, Linked Data crawlers, Web of Data search engines and other applications that consume Linked Data from the Web.

The DBpedia knowledge base is served as Linked Data on the Web. As DBpedia defines Linked Data URIs for millions of concepts, various data providers have started to set RDF links from their data sets to DBpedia, making DBpedia one of the central interlinking-hubs of the ermerging Web of Data.

*The DBpedia Ontology*

The DBpedia Ontology is a shallow, cross-domain ontology, which has been manually created based on the most commonly used infoboxes within Wikipedia. The ontology currently covers over 170 classes which form a subsumption hierarchy and has 940 properties.

With the DBpedia 3.2 release, it introduced a new infobox extraction method which is based on hand-generated mappings of Wikipedia infoboxes to the DBpedia ontology. The mappings define fine-granular rules on how to parse infobox values. The mappings also adjust weaknesses in the Wikipedia infobox system, like having different infoboxes for the same class (currently 350 Wikipedia templates are mapped to 170 ontology classes), using different property names for the same property (currently 2350 template properties are mapped to 940 ontology properties), and not having clearly defined datatypes for property values (the ontology used 55 different datatypes). Therefore, the instance data within the infobox ontology is much cleaner and better structured than the infobox data within the DBpedia infobox dataset which is generated using the old infobox extraction code.

Overview of the class hierarchy of the DBpedia Ontology.

The DBpedia Ontology currently contains about 882.000 instances. The table1 below lists the number of instances for several classes within the ontology:

**Table 1.** DBpedia Ontology

| Class | Instances |
| --- | --- |
| Resource(overall) | 882,000 |
| Place | 248,000 |
| Person | 214,000 |
| Work | 193,000 |
| Species | 90,000 |
| Organisation | 76,000 |
| Building | 23,000 |

*The Architecture of DBpedia*

The DBpedia RDF Data Set is hosted and published using OpenLink Virtuoso. The Virtuoso infrastructure provides access to DBpedia's RDF data via a SPARQL endpoint, alongside HTTP support for any Web client's standard GETs for HTML or RDF representations of DBpedia resources.

*Illustration of Current DBpedia Architecture*

Fig.1 gives the Current DBpedia Architecture as below:

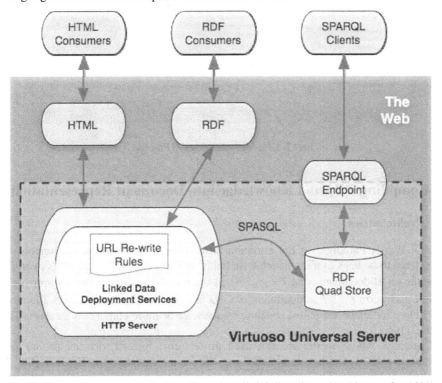

**Fig. 1.** Current DBpedia Architecture (From http://wiki.dbpedia.org/Architecture?v=1411)

Though the DBpedia RDF Data has always been housed in Virtuoso, which has supported all desired means of access since the DBpedia project began, early DBpedia releases used Pubby Linked Data Deployment services in front of the Virtuoso SPARQL endpoint.

As the project gained traction, the HTTP demands on Pubby's out-of-process Linked Data Publishing services increased, and the natural option was to take advantage of Virtuoso's SPASQL (SPARQL inside SQL) and other Linked Data Deployment features, by moving these services in-process with Virtuoso.

Fig.2 shows the DBpedia ontology imported in Protégé.

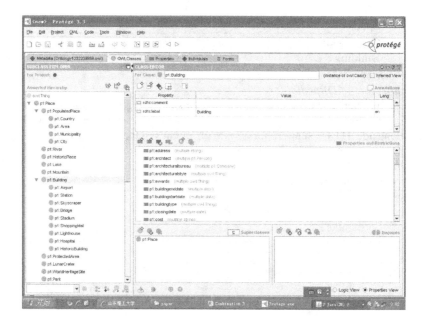

**Fig. 2.** DBpedia's ontology in Protégé

# 3   Compiling DBpedia Knowledge into Document Representation

## 3.1  Preliminaries

Bag-Of-Words Paradigm in the common term-based representation, documents are considered to be bags of terms, each term being an independent feature of its own. Let D be the set of documents and $T = \{t_1, \cdots, t_m\}$ the set of all different terms occurring in D. For each term $t \in T$ in document $d \in D$ one can define feature values functions like binary indicator variables, absolute frequencies or more elaborated measures like TFIDF [10].

Typically, whole words are not used as features. Instead, documents are first processed with stemming algorithms, e.g. the Porter stemmer for English [11]. In addition, Stopwords, i.e. words which are considered as non–descriptive within a bag–of–words approach, are typically removed. In our experiments later on, we removed stopwords from $T$, using a standard list with 571 stopwords.

*Ontologies.* The background knowledge we have exploited is given through ontologies which extracted form DBpedia. We will discuss the usage for the extraction of conceptual feature representations for text documents. The background knowledge we will exploit further on is encoded in a core ontology. For the purpose of this paper, we present some ontology definitions.

**Definition 1 (Core Ontology)**
A core ontology is a structure $O := (C, <c)$ consisting of a set C, whose elements are called concept identifiers, and a partial order $<c$ on C, called concept hierarchy or taxonomy.

**Definition 2 (Subconcepts and Superconcepts)**
If $c1 <c c2$ for any $c1, c2 \in C$, then $c1$ is a subconcept (specialization) of $c2$ and $c2$ is a superconcept (generalization) of $c1$. If $c1 <c c2$ and there exists no $c3 \in C$ with $c1 <c c3 <c c2$, then $c1$ is a direct subconcept of $c2$, and $c2$ is a direct superconcept of $c1$, denoted by $c1 < c2$.

These specialization/generalization relationships correspond to what we know as is-a vs. is-a-special-kind-of, resulting in a hierarchical arrangement of concepts. In ontologies that are more loosely defined, the hierarchy may, however, not be as explicit as is-a relationships but rather correspond to the notion of narrower-than vs. broaderthan

According to the international standard ISO 704, we provide names for the concepts (and relations). Instead of 'name', we here call them 'sign' or 'lexical entries' to better describe the functions for which they are used.

**Definition 3 (Lexicon for an Ontology)**
A lexicon for an ontology O is a tuple $Lex := (SC; RefC)$ consisting of a set SC, whose elements are called signs for concepts (symbols), and a relation $RefC \subseteq SC \times C$ called lexical reference for concepts, where $(c, c) \in RefC$ holds for all $c \in C \cap SC$. Based on RefC, for $s \in SC$ we define $RefC(s) := \{c \in C | (s,c) \in RefC\}$. Analogously, for $c \in C$ it is $Ref_C^1(c) := \{s \in SC | (s, c) \in RefC\}$. An ontology with lexicon is a pair $(O, Lex)$ where O is an ontology and Lex is a lexicon for O.

**Definition 4. Homographic concepts H**
$H := \{(c1, c2) | c1 \in O1 \wedge c2 \in O2 \wedge O1 \neq O2 \wedge (name(c1)=name(c2) \vee name(c1)$
$synonyms(c2) \vee synonyms(c1) \cap synonyms(c2) \neq )\}$
where name(c) is a function that returns the concept name, and synonyms(c) is a function that returns a set of all synonyms of a concept.

Equivalent concepts are concepts that represent the same real world entity. Homographic concepts may still contain words that refer to different real world entities, such as mouse (pointing device) vs. mouse (animal). For the scope of this work, concepts are considered to be equivalent, if they are homographic, and if their sub- or superconcepts are homographic:

**Definition 5. Equivalent concepts S**
$S : \{(c1, c2) | c1 \in O1 \wedge c2 \in O2 \wedge O1 \neq O2 \wedge (subconcepts(c1, t)$ and $subconcepts(c2, t)$ is homographic $\vee$ superconcepts(c1,t) and superconcepts(c2, t) is homographic$)\}$

where superconcepts(c, t) and subconcepts(c, t) are functions that return the set of all direct super- and sub-concepts of a given concept (with relation type t).

**Definition 6. Controlled vocabulary CV**

CV := named set of concepts c with c
: (name, definition, identifier, synonyms)

Controlled vocabularies are named lists of terms that are well defined and may have an identifier. The elements of a controlled vocabulary are called concepts.

In ontologies the concepts are linked by directed edges, thus forming a graph. The edges of an ontology specify in which way concepts are related to each other, e.g. 'is-a' or 'part-of'.

**Definition 6. Context of a concept c**

Context ccont :=synonyms(c) $\cup$

name(subconcepts(c; t)) $\cup$

name(superconcepts(c; t)) $\cup$

synonyms(subconcepts(c; t)) $\cup$

synonyms(superconcepts(c; t))

The context wcont of a word w is defined as the set of all stems for all the words that occur in the same document as w. The context also does not contain stopwords, which were already filtered out.

## 3.2 Conceptual Document Representation

To extract concepts from texts, we have developed a detailed process, that can be used with DBpedia. The overall process comprises five processing steps that are described in this section.

*Candidate Term Detection.* Due to the existence of multi-word expressions, the mapping of terms to concepts cannot be accomplished by querying the lexicon directly for the single words in the document.

We have addressed this issue by defining a candidate term detection strategy that builds on the basic assumption that finding the longest multi-word expressions that appear in the text and the lexicon will lead to a mapping to the most specific concepts. The candidate expression detection algorithm we have applied for this lookup procedure is given in algorithm 1.

The algorithm works by moving a window over the input text, analyze the window content and either decrease the window size if unsuccessful or move the window further. For English, a window size of 4 is sufficient to detect virtually all multi-word expressions.

*Syntactical Patterns Querying.* The lexicon directly for any expression in the window will result in many unnecessary searches and thereby in high computational requirements. Luckily, unnecessary search queries can be identified and avoided through an analysis of the part-of-speech (POS) tags of the words contained in the current window. Concepts are typically symbolized in texts within noun phrases. By defining appropriate POS patterns and matching the window content against these, multi-word combinations that will surely not symbolize concepts can be excluded in the first hand and different syntactic categories can be disambiguated.

**Algorithm 1.** The candidate expression detection algorithm

```
Input: document d = {w1,w2, …,wn},
Lex = (SC;RefC) and window size k ≥ 1.
i ← 1
list Ls
index-term s
while i≤n do
for j = min(k, n - i + 1) to 1 do
s ← {wi…wi+j-1}
if s ∈ SC then
save s in Ls
i ← i + j
break
else if j = 1 then
i ← i + j
end if
end for
end while
return Ls
```

*Morphological Transformations.* Typically the lexicon will not contain all inflected forms of its entries. If the lexicon interface or separate software modules are capable of performing base form reduction on the submitted query string, queries can be processed directly. For example, if the lexicon, as in most cases, does not contain such functionalities, a simple fallback strategy can be applied. Here, a separate index of stemmed forms is maintained. If a first query for the inflected forms on the original lexicon turned out unsuccessful, a second query for the stemmed expression is performed.

*Word Sense Disambiguation.* Having detected the lexical entry for an expression, this does not necessarily imply a one-to-one mapping to a concept in the ontology. Although multi-word-expression support and pos pattern matching reduce ambiguity, there may arise the need to disambiguate an expression versus multiple possible concepts. The word sense disambiguation (WSD) task is a problem in its own right and was not the focus of our work.

In our experiments, we have used three simple strategies proposed in [12] to process polysemous terms:

– The "all" strategy leaves actual disambiguation aside and uses all possible concepts.

– The "first" strategy exploits WordNet's capability to return synsets ordered with respect to usage frequency. This strategy chooses the most frequent concept in case of ambiguities. Here we replace WordNet with DBpedia.

– The "context" strategy performs disambiguation based on the degree of overlap of lexical entries for the semantic vicinity of candidate concepts and the document content as proposed in [12].

*Generalization.* The last step in the process is about going from the specific concepts found in the text to more general concept representations. Its principal idea is that if a term like 'beef' appears, one does not only represent the document by the concept corresponding to 'arrythmia', but also by the concepts corresponding to 'heart disease' and 'cardiovascular Diseases' etc. up to a certain level of generality. This is realized by compiling, for every concept, all superconcept up to a maximal distance h into the concept representation. Note that the parameter h needs to be chosen carefully as climbing up the taxonomy too far is likely to obfuscating the concept representation.

## 4   Experiments

The focus of our evaluation experiments was directed towards comparing whether SVM using the enhanced document representation would outperform the classical term representation.

### 4.1   Experimental Framework: Design and Architecture

The design of our system has the components outlined below.

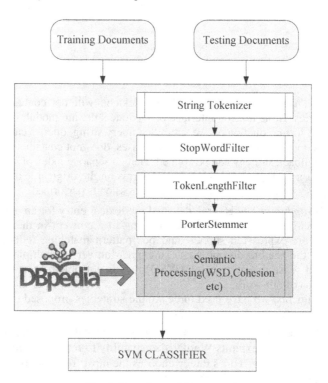

**Fig. 3.** Experimental Framework

## 4.2  Datasets and Platform

Our goal is to obtain a high performance for closely related categories. Therefore, in order to test our approach, we designed a robot to crawler a data set from Yahoo! Website. It is contained the closely related (ambiguous) categories under Science->Biology. The test categories under Science->Biology considered here for Training and Testing are: Bio-Archaeology, Bio-Informatics, Genetics, Food Science and Microbiology.

The experiments run on Pentium IV 3.0GHZ CPU, 2GB RAM platform.

The introduced method requires word stemming and POS tagging. Therefore, appropriate methods/tools for stemming and POS tagging had to be selected. This work we decided to use QTag 3.1[14] for several reasons: good accuracy (97%), performance (several MB of text per second on a Pentium 2400 MHz), Java API and the availability which is free of charge for non-commercial purposes. QTag uses a variant of the Brown/ Penn-style tagsets [15]. QTAG is in principle language independent, although this release only comes with resource files for English and German. If there is the need to use it with other languages, it can be trained using pretagged sample texts for creating the required resource files.

For word stemming different approaches exist. We used an implementation according to the Paice/Husk algorithm [16] also known as Lancaster algorithm, which is an affixremoval stemmer. Those stemmers are widely used and different implementations are available. As it's the best known implementation we used the Java adaption of the original located at the Lancaster University.

## 4.3  Results and Discussion

We have selected total of 100 documents that are not directly related but have words with cross-domain references; 20 documents fall in each of the above-mentioned categories. 50 documents have been used for training and 50 for testing in which, 10 documents from each category have been used for testing using SVM classifier without applying semantic process.

Correct: 35 out of 50 (70.00 percent accuracy)

- Confusion details, row is actual, column is predicted

**Table 2.** Confusion Matrix before Applying Semantic Processing

|   | ClassName | 0 | 1 | 2 | 3 | 4 | Total | Accuracy % |
|---|---|---|---|---|---|---|---|---|
| 0 | Bio-archaeology | 8 | . | . | 2 | . | 10 | 80.00% |
| 1 | Bio-informatics | . | 8 | 1 | 1 | . | 10 | 80.00% |
| 2 | FoodScience | . | . | 7 | 3 | . | 10 | 70.00% |
| 3 | Genetics | 2 | 1 | 2 | 5 | . | 10 | 50.00% |
| 4 | Microbiology | 2 | 1 | . | . | 7 | 10 | 70.00% |

The confusion matrix table clearly shows that because of the highly ambiguous terminologies present in Genetics category, the word probabilities are very low and hence the classifier could not find more distinctive information. Similarly, mutually distinctive words between the classes Genetics, Bio-Archaeology and Food Science are missing because of the redundant discussions or details about DNA and other genetics related information widespread in all these three categories.

Now, we have represent the document with semantic information (discussed in section 3) for all these 100 documents and repeated the same test with classifier. The same set of documents was used for training and testing.

Correct: 42 out of 50 (84.00 percent accuracy)

- Confusion details, row is actual, column is predicted

**Table 3.** Confusion Matrix after Applying Semantic Processing

|   | Class Name | 0 | 1 | 2 | 3 | 4 | Total | Accuracy % |
|---|---|---|---|---|---|---|---|---|
| 0 | Bio-archaeology | 9 | . | . | 1 | . | 10 | 90.00% |
| 1 | Bio-informatics | . | 10 | . | . | . | 10 | 100.00% |
| 2 | FoodScience | . | . | 8 | 2 | . | 10 | 80.00% |
| 3 | Genetics | 1 | . | 1 | 8 | . | 10 | 80.00% |
| 4 | Microbiology | 2 | 1 | . | . | 7 | 10 | 70.00% |

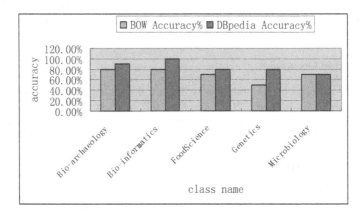

**Fig. 4.** Accuracy from Semantic Representation Terms vs. Bag of Words

The results indicate that there is a significant improvement in the classification process. We have repeated the tests 4 times with different set of documents in different categories. The percentage accuracies were 70, 62, 72 and 56 (rounded off) for all the four tests respectively when semantic processing was not applied. When semantic processing was applied, the accuracies turned out were 84, 70, 72 and 68 respectively.

It is interesting to note that all the test results show significant improvement in the accuracy, one of the cases reflects same results for experiments with-and-without using DBpedia background knowledge; that is, even after applying semantic processing, the accuracy did not differ.

We have also observed the Mutual Information displayed by our classifier platform for all the training and test cases above. Before applying semantic mapping, system has identified the words such as health, evidence and technology in mutual information though they are semantically irrelevant to the categories. When applied semantic tagging, the words such as disease, genes and infection that were more specific to the categories were picked.

## 5 Conclusion

In this paper, we have discussed a novel approach to applying DBpedia's background knowledge represent documents for boosting text categorization performance. We presented an experimental framework for applying semantic processing for classification. Although several previous works were carried on applying semantics and word sense disambiguation for information retrieval applications such as improving web searches[13], no similar experiments were done for text classification techniques. Our approach and experiments prove that applying semantic level processing and normalization help in achieving higher accuracies over classification of documents, which have words with cross category references. However, the quality of the results will be affected if the semantic mapping is done inappropriately or wrongly. The semantic mapping process is the most challenge of our current implementation. Experimentation with larger volumes of documents spanning different categories with different levels of cross category references remains an important task. For future work, we will improve our mapping Algorithm to identify positive and negative impact on the accuracy.

## References

1. de Buenaga Rodriguez, M., Gomez Hidalgo, J.M., Agudo, B.D.: Using WordNet to complement training information in text categorization. In: The 2nd international conference on recent advances in natural language processing, RANLP 1997 (1999)
2. Urena-Lopez, L.A., Buenaga, M., Gomez, J.M.: Integrating linguistic resources in TC through WSD. Comput. Hum. 35, 215–230 (2001)
3. Reuters-21578 text categorization test collection, Distribution 1.0. Reuters (1997), http://www.daviddlewis.com/resources/testcollections/reuters21578/
4. Dave, K., Lawrence, S., Pennock, D.M.: Mining the peanut gallery: opinion extraction and semantic classification of product reviews. In: Proceedings of the 12th international World Wide Web conference WWW 2003 (2003)
5. Hotho, A., Staab, S., Stumme, G.: Wordnet improves text document clustering. In: Proceedings of the semantic web workshop at SIGIR 2003 (2003)
6. Gabrilovich, E., Markovitch, S.: Feature generation for text categorization using world knowledge. In: Proceedings of the 19th international joint conference on artificial intelligence, IJCAI 2005 (2005)
7. Gabrilovich, E., Markovitch, S.: Overcoming the brittleness bottleneck using DBpedia: enhancing text categorization with encyclopedic knowledge. In: Proceedings of the 21nd AAAI conference on artificial intelligence, AAAI 2006 (2006)
8. http://dbpedia.org/
9. Vapnik, V.N.: The nature of statistical learning theory. Springer, New York (1995)

10. Salton, G.: Automatic Text Processing. Addison-Wesley Publishing Inc., Boston (1989)
11. Porter, M.F.: An algorithm for suffix stripping. Program 14(3), 130–137 (1980)
12. Hotho, A., Staab, S., Stumme, G.: Wordnet improves Text Document Clustering. In: Proc. of the Semantic Web Workshop of the 26th Annual International ACM SIGIR Conference, Toronto, Canada (2003)
13. Moldovan, D.I., Mihalcea, R.: Improving the Search on the Internet by using WordNet and lexical operators. IEEE Internet Computing 4(1), 34–43 (2000)
14. Marcus, M.P., Santorini, B., Marcinkiewicz, M.A.: Building a large annotated corpus of English: The Penn Treebank. Comput. Linguist. 19(2), 313–330 (1993)
15. Paice, C.D.: Another stemmer. SIGIR Forum 24(3), 56–61 (1990)
16. Reuters-21578 text categorization test collection, Distribution 1.0. Reuters (1997), `http://www.daviddlewis.com/resources/testcollections/reuters21578/`
17. Hersh, W., Buckley, C., Leone, T., Hickam, D.: OHSUMED: an interactive retrieval evaluation and new large test collection for research. In: Proceedings of the 17th annual internationalACM-SIGIR conference on research and development in information retrieval (SIGIR 1994), pp. 192–201 (1994)
18. Lang, K.: Newsweeder: learning to filter netnews. In: Proceedings of the 12th international conference on machine learning (ICML 1995), pp. 331–339 (1995)
19. Joachims, T.: Text categorizationwith support vectormachines: learning with many relevant features. In: Nédellec, C., Rouveirol, C. (eds.) ECML 1998. LNCS, vol. 1398, pp. 137–142. Springer, Heidelberg (1998)
20. Stumme, G., Maedche, A.: FCA-Merge: A Bottom Up Approach for Merging Ontologies. In: Proceedings of the International Joint Conference on Artificial Intelligence, Seattle, Washington, USA, pp. 225–234 (2001)
21. Noy, N.F., Musen, M.A.: SMART: Automated Support for Ontology Merging and Alignment. In: Proceedings of the KAW 1999, Banff, Alberta, Canada, Saturday 16 to Thursday 21 October (1999)
22. Noy, N.F., Musen, M.A.: Algorithm and Tool for Automated Ontology Merging and Alignment. In: Proceedings of the Seventeenth National Conference on Artificial Intelligence (AAAI-2000), Austin, TX, USA (2000)

# Study on the Performance Support Vector Machine by Parameter Optimized

Junhua Liao and Rujiang Bai

Shandong University of Technology Library Zibo 255049, China
{ljhbrj,brj}@sdut.edu.cn

**Abstract.** With the quick increase of information and knowledge, automatically classifying text documents is becoming a hotspot of knowledge management. Standard machine learning techniques like support vector machines(SVM) and related large margin methods have been successfully applied for this task. Unfortunately, the high dimensionality of input feature vectors impacts on the classification speed. The kernel parameters setting for SVM in a training process impacts on the classification accuracy. Feature selection is another factor that impacts classification accuracy. The objective of this work is to reduce the dimension of feature vectors, optimizing the parameters to improve the SVM classification accuracy and speed. In order to improve classification speed we spent rough sets theory to reduce the feature vector space. We present a genetic algorithm approach for feature selection and parameters optimization to improve classification accuracy. Experimental results indicate our method is more effective than traditional SVM methods and other traditional methods.

**Keywords:** Document Classification; Support Vector Machine; Rough Sets; Genetic Algorithms.

## 1 Introduction

Due to the rapid growth in textual data, automatic methods for organizing the data are needed. Automatic document categorization is one of these methods. It automatically assigns the documents to a set of pre-defined classes based on its textual content. Document categorization is a crucial and well-proven instrument for organizing large volumes of textual information. There are many classification methods for textual data. A support vector machine, named SVM, was suggested by Vapnik (1995) and have recently been used in a range of problems including pattern recognition (Pontil and Verri, 1998), bioinformatics (Yu, Ostrouchov, Geist, & Samatova, 1999), and text categorization (Joachims, 1998).

When using SVM, three problems are confronted: (1)how to reduce the high dimension of feature vectors; (2)how to choose the optimal input feature subset for SVM, (3)and how to set the best kernel parameters. These three problems are crucial, because the feature subset choice influences the appropriate kernel parameters and vice versa (Frohlich and Chapelle, 2003). Therefore, obtaining the optimal feature subset and SVM parameters is important.

T.-h. Kim et al. (Eds.): ASEA 2008, CCIS 30, pp. 79–92, 2009.

In the literature, only a few algorithms have been proposed for SVM feature selection (Bradley, Mangasarian, & Street, 1998; Bradley and Mangasarian, 1998; Weston et al., 2001; Guyon, Weston, Barnhill, & Bapnik, 2002; Mao, 2004). Some other genetic algorithms(GA)-based feature selection methods were proposed (Raymer, Punch, Goodman, Kuhn, & Jain, 2000; Yang and Honavar, 1998; Salcedo-Sanz, Prado-Cumplido, Perez-Cruz, & Bousono-Calzon, 2002). However, these papers focused on feature selection and did not deal with attribute reduce and parameters optimization for the SVM classifier.

In addition to the feature selection, proper parameters setting can improve the SVM classification accuracy. The parameters that should be optimized include penalty parameter C and the kernel function parameters such as the gamma ($\gamma$) for the radial basis function (RBF) kernel. To design a SVM, one must choose a kernel function, set the kernel parameters and determine a soft margin constant C (penalty parameter). The Grid algorithm is an alternative to finding the best C and gamma when using the RBF kernel function. However, this method is time consuming and does not perform well (Hsu and Lin, 2002; LaValle and Branicky, 2002).

In order to improve SVM classification speed and accuracy, we proposed a new method. First, Rough Sets Theory(RST) is used to reduce feature vectors after data preprocess. Second, using genetic algorithms to select feature and optimize the parameter for SVM.

This paper is organized as follows: a brief introduction to the SVM is given in Section 2. Section 3 describes Rough Sets Theory. Section 4 describes basic GA concepts. Section 5 describes the system overview. Include:(1)algorithm of RST-based attribute reduce;(2)GA-based feature selection and parameter optimization. Section 6 presents the experimental results from using the proposed method to classify test datasets. Section 7 draws a general conclusion and describes the future work.

## 2  Brief Introduction of Support Vector Machine[1~3]

The primary idea of support vector machine (SVM) is using a high dimension space to find a hyper plane to do binary division, where the achieved error rate is minimum. An SVM can handle the problem of linear inseparability.

An SVM uses a portion of the data to train the system and finds several support vectors that represent training data. These support vectors will be formed into a model by the SVM, representing a category. According this model, the SVM will classify a given unknown document by the following classification decision formula

$$(x_i, y_i), \cdots, (x_n, y_n), x \in R^m, y \in \{+1, -1\}. \tag{1}$$

Where $(x_i, y_i), \cdots, (x_n, y_n)$ are training samples, n is the number of samples, m is the input dimension, and y belongs to the category of +1 or -1, respectively.

In a linear problem, a hyper plane is divided into two categories. Fig. 1 shows a high dimension space divided into two categories by a hyper plane. The hyper plane formula is: (w·x)+b=0.

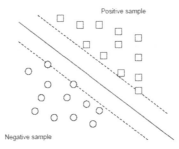

**Fig. 1.** The hyper plane of SVM

The classification formula is:

$$(w \bullet x_i) + b > 0 \ if \ y_i = +1 \quad (w \bullet x_i) + b < 0 \ if \ y_i = -1 \tag{2}$$

However, for many problems it is not easy to find a hyper plane to classify the data. The SVM has several kernel functions that users can apply to solve different problems, such as radial basis function, sigmoid, Polynomial etc.

Radial basis function kernel is:

$$k(x_i, x_j) = \exp(-\gamma \|x_i - x_j\|^2) \tag{3}$$

## 3  Rough Sets Theory

The rough sets theory has been developed for knowledge discovery in databases and experimental data sets [4~8]. The rough sets theory deals with information represented by a table called information system. This table consists of objects (or cases) and attributes. The entries in the table are the categorical values of the features and possibly categories. It also denoted to attribute reduce.

An information system is a 4-tuple $S = \langle U, A, V, f \rangle$, where U is a finite set of objects, called the universe, A is a finite set of attributes. $V = U_{a \in A} V_a$ is a domain of attribute a, and $f := U \times A \rightarrow V$ is called an information function such that $f(x, a) \in V_a$ ,for $\forall a \in A, \forall x \in U$ .

In the classification problems, an information system is also seen as a decision table assuming that $A = C \cup D$ and $C \cap D = \emptyset$, where C is a set of condition attributes and D is a set of decision attributes.

Let $S = \langle U, A, V, f \rangle$ be an information system, every $P \subseteq A$ generates a indiscernibility relation IND(P) on U, which is defined as follows:

$$IND(P) = \{(x, y) \in U \times U : f(x, a) = f(y, a), \forall a \in P\} \tag{4}$$

$U / IND(P) = \{C_1, C_2, \cdots C_k, \}$ is a partition of U by P, every $C_i$ is an equivalence class. For $\forall x \in U$ , the equivalence class of x in relation $U / IND(P)$ is defined as follows:

$$[x]_{IND(P)} = \{y \in U : f(y,a) = f(x,a), \forall a \in P\} \tag{5}$$

Let $s = \langle U, C \cup D, V, f \rangle$ be a decision table, the set of attributes $P(P \subseteq C)$ is a reduction of attributes C, which satisfies the following conditions:

$$P\_X = \{y \in U : [y]_{IND(P)} \subseteq X\}, \tag{6}$$

$$P^-X = \{y \in [y]_{IND(P)} \cap X \neq \phi\} \tag{7}$$

$P\_X$ is the set of all objects from U which can be certainly classified as elements of X employing the set of attributes P. $P^-X$ is the set of objects of U which can be possibly classified as elements of X using the set of attributes P.

Let $P, Q \subseteq A$, the positive region of classification $U / IND (Q)$ with respect to the set of attributes P, or in short, P-positive region of Q, is defined as

$$pos_P(Q) = \bigcup_{X \in U / IND(Q)} P\_X \tag{8}$$

$pos_P(Q)$ contains all objects in U that can be classified to one class of the classification $U / IND (Q)$ by attributes P. The dependency of Q on P is defined as

$$\gamma_P(Q) = \frac{card(POS_P(Q)}{card(U)}. \tag{9}$$

An attribute a is said to be dispensable in P with respect to Q, if $\gamma_P(Q) = \gamma_{P-\{a\}}(Q)$ ;otherwise a is an indispensable attribute in P with respect to Q. Let $s = \langle U, C \cup D, V, f \rangle$ be a decision table, the set of attributes $P(P \subseteq C)$ is a reduct of attributes C, which satisfies the following conditions:

$$\gamma_P(D) = \gamma_C(D) \text{ and } \gamma_P(D) \neq \gamma_{P'}(D), \forall P' \subset P. \tag{10}$$

A reduction of condition attributes C is a subset that can discern decision classes with the same discriminating capability as C, and none of the attributes in the reduction can be eliminated without decreasing its discriminating capability.

## 4  Genetic Algorithms[9~11]

GAs(Genetic Algorithms) are stochastic and evolutionary search techniques based on the principles of biological evolution, natural selection, and genetic recombination. They simulate the principle of 'survival of the fittest' in a population of potential solutions known as chromosomes. Each chromosome represents one possible solution to the problem or a rule in a classification. The population evolves over time through a process of competition whereby the fitness of each chromosome is evaluated using a fitness function. During each generation, a new population of chromosomes is formed in two steps. First, the chromosomes in the current population are selected to reproduce on the basis of their relative fitness. Second, the selected chromosomes are recombined using idealized genetic operators, namely crossover and mutation, to form a new set of chromosomes that are to be evaluated as the new solution of the problem. GAs are conceptually simple but computationally powerful. They are used to solve a wide variety of problems, particularly in the areas of optimization and machine learning (Davis, 1991; Grefenstette, 1994).

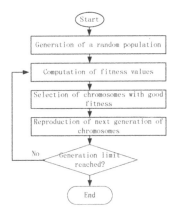

**Fig. 2.** A typical GA program flow

Fig. 2 shows the flow of a typical GA program. It begins with a population of chromosomes either generated randomly or gleaned from some known domain knowledge. Subsequently, it proceeds to evaluate the fitness of all the chromosomes, select good chromosomes for reproduction, and produce the next generation of chromosomes. More specifically, each chromosome is evaluated according to a given performance criterion or fitness function, and is assigned a fitness score. Using the fitness value attained by each chromosome, good chromosomes are selected to undergo reproduction. Reproduction involves the creation of offspring using two operators, namely crossover and mutation (Fig. 3). By randomly selecting a common crossover site on two parent chromosomes, two new chromosomes are produced. During the process of reproduction, mutation may take place. For example, the binary value of Bit 2 in Fig. 3 has been changed from 0 to 1. The above process of fitness evaluation, chromosome selection, and reproduction of the next generation of chromosomes continues for a predetermined number of generations or until an acceptable performance level is reached.

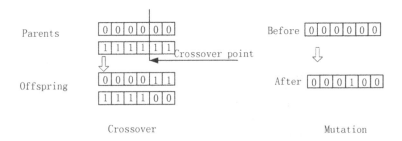

**Fig. 3.** Genetic crossover and mutation operation

## 5  System Overview

To improve classification accuracy and speed we proposed a hybrid solution called RGSC(Rough sets and Genetic algorithms for SVM classifier).The system architectures shown in Fig.4. The detailed explanation is as follows:

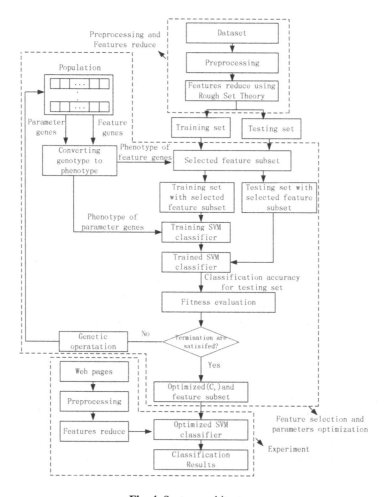

**Fig. 4.** System architectures

(1) Preprocessing: preprocessing includes remove HTML tags, segment word and construct Vector Space Model.

(2) Feature reduction by rough sets. Our objective is to find a reduction with minimal number of attributes, describes in Alg. 1.

(3) Converting genotype to phenotype. This step will convert each parameter and feature chromosome from its genotype into a phenotype.

(4) Feature subset. After the genetic operation and converting each feature subset chromosome from the genotype into the phenotype, a feature subset can be determined.

(5) Fitness evaluation. For each chromosome representing C, $\gamma$ and selected features, training dataset is used to train the SVM classifier, while the testing dataset is used to calculate classification accuracy. When the classification accuracy is obtained, each chromosome is evaluated by fitness function— formula (8).

(6) Termination criteria. When the termination criteria are satisfied, the process ends; otherwise, we proceed with the next generation.

(7) Genetic operation. In this step, the system searches for better solutions by genetic operations, including selection, crossover, mutation, and replacement.

(8) Input the preprocessed data sets into the obtained optimized SVM classifier.

## 5.1  Algorithm of RST-Based Feature Reduce

Based on section 3 described. We proposed rough set feature reduction algorithm of finding a reduction of a decision table, which is outlined below.

---

**Algorithm 1. Rough Sets Attribute Reduction algorithm**

Input: a decision table $T = \langle U, C \cup D, V, f \rangle$, $U = \{x_1, x_2, \cdots x_m\}$, $C = \{C_1, C_2, \cdots C_n\}$

Output: a reduction of $T$, denoted as *Redu*.

1: construct the binary discernibility matrix $M$ of $T$;

2: delete the rows in the M which are all 0's, Redu= $\phi$

/* delete pairs of inconsistent objects*/

3: while $(M \neq \phi)$

4:    {(1) select an attribute ci in the M with the highest discernibility degree (if there are several

$c_j$ (j=1,2,…,m) with the same highest discernibility degree, choose randomly an attribute from them);

5:    (2) Redu $\leftarrow$ Redu $\cup \{c_i\}$;

6:    (3) remove the rows which have "1" in the $c_i$ column from M;

7:    (4) remove the $c_i$ column from M; }endwhile

/* the following steps remove redundant attributes from *Redu* */

8: suppose that Redu $= \{r_1, r_2, \cdots r_k\}$ contains $k$ attributes which are sorted by the order of entering

*Redu*, $r_k$ is the first attributes chosen into *Redu*, $r_1$ is the last one chosen into *Redu*.

9: get the binary discernibility matrix $MR$ of decision table $TR = \langle U, Redu \cup \{d\}, V, f \rangle$;

10: delete the rows in the $MR$ which are all 0's;

11: for i = 2 to k{

12:       remove the $r_i$ column from $MR$;

---

| 13: | if (no row in the *MR* is all 0's){ |
|---|---|
| 14: | Redu $\leftarrow$ Redu $-$ { $r_i$ }; |
| 15: | else |
| 16: | Put the $r_i$ column back to MR; |
| 17: | Endif ;} |
| 18: | Endfor;} |

## 5.2 Chromosome Design

To implement our proposed approach, this research used the RBF kernel function for the SVM classifier because the RBF kernel function can analysis higher-dimensional data and requires that only two parameters, C and γ be defined (Hsu, Chang, & Lin, 2003; Lin and Lin, 2003). When the RBF kernel is selected, the parameters (C and γ) and features used as input attributes must be optimized using our proposed GA-based system. Therefore, the chromosome comprises three parts, C, γ, and the features mask. However, these chromosomes have different parameters when other types of kernel functions are selected. The binary coding system was used to represent the chromosome.

$$\boxed{g_C^1 \cdots g_C^i \cdots g_C^{n_C}} \boxed{g_\gamma^1 \cdots g_\gamma^j \cdots g_\gamma^{n_\gamma}} \boxed{g_f^1 \cdots g_f^k \cdots g_f^{n_f}}$$

**Fig. 5.** The chromosome comprises three parts, C, γ, and the features mask

Fig. 5 shows the binary chromosome representation of our design. In Fig. 5, $g_C^1 \sim g_C^{n_C}$ represents the value of parameter C, $g_\gamma^1 \sim g_\gamma^{n_\gamma}$ represents the parameter value γ, and $g_f^1 \sim g_f^{n_f}$ represents the feature mask. nc is the number of bits representing parameter C, nr is the number of bits representing parameter γ, and nf is the number of bits representing the features. Note that we can choose nc and nγ according to the calculation precision required, and that nγ equals the number of features varying from the different datasets.

In Fig. 5, the bit strings representing the genotype of parameter C and γ should be transformed into phenotype by Eq. (7). Note that the precision of representing parameter depends on the length of the bit string (nc and nγ); and the minimum and maximum value of the parameter is determined by the user. For chromosome representing the feature mask, the bit with value '1' represents the feature is selected, and '0' indicates feature is not selected.

$$p = \min_p + \frac{\max_p + \min_p}{2^l - 1} \times d \qquad (7)$$

*P*  phenotype of bit string
*minp*  minimum value of the parameter
*maxp*  maximum value of the parameter
*d*  decimal value of bit string
*l*  length of bit string

### 5.3 Fitness Function

Classification accuracy, the number of selected features, and the feature cost are the three criteria used to design a fitness function. Thus, for the individual (chromosome) with high classification accuracy, a small number of features, and low total feature cost produce a high fitness value. We solve the multiple criteria problem by creating a single objective fitness function that combines the three goals into one. As defined by formula (23), the fitness has two predefined weights: (i) WA for the classification accuracy; (ii) WF for the summation of the selected feature (with nonzero Fi) multiplying its cost. The weight accuracy can be adjusted to 100% if accuracy is the most important. Generally, WA can be set from 75 to 100% according to user's requirements. If we do not have the feature cost information, the cost Ci can be set to the same value, e.g. '1' or another number. The chromosome with high fitness value has high probability to be preserved to the next generation, so user should appropriately define these settings according to his requirements.

$$fitness = W_A \times SVM\_accuracy + W_F \times (\sum_{i=1}^{n_f} C_i \times F_i)^{-1} \tag{8}$$

*WA*  SVM classification accuracy weight
*SVM_accuracy*  SVM classification accuracy
*WF*  weight for the number of features
*Ci*  cost of feature *i*
*Fi*  '1' represents that feature *i* is selected; '0' represents that feature *i* is not selected

## 6 Experiments

In this section, we designed an experiment to test the performance of the proposed RGSC. We also investigated k-NN and Decision tree to compare their classification performances. The experiments are described below.

### 6.1 Experiment Environment

Our implementation was carried out on the YALE(Yet Another Learning Environment) 3.3 development environment(Available at:http://rapid-i.com/). Feature reduction by Rough Sets Theory carried out on ROSETTA(you can download it from http://rosetta.sourceforge.net/). The empirical evaluation was performed on Intel Pentium IV CPU running at 3.0 GHz and 1GB RAM.

## 6.2  Data Set

To provide an overview on the base line accuracy of the classifiers and to compare them with various studies, the Reuters 21578 corpus was taken in our experiments (this collection is publicly available at: http://www.research.att.com/~lewis/reuters21578.html). These stories average about 200 words in length. Various splits of the Reuters 21578 can be used, whereas we followed the ModApte split in which 75% of the stories (9603 stories) are used to build classifiers and the remaining 25% (3299 stories) to test the accuracy of the resulting models in reproducing the manual category assignments. From this split, all categories (including the documents not assigned to any category), which have no training or test document were deleted. The resulting data set has 90 different categories and is the same as that used by Joachims (1998).

## 6.3  The Performance Measure

Given a binary-classification problem of topic versus not-topic, recall is the ratio of the correct topic cases to the total topic cases. Precision is the ratio of correct topic cases to the total predicted topic cases. The standard evaluation criterion for the Reuters benchmark is the breakeven point, at which precision equals recall, and the F1 measure, which is defined as $(2 \times \text{precision} \times \text{recall})/(\text{precision} + \text{recall})$.

## 6.4  Simulate

Figure 6, Figure 7 and Figure 8 show the performance of our proposed method against to the decision tree (Weiss et al., 1999) and the k-NN classifiers (Aas & Eikvil, 1999) for the ten most frequent categories.

The precision of the k-NN, Decision tree, and RGSC is shown in Figure 6, the recall of the k-NN, Decision tree, and RGSC is shown in Figure 7, the F1-value of the k-NN, Decision tree, and RGSC is shown in Figure 8, and the speed of the k-NN, Decision tree, and RGSC is shown in Figure 9.

The average precision for k-NN, Decision tree and RGSC are 75.6, 84.9 and 90.7% respectively. With the exception of category Grain, Crude, Wheat, Corn, the precision of each category for RGSC is higher than other two methods. This indicates that the RGSC methods perform generally high precision.

The average recall results for the RGSC, k-NN and the Decision tree are 95.1, 82.3, and 87.8%, respectively. The recall of k-NN and Decision tree are nearly the same and both are lower than the RGSC. The RGSC can classify documents into the correct category mapping to precision, with a high recall ratio (Fig. 6).

The simulated result shows that the average F1-values of the RGSC, k-NN and the Decision tree are 92.5, 78.8 and 87.9%, respectively. This indicates that the RGSC yields a better classification result than the other two methods. But RGSC classification performs lower than Decision tree for the "Grain", "Crude", "Sheep" and "Wheat" categories. We now try to explain why the performance of those four categories is poorer than other categories. We find that the "Grain", "Crude", "Sheep" and "Wheat" categories contain a smaller number of documents in Reuters 21578. This indicates that the RGSC is able to effectively process categories with large documents. But poorer with smaller documents. Fig. 7 shows that among the three methods, the RGSC has the average highest classification result.

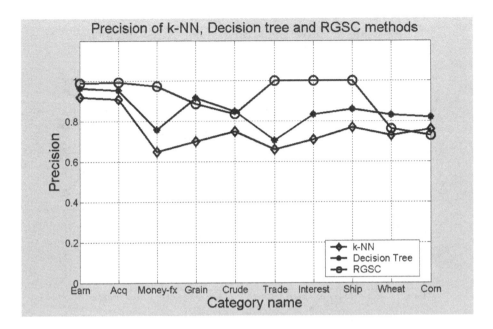

**Fig. 6.** The precision of the k-NN, Decision tree, and RGSC

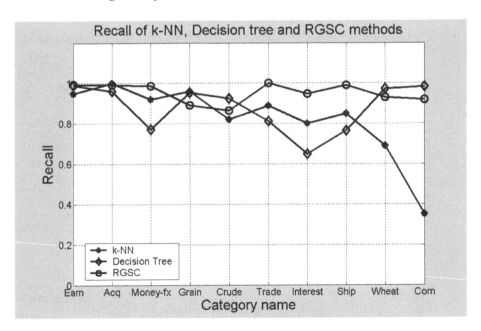

**Fig. 7.** The recall of the k-NN, Decision tree, and RGSC

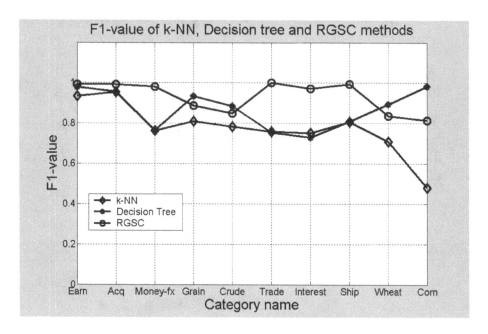

**Fig. 8.** The F1-value of the k-NN, Decision tree, and RGSC

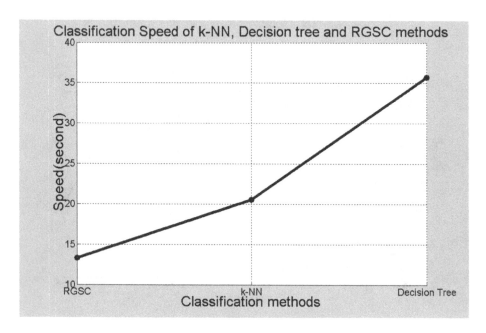

**Fig. 9.** The speed of the k-NN, Decision tree, and RGSC

The speed for RGSC, k-NN and Decision tree are 13.3, 20.5 and 35.7 seconds respectively. This indicates that the RGSC is more effective than the other two methods. It easily explain that the feature is reduced by Rough Set Theory before input the SVM classifier.

In general the performance of our approach is best in average.

## 7 Conclusion

In this paper, we have proposed a document classification method using an SVM based on Rough Sets Theory and Genetic Algorithms. The feature vectors are reduced by Rough Set Theory. The feature vectors are selected and parameters optimization by Genetic Algorithms. The experimental results show that the RGSC we proposed yields the best result of these three methods. The experiment also demonstrated that the RGSC yields better accuracy even with a large data set. When the larger category has more training data, the RGSC is able categorize documents more accuracy. In future research, we will emphasis on the kernel function selection and parameters optimization for the Genetic Algorithms to improve the performance of RGSC.

## References

1. Burges, C.: A tutorial on support vector machines for pattern recognition. Data Mining and Knowledge Discovery 2(2), 121–167 (1998)
2. Chang, C.C., Lin, C.J.: LIBSVM: A library for support vector machines (2001), http://www.csie.ntu.edu.tw/~cjlin/libsvm
3. Cristianini, N., Shawe-Taylor, J.: An introduction to support vector machines, pp. 100–103. Cambridge University Press, Cambridge (2000)
4. Pal, S.K., Skowron, A.: Rough Fuzzy Hybridization: A New Trend in Decision-Making, pp. 36–70. Springer, Singapore (1983)
5. Pawlak, Z.: Rough sets. Int. J. Comput. Sci. 11, 341–356 (1982)
6. Pawlak, Z.: Rough Sets, Theoretical Aspects of Reasoning About Data, pp. 10–50. Kluwer, Dordrecht (1991)
7. Pawlak, Z., Skowron, A.: Rough membership functions. In: Yaeger, R.R., Fedrizzi, M., Kacprzyk, J. (eds.) Advances in the Dempster Shafer Theory of Evidence, pp. 251–271. Wiley Inc., Chichester (1994)
8. Pawlak, Z., Wong, S.K.M., Ziarko, W.: Rough sets: probabilistic versus deterministic approach. Int. J. Man-Mach. Stud. 29, 81–85 (1988)
9. Davis, L.: Handbook of genetic algorithms, pp. 55–61. Nostrand Reinhold, New York (1991)
10. Goldberg, D.E.: Genetic algorithms in search, optimization and machine learning, pp. 23–32. Addison-Wesley, Reading (1989)
11. Grefenstette, J.J.: Genetic algorithms for machine learning, pp. 100–106. Kluwer, Boston (1994)
12. Vapnik, V.N.: The nature of statistical learning theory, pp. 61–70. Springer, New York (1995)
13. Frohlich, H., Chapelle, O.: Feature selection for support vector machines by means of genetic algorithms. In: Proceedings of the 15th IEEE international conference on tools with artificial intelligence, Sacramento, CA, USA, pp. 142–148 (2003)

14. Yu, G.X., Ostrouchov, G., Geist, A., Samatova, N.F.: An SVMbased algorithm for identification of photosynthesis-specific genome features. In: Second IEEE computer society bioinformatics conference, CA, USA, pp. 235–243 (2003)
15. Bradley, P.S., Mangasarian, O.L., Street, W.N.: Feature selection via mathematical programming. INFORMS Journal on Computing 10, 209–217 (1998)
16. Hsu, C.W., Chang, C.C., Lin, C.J.: A practical guide to support vector classification (2003),
    http://www.csie.ntu.edu.tw/~cjlin/papers/guide/guide.pdf
17. LaValle, S.M., Branicky, M.S.: On the relationship between classical grid search and probabilistic roadmaps. International Journal of Robotics Research 23, 673–692 (2002)
18. Joachims, T.: Text categorization with support vector machines. In: Proceedings of European conference on machine learning (ECML), Chemintz, DE, pp. 137–142 (1998)
19. Pontil, M., Verri, A.: Support vector machines for 3D object recognition. IEEE Transactions on Pattern Analysis and Machine Intelligence 20(6), 637–646 (1998)

# A Tiling Bound for Pairwise Global Sequence Alignment

Paul Horton* and Martin Frith

AIST, Computational Biology Research Center,
2-42 Aomi, Koutou-ku, Tokyo
horton-p@aist.go.jp

**Abstract.** In this paper we motivate the need to develop new techniques to accelerate pairwise global sequence alignment and then propose a *tiling* bound to achieve this. The bounds involve a problem relaxation in which alignment scores of sequence fragments are combined to give a bound on the distance of any alignment passing through any particular point in the edit graph. We prove the correctness of the bound and briefly discuss possible implementation strategies.

## 1 Introduction

Global pairwise sequence alignment is a well established problem in computational biology. It is usually solved with dynamic programming [10] which can be performed in $O(l_1 l_2)$ time, for two input sequences of length $l_1$ and $l_2$ respectively. Although only quadratic in sequence length, for some applications the computation time can be prohibitive. As sequence data began to accumulate in the 1980's, some score bounding techniques were suggested to speed-up the dynamic programming calculation without sacrificing any accuracy in the computed result[3, 16]. These techniques and were extended and described under a unified framework by Spouge[14]. The bounds described were very simple, either simply the constant zero[3] or bounds based on the minimum number of indels needed to return an alignment to the diagonal of the edit graph, otherwise assuming perfect matches[14, 16].

However, around this time the focus of the research community shifted almost exclusively to the development of heuristic algorithms to accelerate local alignment based sequence similarity search[1, 13].

Heuristics were invoked because the exponentially expanding sequence data made full dynamic programming impractical. The shift to local alignment reflected: the realization that for database search, local sequence similarity is generally more useful than global similarity; and the amenability of local sequence similarity search to acceleration through the use of simple tables of short subsequences (*e.g.* as in BLAST[1]).

Arguably, accelerating global alignment computation is less important than accelerating local alignment was *circa* 1990 – but this is true for nearly all

---

* Corresponding author.

T.-h. Kim et al. (Eds.): ASEA 2008, CCIS 30, pp. 93–98, 2009.

research topics (BLAST is one of the most highly cited software tools in all of science).

In fact the computation of global alignment scores is commonly desired in circumstances in which the time complexity presents a practical problem. Two major applications are:

1. Construction of so-called "non-redundant" databases.
2. All pairs global alignment similarity computation as a pre-processing step for multiple alignment.

These tasks are computationally intensive because they require computing or bounding the global alignment score of each pair from a set of $n$ sequences, requiring a worst case computation time of $O(n^2 l^2)$, where $l$ is the harmonic average of the sequence lengths – around 1000 for proteins and possibly much larger for RNA or DNA sequences – and $n$ can be larger than $10^6$ (for example Uniprot[2]).

Sequence clustering is the task of partitioning a set of sequences into the maximum number of partitions possible, under the constraint that no pair of sequences from different partitions are more similar (usually defined as the fraction of identical residues in the global sequence alignment) than a given threshold. This is useful to accelerate subsequence database search, and to reduce biases from large numbers of similar sequences when performing statistical analysis.

Fortunately, sequence clustering does not require that the exact alignment score of all pairs is computed, since it is enough to know whether or not the score is below the similarity threshold. Considerable effort has been invested to exploit this fact by avoiding the alignment of pairs of sequences which can be proven to have alignment scores below the threshold by a quickly computable upper bound[5, 7, 8]. These technique are very useful. However they lose their effectiveness when strict (*e.g.* 35% identity for protein sequences) thresholds are desired, because too many sequence pairs survive the bounding procedure.

Multiple alignment is a central task in computational biology. Despite its long history, it remains an area of intensive development[9, 12]. Multiple alignment is typically performed globally and many popular multiple alignment programs start with the computation of the pairwise global alignment scores for each possible pairing of the input sequences[6, 11, 15]. Unlike sequence clustering, it is not possible to avoid computing an alignment score for each pair. To save time, in practice heuristic estimates are often used in *in lieu* of the desired alignment score.

## 2   Method

In this section we propose a technique to bound the score of aligning suffices of the input sequence pair, which can be used to avoid expanding hopeless sections of the dynamic programming table as describe by Spouge[14] or as a bound on the distance to the goal in an $A^*$ algorithm[4] implementation of global sequence alignment. In either case, the key to reducing computational work is to quickly and effectively bound the alignment score of any pair of suffices of the sequences being aligned.

The usual formulation of sequence alignment is a special case of the shortest path problem from graph theory. Like path costs in graph theory, alignment scores are additive (this is not strictly true for affine or concave gap costs, but the bounds presented here can be modified to handle this detail). In other words, if an alignment is partitioned into two or more contiguous blocks of columns, the score of the whole alignment is equal to the sum of the score of each block.

This fact suggests a useful theorem. First some notation and definitions are needed. We consider strings over a fixed alphabet, which we simply refer to as "the alphabet". We denote the optimal pairwise global alignment (breaking ties arbitrarily) of two strings $r$ and $t$ as $A_G(r,t)$ and its score as $G(r,t)$. We use $A_g(r,t)$ and $g(r,t)$ to denote the semi-global variant of $G(r,t)$ in which the cost of terminal gaps in the second string ($t$ in this case) are assigned zero cost.

**Definition 1 (Tile).** *A set of strings $T = \tau_1, \ldots$ tiles a string $t$, iff the strings in $T$ can be concatenated in some order such that the concatenated string is equal to $t$.*

**Theorem 1.** *Assuming the scoring function used never assigns a positive score to a gap (i.e. non-negative gap costs); let $r$, $t$ be two strings and $T = \tau_1, \ldots$ be a set of strings which tiles $t$. Then*

$$G(r,t) \le \sum_i g(r, \tau_i) \tag{1}$$

**Proof:** *Observe that $A_G(r,t)$ consists of the concatenation of*

- *feasible alignments between $r$ and the elements of $T$, with each element appearing exactly once.*
- *zero or more blocks with parts of $r$ aligned to a gap*

*The theorem follows from the additivity of alignments and the assumption of non-positive gap scores.* Note regarding non-constant gap costs: *affine gap-costs violate the additivity property of alignment. This case can be handled by halving the gap cost of terminal gaps in $r$ when computing $g(r, \tau)$.*

**Definition 2 (Tiling Set).** *Let $R$ and $T$ be sets of strings. $T$ is a tiling set with respect to $R$, iff $\forall\, r \in R$, every suffix of $r$ is tiled (or "almost tiled") by some subset of $T$. A set of strings is a universal tiling set if it is a tiling set with respect to all possible sets of strings. For example, if "almost tiled" is defined as meaning that every suffix with length $l = 0 \pmod 3$ must be tiled, then the set of all possible 3-mers over the alphabet is a universal tiling set.*

computeGlobalAlignmentScoresOneVsMany( string $r$, string[] $D = d_1, \dots$ )
    Let $T$ be a tiling set with respect to $D$
    *// either compute $T$ from $D$ or use a universal tiling set.*

    For each string $\tau \in T$, compute $S(r, \tau)$
    Store $g(r, \tau)$ in table (or trie) $H$ with $\tau$ as the key.

    For each string $d_i \in D$
        $B \leftarrow$ computeSuffixBounds( $H$, $d_i$ )
        Perform standard bounded global alignment computation (Spouge[14]) using
        $B$ for suffix bounds.

computeSuffixBounds( table $H$, string $s$ )
    $l_s \leftarrow$ length( $s$ )
    $B[l_s] = 0$
    $i \leftarrow l_s$
    **while**( $\exists h \in H : h$ is an exact match of a suffix of $s_1 \dots s_i$ )
    *// for a k-mer tiling set, this loop continues until $i < k$*

        $l_h \leftarrow$ length( $h$ )
        $i \leftarrow i - l_h$         *// $i$ holds the length of the current suffix of $s$*
        $B[i] \leftarrow B[i + l_h] + H\{h\}$   *// $H\{h\}$ holds $g(r, h)$*
    Fill in the "holes" in $B$,
      *i.e.* $\forall i : B[i] =$ **undefined**, extrapolate from the nearest defined index of $B$,
      assuming perfect matches for the untiled end portion.
    return $B$

**Fig. 1.** Pseudo-code illustrating how the tiling bound could be used to accelerate global alignment score computation

When computing the alignment of some string $s$ against many other strings, this relationship can be used to compute an upper bound on the alignment score of suffices as shown in figure 1.

## 2.1   Computation Time and Tiling Set Choice

The computation we propose has two parts: The computation of $H$ in figure 1, performed once for each sequence; and the computation of computeSuffixBounds, performed for each pair of sequences.

The computation time of the former can be adjusted by choosing smaller or larger tiling sets. Larger tiling sets cost more to pre-compute – but may save time overall by providing tighter bounds. To maximize gain in computation time, the elements of the tiling set should appear repeatedly in the sequence collection, so substring counting data structures such as suffix trees may be useful to optimize the choice of tiling set for a particular sequence collection.

The computation of computeSuffixBounds can be performed in linear time, as long as the value of $g(r, \tau)$ can be can be obtained from $H$ in time linear in the size of the tiling substring ($\tau$). We expect that a trie constructed with the tiling substrings reversed will be one convenient way to implement this.

# Summary

In this paper, we motivated the need for techniques to accelerate pair-wise global alignment score computation for applications in which the alignment score of a sequence needs to be computed against many other sequences. To this end, we introduced a *tiling* bound to replace the naïve perfect match bounds used in earlier work. When many computations are performed involving the same sequence, we speculate that the time needed to pre-compute the alignment scores of the substrings in the tiling set will more than repay itself in the speed-up gained from tighter upper bounds on the alignment of suffices. The implementation of the pseudo-code shown in figure 1 should be simple and efficient.

We close with a quotation. Although the work of Spouge[14] employed relatively simple bounds, he did make a rather enticing statement regarding such bounds:

... with some thought almost any inequality can be improved.

We agree strongly. We hope this manuscript inspires further "thought" on the issue.

# Acknowledgement

P.H. was supported by a Japanese Ministry of Education, Culture, Sport, Science and Technology, Grant-in-Aid for Scientific Research (B).

# References

1. Altschul, S.F., Gish, W., Miller, W., Myers, E.W., Lipman, D.J.: Basic local alignment search tool. JMB 215, 403–410 (1990)
2. Bairoch, A., Apweiler, R., Wu, H.C., Barker, C.W., Boeckmann, B., Ferro, S., Gasteiger, E., Huang, H., Lopez, R., Magrane, M., Martin, J.M., Natale, A.D., O'Donovan, C., Redaschi, N., Yeh, S.L.: The universal protein resource (UniProt). NAR 33, D154–D159 (2005)
3. Ficket, J.W.: Fast optimal alignment. Nucleic Acids Research 12, 175–180 (1983)
4. Hart, P.E., Nilsson, N.J., Raphael, B.: A formal basis for the heuristic determination of minimum cost paths. IEEE Transactions on Systems Science and Cybernetics SSC 4(2), 100–107 (1968)
5. Holm, L., Sander, C.: Removing near-neighbour redundancy from large protein sequence collections. Bioinformatics 14, 423–429 (1998)
6. Katoh, K., Toh, H.: Recent developments in the MAFFT multiple sequence alignment program. Briefings in Bioinformatics 9, 286–298 (2008)
7. Li, W., Godzik, A.: Cd-hit: a fast program for clustering and comparing large sets of protein or nucleotide sequences. Bioinformatics 22(13), 1658–1659 (2006)
8. Li, W., Jaroszewski, L., Godzik, A.: Clustering of highly homologous sequences to reduce the size of large protein databases. Bioinformatics 17(3), 282–283 (2001)
9. Löytynoja, A., Goldman, N.: Phylogeny-aware gap placement prevents errors in sequence alignment and evolutionary analysis. Science 320, 1632–1635 (2008)

10. Needleman, S.B., Wunsch, C.D.: A general method applicable to the search for similarities in the amino acid sequences of two proteins. Journal of Molecular Biology 48, 444–453 (1970)
11. Notredame, C., Holm, L., Higgins, D.G.: COFFEE: an objective function for multiple sequence alignments. Bioinformatics 14, 407–422 (1998)
12. Notredame, C.: Recent evolutions of multiple sequence alignment algorithms. PLoS Comput. Biol. 3(8), e123 (2007)
13. Pearson, W.R., Lipman, D.J.: Improved tools for biological sequence comparison. Proc. Natl. Acad. Sci. USA 85, 2444–2448 (1988)
14. Spouge, J.L.: Fast optimal alignment. CABIOS 7(1), 1–7 (1991)
15. Thompson, J.D., Higgins, D.G., Gibson, T.J.: CLUSTAL W: improving the sensitivity of progressive multiple sequence alignment through sequence weighting, position-specific gap penalties and weight matrix choice. Nucleic Acids Research 22, 4673–4680 (1994)
16. Ukkonen, E.: On approximate string matching. LNCS, vol. 158, pp. 487–495. Springer, Heidelberg (1984)

# Discovering Decision Tree Based Diabetes Prediction Model

Jianchao Han, Juan C. Rodriguez, and Mohsen Beheshti

Department of Computer Science
California State University Dominguez Hills
1000 E. Victoria Street, Carson, CA 90747, USA
jhan@csudh.edu, jrodriguez236@cp.csudh.edu, mbeheshti@csudh.edu

**Abstract.** Data mining techniques have been extensively applied in bioinformatics to analyze biomedical data. In this paper, we choose the Rapid-I's RapidMiner as our tool to discover decision tree based diabetes prediction model from a Pima Indians Diabetes Data Set, which collects the information of patients with and without developing diabetes. Following the data mining process, our discussion will focus on the data preprocessing, including attribute identification and selection, outlier removal, data normalization and numerical discretization, visual data analysis, hidden relationships discovery, and a diabetes prediction model construction.

**Keywords:** Decision tree, data mining, prediction model, bioinformatics and biomedicine, diabetes.

## 1 Introduction

Modern computers have made it so that every field of study is generating data at an unprecedented rate. Computers can process data in ways and speeds humans could never achieve. Data mining is the entire process of applying a computer-based methodology for developing knowledge from data.

Data mining is an iterative process in which progress is defined by discovery, through either manual or automatic methods. Data mining is most useful in an exploratory analysis scenario in which there are no predetermined ideas about what will constitute an "interesting" outcome. Data mining is the search for new, valuable, and nontrivial information in large volumes of data.

In practice, the two primary goals of data mining tend to be prediction and description [1]. Prediction involves using some attributes or fields in the data set to predict unknown or future values of other attributes of interest. On the other hand, description focuses on finding patterns for describing the data so that humans can interpret it. Therefore, it is possible to put data mining activities into one of two categories:

- Predictive data mining produces the model described by the data set; and
- Descriptive data mining produces nontrivial information based on the data set.

T.-h. Kim et al. (Eds.): ASEA 2008, CCIS 30, pp. 99–109, 2009.
© Springer-Verlag Berlin Heidelberg 2009

To achieve the goals of prediction and description one must follow a data mining process. There are many different versions of data mining processes and many opinions on how to approach them. This paper focuses on the RapidMiner software package, and follows the process below to analyze diabetes data and mine a diabetes prediction model:

- Preprocessing the data, including attribute selection and identification, outlier removal, data normalization, and numeric data discretization;
- Analyzing the data using tables, charts, statistics, and algorithms;
- Finding hidden relationships that were not or could not be found using standard analysis; and
- Constructing a diabetes prediction model.

## 1.1 RapidMiner

Progress in the field of data mining has lead to the creation of many software packages such as DataMiner, Clementine, Intelligent Miner, 4Though, and See5. These packages attempt to make the tedious work of the data mining process more straightforward. However, regardless of the simplicity of the software, one must understand the steps needed to find the data in order to achieve optimal results.

Rapid-I's RapidMiner software package was developed in Yale University and supports all steps of data mining process [2]. It is a Java-based open-source software and can be used as a Java API. It also provides a simple and friendly GUI. RapidMiner uses internal XML representations to ensure standardized interchange format of data mining experiments. One can email the XML file of the project and the person receiving email will be able to duplicate the exact project without having to redo the steps.

In RapidMiner, all data mining steps are designed as operator trees. Unlike other data mining suits, the operators in RapidMiner are not defined in a graph layout where components are positioned and connected by the user. The data flow is always the same and follows the concept of a depth first search. This drastically eases the design of data mining processing. Child operators are invoked by their parents and work on the data their parents provide. This also allows for-loops which are controlled by the parent operators.

Not every step will lead to results. Those that do not will only be mentioned to provide a complete view of the process. The focus will be on documenting and explaining the steps that do lead to results.

## 1.2 Project Plan and Data Set

"Kidney failure is a deadly complication of diabetes, and Pimas, so far as scientists can tell, have the world's heightest rate of type 2 diabetes." [3] The objective of this analysis is to understand any general relationships between different patient characteristics and the propensity to develop diabetes. In particular it would help to:

- Understand relationships between different patient characteristics and likelihood of developing diabetes;

- Understand the differences between the patients that develop diabetes and those who did not;
- Develop predictive model to estimate whether a patient will develop diabetes within an acceptable percentage of certainty.

Using RapidMiner, we will easily deliver an analysis report and a prediction model. The analysis report will summarize the data and their associations to developing diabetes. The prediction model will be a decision tree that should help in predicting whether a patient will develop diabetes using the data gathered.

The data set used in this project is excerpted from the UCI Machine Learning Repository [4]. The Pima Indians Diabetes Data Set contains 8 categories and 768 instances gathered from a larger databases belonging to the National Institute of Diabetes and Digestive and Kidney Diseases. The constraints placed on the selection of these instances are as follow: All patients are females at least 21 years old of Pima Indian heritage.

This paper is organized as follows: The data preprocessing is described in Section 2, including attribute selection and identification, outlier removal, data normalization, and numeric data discretization. Data analysis such as comparing variable values and visualizing attribute relationships, represented as tables, plots, statistics and charts, will be reported in Section 3. Hidden relationships between attributes will be discovered and represented as a decision tree in Section 4. A diabetes prediction model will be constructed in Section 5. Section 6 is the conclusion and future work.

## 2 Data Preprocessing

Most of the data sets used in data mining were not necessarily gathered with a specific goal in mind. Some of them may contain errors, outliers or missing values. In order to use those data sets in the data mining process, the data needs to undergo preprocessing, using data cleaning, discretization and data transformation [5]. It has been estimated that data preparation alone accounts for 60% of all the time and effort expanded in the entire data mining process [6].

### 2.1 Feature Identification and Categorization

Attributes are usually described by a set of corresponding values. Features described by both numerical and symbolic values can be either discrete (categorical) or continuous. Discrete features concern a situation in which the total number of values is relatively small (finite), while with continuous features the total number of values is very large (infinite) and covers a specific interval (range) [7]. The scale of measurements describes the actual numerical value. Ordinal variables are similar to nominal variables, except that an ordinal variable has values that can be arranged in a meaningful order, e.g., small, medium, and large. Ratio describes values where the same difference between values has the same meaning (as in interval) but where a double, tripling, etc. of the values implies a double, tripling, etc. of the measurement. Once it is all gathered, all this information is put into a categorical table. The categorization table is then observed and analyzed in search of errors or inconsistencies.

The following attribute information can be gathered from the data set web site [2]:

- Pregnant: Number of times a patient has been pregnant
- Plasma-Glucose: Plasma glucose concentration measured using a two-hour oral glucose tolerance test. Blood sugar level.
- DiastolicBP: Diastolic blood pressure (mmHg)
- TricepsSFT: Triceps skin fold thickness (mm)
- Serum-Insulin: Two-hour serum insulin (mu U/mt)
- BMI: Body mass index (weight in kg/(height in m)$^2$)
- DPF: Diabetes pedigree function
- Age: Age of the patient (years)
- Class: Diabetes onset within five years (0 or 1)

These characteristics need to be kept in mind as the data set is cleaned. Most of this work can be done in RapidMiner itself. After importing samples of the Pima Indian Data Set, changing default attribute titles, and renaming the values of attribute Class from (0, 1) to (No, Yes), one can obtain a proper categorized attribute table, shown in Table 1.

**Table 1.** Attribute Categorization

| Variables | Description | Continuous/ Discrete | Scale of Measure | Role? |
|---|---|---|---|---|
| Pregnant | # of times pregnant | Continuous | | |
| Plasma-Glucose | Plasma-Glucose concentration in blood in a 2 hour oral glucose tolerance test | Continuous | Ratio | Descriptor |
| DiastolicBP | Diastolic blood pressure | Continuous | Ratio | Descriptor |
| TricepsSFT | Triceps skin fold thickness | Continuous | Ratio | Descriptor |
| Serum-Insulin | 2-hour serum insulin | Continuous | Ratio | Descriptor |
| BMI | Body mass index | Continuous | Ratio | Descriptor |
| DPF | Diabetes pedigree function | Continuous | Ratio | Descriptor |
| Age | Of patient | Continuous | Ratio | Descriptor |
| Class | No == Does not contract diabetes in five years Yes = contracts diabetes in five years | Discrete | Ordinal | Response |

## 2.2  Outlier Removal and Feature Selection

Using the Data View in RapidMiner, the attributes can be sorted in different ways to view patterns and values. Some attributes have values of zero even though it cannot be a proper value (missing value). Those rows should be removed for the attributes Plasma-Glucose, DiastolicBP, and BMI.

Outliers are extreme values that lie near the limits of the data range or go against the trend of the remaining data. Identifying outliers is important because they may represent errors in data entry. In addition, even if an outlier is a valid data point and not in error, certain statistical methods are sensitive to the presence of outliers and may deliver unstable results [5]. The Density Plotter in RapidMiner helps to easily discover outliers like one with value 99 found in the TricesSFT attribute. The DistanceBasedOutlierDetection operator can be used to verify it.

The Plot View can also be used to view the data using different plotters. One plotter used was the Scatter Matrix, which helps to visually observe the correlation between two attributes. This plotter illustrates the need to focus on the correlation between BMI vs. TricepsSFT. It shows that two attributes correlate each other. One should take care to avoid feeding correlated attributes to one's data mining and statistical models. At best, using correlated variables will overemphasize one data component; at worst, it will cause the model to become unstable and deliver unreliable results [5]. TricepsSFT has 227 missing values (zero values). Therefore, this attribute could be removed based on the number of missing values and its relationship to BMI. The variable Serum-Insulin was also removed from the data set because of the number of missing values. The Histogram Plotter can be used to check the rest of the attributes for correlations.

## 2.3  Data Normalization

Numerical attributes usually have ranges that vary greatly from each other. This data set is no exception. For example, compare the range of variables of BMI, which range from 18.2 to 67.1, to those of Plasma-Glucose, which range from 44.0 to 199.0. These types of differences in the ranges can lead to a tendency for the variable with greater range to have undue influence on the results. Therefore, data sets should normalize their numerical variables, to standardize the scale of effect each variable has on the results [5].

The RapidMiner software provides tools to quickly normalize numerical attributes without the risk of human error. In this project, the simplest Min-Max normalization model was applied to transform the attribute's values to a new range, 0 to 1. Basically, the formula that are used to normalize attribute X can be generally described as follows:

$$NormalizedX = \frac{X - \min(X)}{\max(X) - \min(X)}.$$

## 2.4  Numerical Data Discretization

After normalizing the numerical attributes, it becomes clear that it would be easier to associate diabetes with other attributes by grouping them, which can be done by discretizing these attributes. The discretization of numerical attributes can be performed before or after normalization. RapidMiner supports to enable or disable operators generated previously whenever needed. Therefore, if normalization has been done, it can be disabled so that the attributes are more recognizable and easier to be discretized and then re-enabled afterwards. For easy understanding, we choose to discretize numerical attributes before normalization or disabling normalization.

Discretization of numerical attributes can be either manually done based on user specification, called UserBasedDiscretization, or automatically done, called BinDiscretization. We discretize the attributes Pregnant, Plasma-Glucose, DiastolicBP and BMI manually, and DPF and Age automatically, respectively.

The attribute Pregnant is discretized into three bins: low (0,1), medium (2, 3, 4, 5), and high (>6).

Using the information on WebMD, one can discretize the following attributes easily. The attribute Plasma-Glucose is grouped into low (<95), medium (95-140), and high (>140) [8]. The attribute DiastolicBP is divided into normal (<80), prehypertension (80-89), and high (>90) [9]. The attribute BMI is mapped into three intervals: low (<18.5), healthy (18.5-24.9), overweight (25-29.9), obese (30-34.9), and severely-obese (>35) [10].

The attribute DPF is discretized using the average value as follows: low (<0.42), medium (0.42-0.82), and high (>0.82). Finally, the attribute Age is automatically discretized into three ranges: range1 (<41), range2 (41-61), and range3 (>61).

## 3  Data Analysis

Data analysis that can be done with the RapidMiner software includes graphs and tables, as well as various charts and plots. The RapidMiner Histogram Color Matrix was used to visually compare the values of the attributes and see the relationships with the Class attribute values (Yes, No). This chart is illustrated in Figure 1. One can easily notice that the patients with higher Plasma-Glucose values are very likely to develop diabetes and most with low Plasma-Glucose values do not develop diabetes within five years.

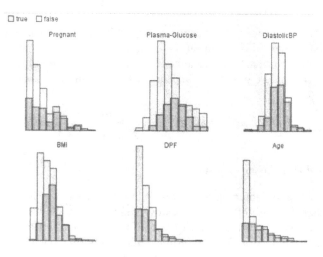

**Fig. 1.** Histogram Color Matrix for various variables with the Class attribute values (Yes and No)

Further analyzing this relationship between Plasma-Glucose and Class by using a box plot, which RapidMiner calls a Quartile Color Plot affirms the above observation. To help clarify whether the observation might be of value, a Naïve Bayes learning tool is applied. In Bayesian statistics, the attributes are considered to be random variables, and the data are considered to be known. The parameters are regarded as coming from a distribution of possible values, and Bayesians look to the observed data to provide information on likely parameter values [5]. This verifies that the initial observation appears to be correct.

## 4  Finding Hidden Relationships

After the data preprocessing, our next goal is to find generally associations in the data in order to understand the relationships between the attributes and whether the patients go on to develop diabetes. With the discretization of numerical attributes, we will focus on the sub-groups (bins) created instead of the individual values of the attributes to minimize the complexity of the analysis without losing accuracy.

RapidMiner provides a very useful tool, BasicRuleLearner, for helping narrow observation down, which sifts through the data and finds general relationship rules. With the discretization enabled, the following rules are achieved:

- If Plasma-Glucose = high then Yes (124/60)
  o  If Plasma-Glucose is high, patient develops diabetes 67% of the time.
- If Plasma-Glucose = low then No (9/97)
  o  If Plasma-Glucose is low, patient does not develop diabetes 92% of the time.
- If BMI = low then No (0/4)
  o  If BMI is low, patient does not develop diabetes 100% of the time. Only four samples.
- If BMI = healthy then No (2/89)
  o  If BMI is healthy, patient does not develop diabetes 98% of the time.
- If  BMI = overweight then No (23/72)
  o  If BMI is overweight, patient does not develop diabetes 76% of the time.
- If Age = range3 [61 - ∞] then No (1/8)
  o  If older than 61, patient does not develop diabetes 89% of the time
- If Pregnant = medium then No (28/65)
  o  If pregnant is medium, patient does not develop diabetes 70% of the time
- If Pregnant = low then No (17/21)
  o  If Pregnant is low, patient does not develop diabetes 55% of the time.
- If DPF = low then No (26/50)
  o  If DPF is low, patient does not develop diabetes 66% of the time.

One may realize that some rules have very low accuracy, thus may be misleading. It would be incorrect to simply look at one attribute and then look at the result. It must be better to see the results when two or more attributes are combined, not to mention to combine all attributes. This can be achieved using CHAID decision tree.

CHAID is a type of decision tree technique. It stands for Chi-squared Automatic Interaction Detector [11]. In practice, it is often used in the context of direct marketing to select groups of consumers and predict how their responses to some variables affect other variables. CHAID detects interaction between variables in the data set by identifying discrete groups of respondents, and seeks to predict what the impact will be on the dependent variables by taking their responses to explanatory variables. Since CHAID requires statistics data, it is not necessary to discretize numerical variables. Therefore the discretization should be disabled.

The CHAID decision tree output by RapidMiner is shown in Figure 2, which once again verifies that Plasma-Glucose plays an important role in the patient developing diabetes. However, this time the tree only shows us the most important attributes and values that lead to the development of diabetes. The exact value of Plasma-Glucose that will lead to diabetes is discovered and BMI is further classified as well. Rapid-Miner can also reveal the quantities of values that lead to this particular tree view. If the values of Plasma-Glucose are less than or equal to 154 (medium or better) then only 154 (25%) patients develop diabetes and 451 (75%) patients do not. When the Plasma-Glucose value is larger than 154 (high) then 94 (80%) patients develop diabetes and 24 (20%) patients do not.

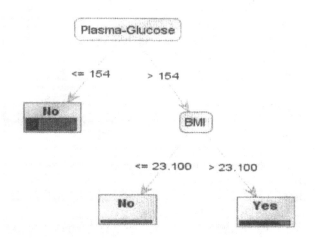

**Fig. 2.** CHAID Tree for Plasma-Glucose

## 5   Constructing the Prediction Model

Data analysis and hidden relationship reveal that have been made so far can be used to either modify the attribute or help get a better understanding of the attribute values. Now we need to construct a predictive model to estimate whether a patient will develop diabetes within an acceptable percentage of certainty, instead of simply shedding light about the data itself. RapidMiner provides means for this purpose. We choose two main options: the ID3 Algorithm and the Decision Tree.

A decision tree can be learned by splitting the source data set into subsets based on an attribute value test [12]. This process is repeated on each derived subset in a recursive manner. The recursion is completed when splitting is either non-feasible or a singular classification can applied to each element of the derived subset. A random forest classifier uses a number of decision trees, in order to improve the classification rate. The decision is not only helpful in representing the current data relationships, but also able to apply other data to the algorithm and test how well it works at predicting the outcome.

RapidMiner supports to generate a decision tree. A part of the decision tree automatically produced by RapidMiner is shown in Figure 3, where the Plasma-Glucose attribute is chosen as the root node. This further reinforces our original observation in the prior section. The decision tree tells us that Plasma-Glucose is the main attribute that will lead us to knowing whether a patient will develop diabetes. The actual data set states that 248 patients develop diabetes and 475 do not. This decision tree predicts that there are 200 patients that develop diabetes and 523 that do not. Of those 200 patients, 19 are wrong, which brings the correct predictions down to 181. This means the decision tree has 72% of accuracy.

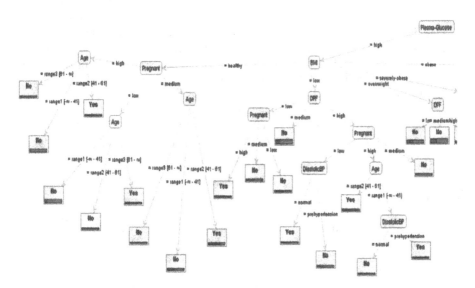

**Fig. 3.** A part of the Decision Tree for the diabetes prediction model

One can also choose the ID3 Algorithm to build the prediction model. The ID3 Algorithm adopts a greedy (i.e., non-backtracking) approach where decision trees are recursively constructed in a top-down divide-and-conquer manner [13]. It starts with a training set of tuples and theirs associated class labels. The training set is recursively partitioned into smaller subsets as the decision tree is being built. The ID3 decision tree predicts that there 231 patients that develop diabetes and 492 that do not. Of those 231 patients, 33 are wrong, which brings the correct predictions down to 198. This means the ID3 decision tree has 80% of accuracy.

Consider the attributes that are predicted incorrectly. We begin with the false positives. We already know that according to the data set, diabetes is often associated with increased levels of Plasma-Glucose. In the false positive examples, the patients have a lower level of Plasma-Glucose than expected. Other characteristics are similar to the average for the data set. This hints at the possibility that we may be missing important attributes to classify these particular observations correctly. There might be other risk factors that the data collections did not consider, like level of exercise, cholesterol, etc.

In the case of false negatives, the patients do have characteristics that would go on to develop diabetes, which are high Plasma-Glucose levels and increased BMI. Again, this hints at the possibility that the data set is missing important fields for the classification of those patients. Considering that we have a well-defined set of false positives and negatives, the proper prediction model would need more data gathering.

## 6 Conclusion and Future Work

A very valuable data mining tool, the Rapid-I's RapidMiner is briefly introduced and applied to mine patterns from a Pima Indian Diabetes Data Set. The discussion follows the data mining process. The diabetes data set is preprocessed by identifying and categorizing attribute, removing outlier removal, normalizing and discretizing numerical attributes. Correlations between attributes are visualized to help understand attributes and their values. Hidden relationships between attributes and class labels are revealed, and a diabetes prediction model is constructed as a decision tree, which is also analyzed against false positives and negatives.

Our future work will focus on the application of RapidMiner in more practical bioinformatics and biomedical data sets to see how the results will vary depending on different types of data.

## References

1. Kantardzic, M.: Data Mining: Concepts, Models, Methods, and Algorithms. John Wiley & Sons, Inc., New Jersey (2002)
2. Rapid-I, Interactive Design. Products: RapidMiner, Yale (2008),
   http://rapidi.com/content/view/13/69/lang.en/
3. Wheelwright, J.: Native America's Alleles. Discover Magazine (2005),
   http://discovermagazine.com/2005/may/native-americas-alleles
4. Asuncion, A., Newman, D.J.: Pima Indians Diabetes Data Set, UCI Machine Learning Repository. University of California, School of Information and Computer Science, Irvine, CA (2007),
   http://archive.ics.uci.edu/ml/datasets/Pima+Indians+Diabets
5. Larose, D.T.: Data Mining Methods and Models. John Wiley & Sons, Inc., Hoboken (2006)
6. Pyle, D.: Data Preparation for Data Mining. Morgan Kaufmann, San Francisco (1999)
7. Cios, K.J., Pedrycz, W., Swiniarski, R.W., Kurgan, L.A.: Data Mining: A Knowledge Discovery Approach. Springer, New York (2007)

8. Seibel, J.A.: Diabetes Guide, WebMD (2007),
   http://diabetes.webmd.com/guide/oral-glucose-tolerance-test
9. Stein, D.W.: Hypertension / High Blood Pressure Guide, WebMD (2006),
   http://www.webmd.com/
   hypetension-diagnosing-high-blood-pressure
10. Zelman, K.M.: How Accurate is Body Mass Index, or BMI? WebMD (2008),
    http://www.webmd.com/diet/features/
    how-accurate-body-mass-index-bmi
11. Kass, G.V.: An Exploratory Technique for Investigating Large Quantities of Categorical Data. Journal of Applied Statistics 29(2), 119–127 (1980)
12. Quinlan, J.R.: C4.5: Programs for Machine Learning. Morgan Kaufmann, San Francisco (1992)
13. Han, J., Kamber, M.: Data Mining: Concepts and Techniques, 2nd edn. Morgan Kaufmann, San Francisco (2006)

# Application of Formal Concept Analysis in Model-Based Testing

Pin Ng[1] and Richard Y.K. Fung[2]

[1] Hong Kong Community College, Hong Kong Polytechnic University, Hong Kong
ccpng@hkcc-polyu.edu.hk
[2] Department of Manufacturing Engineering and Engineering Management,
City University of Hong Kong, Hong Kong
richard.fung@cityu.edu.hk

**Abstract.** Model-based testing is a software testing technique that derives a suite of test cases from a model which represents the behavior of a software system. By executing a set of model-based test cases, the conformance of the implementation of the target system to its specification can be validated. However, as there may be large, sometimes infinite, number of operational scenarios that could be generated from a given model, an important issue of model-based testing is to determine a minimal set of test cases which provides sufficient test coverage. By using the Formal Concept Analysis (FCA) mechanism, we could analyze the coverage of the test cases and eliminate those redundant ones. This systematic approach can help reduce the test suite whilst still maintain the sufficiency of test coverage.

**Keywords:** model-based testing, test suite reduction, formal concept analysis, UML state machine diagram.

## 1 Introduction

Testing is an important part of software development process for the purposes of quality assurance, reliability estimation and verification and validation. However, software testing is an extremely costly and time consuming process. Studies show that more than 50% of the cost of software development is devoted to testing [11]. As a result, many researchers have advocated model-based testing [3][4][5][17][19][24] for improving the efficiency and effectiveness of test cases generation. Model-based testing refers to deriving a suite of test cases from a model that represents the behavior of a software system. By executing a set of model-based test cases, the conformance of the implementation of the target system to its specification can be validated. One commonly used modeling diagram for that purpose is state machine diagram. According to UML (Unified Modeling Language) specification [20], a state machine diagram consists of a set of states and transitions. A transition is triggered when an event occurs and a condition associated with the transition is satisfied. When a transition is triggered, the associated actions will be performed which may lead to a change in the state of the system. These features are useful to the designers for modeling the

T.-h. Kim et al. (Eds.): ASEA 2008, CCIS 30, pp. 110–123, 2009.

dynamic behavior of event-driven systems such as communication protocols or graphical user interface systems [17]. Each feasible path of transitions [4] within a state machine diagram is considered as an operational scenario of the system under test. Thus, the instances of the operational scenarios will form a suite of test cases for model-based testing.

However, since cycles within the state machine diagram will lead to infinite number of feasible paths of transitions, exhaustive testing is usually impossible. Therefore, an important issue is to decide which feasible paths should be selected for testing. A default criterion of adequate testing with a state machine diagram is that all transitions in the diagram are covered by the test executions. This is called all-transitions coverage criterion [13][19][24] which means each transition specified in the state machine diagram is triggered at least once by executing the test cases.

In this paper, we are proposing to apply formal concept analysis (FCA) [9] to analyze the association of a set of feasible paths with a set of transitions specified in the state machine diagram, and to organize them to form a concept lattice. The concept lattice structure can then be used for analyzing the transition coverage of the feasible paths. With the concept analysis mechanism, our approach is able to reduce the test suite whilst satisfying the all-transitions coverage criterion for model-based testing.

The remaining part of this paper is organized as follows. Section 2 reviews the related work. It follows with Section 3 which introduces the basic concepts of FCA. In Section 4, a working example is used to demonstrate the way that FCA is applied in model-based test suite reduction, and finally, Section 5 concludes the paper.

## 2   Related Work

Model-based testing is a software testing technique [2][3] that derives a suite of test cases from a model representing the behavior of a software system. Being the most formalized component of UML, state machine diagrams have been used as a basis for generating test data [7][14][15][19]. Therefore, state machine diagrams can be readily used by system domain experts to express and analyze behavioral requirements and thus provide the software developers with a means for early validation of requirements [18].

A number of researchers have proposed coverage criteria for test data selection from UML state machine diagrams. Some of the well-established criteria [3][19][24] include all-states coverage, full predicate coverage, all-transitions coverage, all-transition-pairs coverage, and complete sequence coverage. Since the all-transitions coverage criterion means every transition is covered at least once, it implies the satisfaction of both all-states coverage and full predicate coverage criteria. The all-transition-pairs coverage criterion in general produces $O(k^2)$ test cases [24] where $k$ is the number of transitions. Thus for large state machine models, this criterion may not be practical because it requires too many test cases. The complete sequence coverage relies on the domain knowledge of the requirements engineers in choosing the testing sequences. There may exists some cases that these testing sequences are redundant or cannot fully exercises all the transitions in a state machine diagram. Therefore, among all these coverage criteria, we choose the all-transitions coverage as the coverage adequacy criterion for selecting the test cases.

Test suite reduction can be considered as a minimum set-covering problem [6]. A classical approach for solving minimum set-covering problem is based on greedy heuristic [8]. By applying that classical greedy heuristic in test cases selection, the test case that covers the most elements will first be selected. Then, the test case that covers the most remaining elements will be selected. The process will be repeated until all the elements have been covered. Harrold et al. [12] developed another greedy heuristic for test suite reduction based on the association between a testing requirement and the test cases that satisfy the requirement. However, these heuristics do not support removing those selected test cases which turn out to be redundant when some other test cases are included at the later stage. Therefore, there are some cases [6] that the test suites derived by these heuristics are not minimal.

Sampath et al. [21] applied FCA for test suite reduction in the situation of web applications testing, in which, the URLs used in a web session are considered as the attributes and each web session as a test case. The reduced test suite is obtained by selecting those test cases associated with the strongest concepts (i.e. the concept nodes that are just above the bottommost concept node in the concept lattice). With this method, although the reduced test suite can provide sufficient test coverage, redundancy can still exist among the strongest concepts. Tallam and Gupta [23] proposed a Delayed-Greedy heuristic based on concept analysis for selecting minimum number of test cases which can exercise the given set of testing requirements. Our proposed method differs from theirs in which (i) our test suite is derived based on a set of feasible paths with reference to a state machine diagram; and (ii) we do not need to go through the attribute reduction procedure as described in their Delayed-Greedy heuristic. Our approach applies concept analysis mechanism to analyze the transition coverage relationship of "feasible path $p$ covers transition $t$". The mechanism can help identify and remove the redundant feasible paths iteratively so that the test suite will be minimal whilst satisfying the all-transitions coverage criterion.

## 3   Formal Concept Analysis

Formal Concept Analysis (FCA) provides a mathematical foundation for systematically combining and organizing individual concepts of a given context into hierarchically ordered conceptual structure [9]. Given a binary relation $R$ between a set of objects $O$ and a set of attributes $A$ (that is, $R \subseteq O \times A$ ), the tuple $(O, A, R)$ forms a *formal context*. For a set of objects, $O_i \subseteq O$, the set of *common attributes*, $\sigma$, is defined as:

$$\sigma(O_i) = \{ a \in A \mid \forall (o \in O_i)\, (o, a) \in R \} \qquad (1)$$

Analogously, the set of *common objects*, $\tau$, for a set of attributes, $A_i \subseteq A$, is defined as:

$$\tau(A_i) = \{ o \in O \mid \forall ( a \in A_i)\, (o, a) \in R \} \qquad (2)$$

A *concept* $c$ is defined as an ordered pair $(O_i, A_i)$ such that $A_i = \sigma(O_i)$ and $O_i = \tau(A_i)$. That means, all and only objects in $O_i$ share all and only attributes in $A_i$.

For a concept $c = (O_i, A_i)$, $O_i$ is called the *extent* of $c$, denoted by $Extent(c)$, and $A_i$ is called the *intent* of $c$, denoted by $Intent(c)$.

For example, a relation $R$ is specified in the sample cross table shown in Table 1 and the set of concepts deduced from relation $R$ is listed in Table 2.

**Table 1.** Sample cross table

| $R$ | a1 | a2 | a3 | a4 | a5 | a6 |
|-----|----|----|----|----|----|----|
| o1  | ×  |    |    |    |    | ×  |
| o2  |    |    | ×  |    |    | ×  |
| o3  | ×  |    | ×  |    | ×  | ×  |
| o4  |    | ×  | ×  | ×  |    | ×  |

**Table 2.** List of concepts

| Concept | Extent( ) | Intent( ) |
|---------|-----------|-----------|
| c1 | { o1, o2, o3, o4 } | { a6 } |
| c2 | { o1, o3 } | { a1, a6 } |
| c3 | { o2, o3, o4 } | { a3, a6 } |
| c4 | { o3 } | { a1, a3, a5, a6 } |
| c5 | { o4 } | { a2, a3, a4, a6 } |
| c6 | { } | { a1, a2, a3, a4, a5, a6 } |

The set of all concepts of a given formal context forms a partial order by:

$$c_1 \leq c_2 \iff Extent(c_1) \subseteq Extent(c_2) \tag{3}$$

or equivalently

$$c_1 \leq c_2 \iff Intent(c_1) \supseteq Intent(c_2) \tag{4}$$

Given two concepts $c_1$ and $c_2$, if $c_1 \leq c_2$ holds, then $c_1$ is called *subconcept* of $c_2$; or equivalently, $c_2$ is called *superconcept* of $c_1$. The set of all concepts of a formal context and the partial ordering can be represented graphically using a *concept lattice*. A concept lattice consists of nodes that represent the concepts and edges connecting these nodes. The nodes for concepts $c_1$ and $c_2$ are connected if and only if $c_1 \leq c_2$ and there is no other concept $c_3$ such that $c_1 \leq c_3 \leq c_2$. Various algorithms for constructing concept lattices can be found in [1][16][22]. In the worst case, there may be $2^n$ concepts in a concept lattice where the value of $n = max \ ( \ |O|, |A| \ )$ and that implies an exponential complexity. In practice, however, it is reported that usually a concept lattices has $O(n^2)$ concepts and sometimes $O(n)$ concepts [10][22].

Fig. 1 shows the concept lattice based on the set of concepts listed in Table 2. The Top concept, c1, of the concept lattice is the most generalized concept (the superconcept to all other concepts); whereas the Bottom concept, c6, is the most specialized concept (the subconcepts to all other concepts). In Fig. 1, the labeling of the lattice nodes is kept simple by only showing the attributes and objects which are most specific to a given concept:

$$AttributeLabels\,(c) = Intent\,(c) - \bigcup_{\forall c_j \geq c} Intent\,(c_j) \tag{5}$$

$$ObjectLabels\,(c) = Extent\,(c) - \bigcup_{\forall c_i \leq c} Extent\,(c_i) \tag{6}$$

That means all attributes that can be reached by ascending paths and all objects that can be reached by descending paths from a given concept are suppressed.

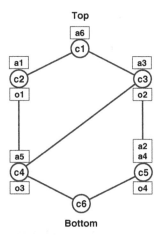

**Fig. 1.** A concept lattice

## 4  Model-Based Test Suite Reduction with FCA

In this section, we use a simplified behavior model of an MP3 player to illustrate the mechanism of reducing model-based test suite with FCA. With reference to the all-transitions coverage criterion, the following questions are to be addressed in this section:

- Sufficiency of test coverage: *Is every transition specified in the state machine diagram triggered at least once by the selected test cases?*

- Reduction of test suite: *How could we keep the test suite minimal whilst maintaining sufficient test coverage?*

Fig. 2 depicts a state machine diagram of a simplified MP3 player. The model comprises of four states: *Off, Ready, Playing,* and *Paused.* It describes the set of events that will trigger the transitions for changing the state of the MP3 player. For the ease of explanation, we labeled each transition with an identifier.

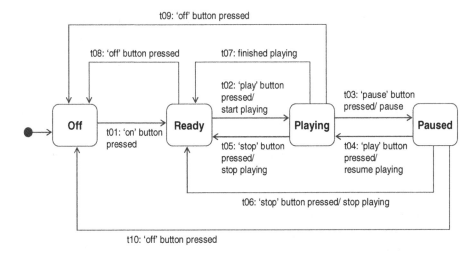

**Fig. 2.** A simplified state machine diagram for a MP3 player

By traversing the state machine diagram, a set of feasible paths of transitions can be obtained. However, because of the iterative nature of the given state machine diagram, there are infinite number of feasible paths. Suppose that we only consider those feasible paths which have depth <= 5 and at most one transition can be traversed twice by the same feasible path. Fig. 3 shows the resultant set of 13 feasible paths in form a transition tree [3].

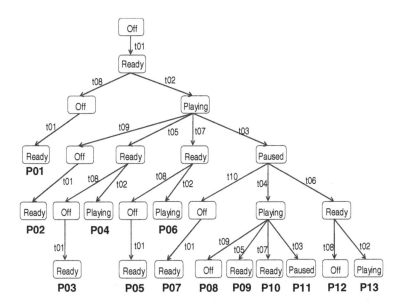

**Fig. 3.** Transition tree with depth <= 5

Each feasible path of transitions represents an operational scenario of the usage of the MP3 player. For example, the feasible path P08: t01→t02→t03→t04→t09 indicates the operational scenario for testing the MP3 player with a series of actions that will cause the state changes with the following sequence: *Off, Ready, Playing, Paused, Playing,* and *Off.*

### 4.1   Formal Context of Transition Coverage

The transition coverage of the feasible paths can be defined in form of a formal context $(P, T, R)$ in which:

- $P$ is a set of *feasible paths* (considered as objects)
- $T$ is a set of *transitions* (considered as attributes)
- a pair (path $p$, transition $t$) is in relation $R$ if transition $t$ is triggered when path $p$ is executed.

With reference to the MP3 player example, we can make use of a relation table (see Table 3) to represent the context of transition coverage by the feasible paths.

**Table 3.** Transition coverage by the feasible paths

| R | t01 | t02 | t03 | t04 | t05 | t06 | t07 | t08 | t09 | t10 |
|---|---|---|---|---|---|---|---|---|---|---|
| P01 | x |   |   |   |   |   |   | x |   |   |
| P02 | x | x |   |   |   |   |   |   | x |   |
| P03 | x | x |   | x |   |   |   | x |   |   |
| P04 | x | x |   | x |   |   |   |   |   |   |
| P05 | x | x |   |   |   |   | x | x |   |   |
| P06 | x | x |   |   |   |   | x |   |   |   |
| P07 | x | x | x |   |   |   |   |   |   | x |
| P08 | x | x | x | x |   |   |   |   | x |   |
| P09 | x | x | x | x | x |   |   |   |   |   |
| P10 | x | x | x | x |   |   | x |   |   |   |
| P11 | x | x | x | x |   |   |   |   |   |   |
| P12 | x | x | x |   |   | x |   | x |   |   |
| P13 | x | x | x |   |   | x |   |   |   |   |

Then, by using the FCA mechanism, a set of 18 concepts (listed in Table 4) is deduced from the relation table and the resultant concept lattice structure is shown in Fig. 4. The feasible paths and transitions are labeled as objects and attributes, respectively, on the nodes of the concept lattice.

**Table 4.** List of concepts

| Concept | Extent( ) | Intent( ) |
|---|---|---|
| c1 | {P01, P02, P03, P04, P05, P06, P07, P08, P09, P10, P11, P12, P13} | {t01} |
| c2 | {P01, P03, P05, P12} | {t01, t08} |
| c3 | {P02, P03, P04, P05, P06, P07, P08, P09, P10, P11, P12, P13} | {t01, t02} |
| c4 | {P03, P05, P12} | {t01, t02, t08} |
| c5 | {P05, P06, P10} | {t01, t02, t07} |
| c6 | {P07, P08, P09, P10, P11, P12, P13} | {t01, t02, t03} |
| c7 | {P02, P08} | {t01, t02, t09} |
| c8 | {P12, P13} | {t01, t02, t03, t06} |
| c9 | {P03, P04, P09} | {t01, t02, t05} |
| c10 | {P08, P09, P10, P11} | {t01, t02, t03, t04} |
| c11 | {P05} | {t01, t02, t07, t08} |
| c12 | {P03} | {t01, t02, t05, t08} |
| c13 | {P12} | {t01, t02, t03, t06, t08} |
| c14 | {P10} | {t01, t02, t03, t04, t07} |
| c15 | {P09} | {t01, t02, t03, t04, t05} |
| c16 | {P08} | {t01, t02, t03, t04, t09} |
| c17 | {P07} | {t01, t02, t03, t10} |
| c18 | { } | {t01, t02, t03, t04, t05, t06, t07, t08, t09, t10} |

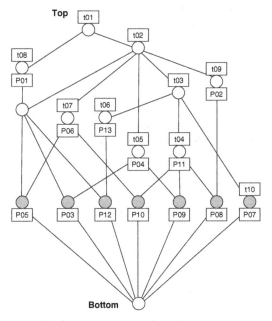

**Fig. 4.** Concept lattice of transition coverage

### 4.2  Sufficiency of Transition Coverage

In the context of transition coverage, the feasible paths can provide sufficient coverage if when test cases are executed according to the sequence specified in the feasible paths, each transition specified in the state machine diagram will be triggered at least once. With reference to a concept lattice structure, a simple indication for sufficiency of transition coverage is:

$AttributeLabels$(Bottom) = $\varnothing$ $\wedge$

$ObjectLabels$(Bottom) = $\varnothing$.

That implies every transition $t$ is covered by some feasible path $p$. Therefore, as shown in Fig. 4, the feasible paths can provide sufficient coverage of all the transitions.

### 4.3  Reduction of Test Suite

A set of feasible paths is considered to be minimal if any of the feasible paths is removed, some transitions in the given state machine diagram are not covered by the remaining feasible paths. With the notion of concept lattice, our approach can determine a minimal set of feasible paths via the following steps.

*Step 1: Identification of the significant feasible paths*

A feasible path is considered to be significant if it can trigger some transitions which are not covered by other feasible paths. With reference to a concept lattice structure, a feasible path $p$ is *significant* if:

(i)   $p \in ObjectLabels(c)$; and

(ii)  there is no other concept $c'$ such that $c \geq c' \geq$ Bottom

In Fig. 4, the concept nodes associated with significant feasible paths (i.e. those nodes that are closest to the Bottom concept) are highlighted on the concept lattice. This set of significant feasible paths {P03, P05, P07, P08, P09, P10, P12} is sufficient enough to cover all the transitions specified in the state machine diagram of the MP3 player. Therefore, those non-significant feasible paths {P01, P02, P04, P06, P11, P13} can be discarded, and the resulting concept lattice is restructured as shown in Fig. 5.

*Step 2: Identification of the redundant feasible paths*

The set of feasible paths can further be reduced by excluding those redundant feasible paths, if they exist.

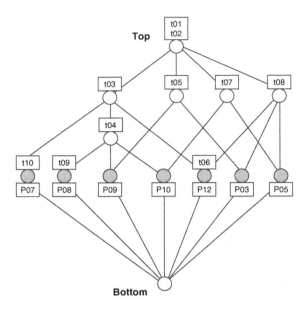

**Fig. 5.** Revised concept lattice with P01, P02, P04, P06, P11, P13 removed

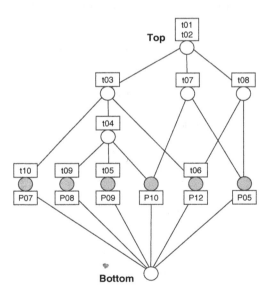

**Fig. 6.** Revised concept lattice with P03 removed

A feasible path *p* is considered to be *redundant* if:

(i)     *p* is *significant*; and

(ii)    $p \in$ *ObjectLabels*(*c*), where

(iii)   *AttributeLabels*(*c*) = $\varnothing$

That means, there is no transition that is solely covered by that feasible path *p*. All the transitions covered by *p* can also be covered by other feasible paths.

In case there is more than one redundant feasible path, the one with least number of intent elements (i.e. covering least number of transitions) will be selected for removal first. This step is repeated until there is no more redundant feasible path.

As revealed from the concept lattice in Fig. 5, there are four potential redundant paths: P03, P05, P09, and P10. We select P03 for removal first and the concept lattice is revised as shown in Fig. 6.

Then, after we further select P05 for removal, there is no more redundant feasible path in the resultant concept lattice as shown in Fig. 7. Therefore the remaining set of feasible paths {P07, P08, P09, P10, P12} is considered to be minimal whilst fulfilling the all-transitions coverage criterion. With that result, we can further develop a specification of test cases (listed in Fig. 8) corresponding to the minimal set of feasible paths.

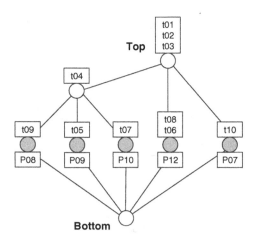

**Fig. 7.** Revised concept lattice for the minimal set of feasible paths

| Path P07 | Step 1 | Step 2 | Step 3 | Step 4 | Step 5 |
|---|---|---|---|---|---|
| Start State | Off | Ready | Playing | Paused | Off |
| Event | 'on' button pressed | 'play' button pressed | 'pause' button pressed | 'off' button pressed | 'on' button pressed |
| Triggered transition | t01 | t02 | t03 | t10 | t01 |
| Next State | Ready | Playing | Paused | Off | Ready |

| Path P08 | Step 1 | Step 2 | Step 3 | Step 4 | Step 5 |
|---|---|---|---|---|---|
| Start State | Off | Ready | Playing | Paused | Playing |
| Event | 'on' button pressed | 'play' button pressed | 'pause' button pressed | 'play' button pressed | 'off' button pressed |
| Triggered transition | t01 | t02 | t03 | t04 | t09 |
| Next State | Ready | Playing | Paused | Playing | Off |

| Path P09 | Step 1 | Step 2 | Step 3 | Step 4 | Step 5 |
|---|---|---|---|---|---|
| Start State | Off | Ready | Playing | Paused | Playing |
| Event | 'on' button pressed | 'play' button pressed | 'pause' button pressed | 'play' button pressed | 'stop' button pressed |
| Triggered transition | t01 | t02 | t03 | t04 | t05 |
| Next State | Ready | Playing | Paused | Playing | Ready |

| Path P10 | Step 1 | Step 2 | Step 3 | Step 4 | Step 5 |
|---|---|---|---|---|---|
| Start State | Off | Ready | Playing | Paused | Playing |
| Event | 'on' button pressed | 'play' button pressed | 'pause' button pressed | 'play' button pressed | finished playing |
| Triggered transition | t01 | t02 | t03 | t04 | t07 |
| Next State | Ready | Playing | Paused | Playing | Ready |

| Path P12 | Step 1 | Step 2 | Step 3 | Step 4 | Step 5 |
|---|---|---|---|---|---|
| Start State | Off | Ready | Playing | Paused | Ready |
| Event | 'on' button pressed | 'play' button pressed | 'pause' button pressed | 'stop' button pressed | 'off' button pressed |
| Triggered transition | t01 | t02 | t03 | t06 | t08 |
| Next State | Ready | Playing | Paused | Ready | Off |

**Fig. 8.** Specification of test cases for the selected feasible paths

## 5  Conclusion

In this paper, we have described an application of FCA to support model-based testing. Fig. 9 summarizes the process of the proposed mechanism. First, we start with a UML state machine model of the target system. By traversing the state machine diagram, a set of feasible paths can be derived. With the notion of concept lattice, the primary contribution of this work is through analyzing the formal context of transition coverage relationship of "feasible path $p$ covers transition $t$", we can determine a minimal set of feasible paths which fulfill the all-transitions coverage criterion.

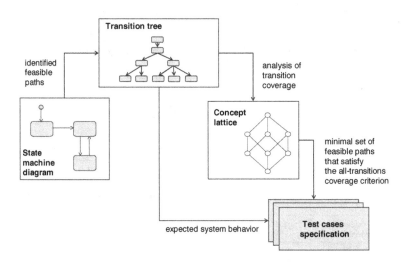

**Fig. 9.** Application of FCA for model-based test suite reduction

## References

1. Arévalo, G., Ducasse, S., Nierstrasz, O.: Lessons learned in applying formal concept analysis to reverse engineering. In: Ganter, B., Godin, R. (eds.) ICFCA 2005. LNCS (LNAI), vol. 3403, pp. 95–112. Springer, Heidelberg (2005)
2. Bertolino, A., Inverardi, P., Muccini, H.: Formal Methods in Testing Software Architectures. In: Bernardo, M., Inverardi, P. (eds.) Formal Methods for Software Architectures, pp. 122–147. Springer, Heidelberg (2003)
3. Binder, R.V.: Testing Object-Oriented Systems-Models, Patterns, and Tools. Addison-Wesley, Reading (1999)
4. Briand, L.C., Labiche, Y., Cui, J.: Automated Support for Deriving Test Requirements from UML Statecharts. Software and Systems Modeling 4(4), 399–423 (2005)
5. Broekman, B., Notenboom, E.: Testing Embedded Software. Addison-Wesley, Reading (2003)
6. Chen, T.Y., Lau, M.F.: A New Heuristic for Test Suite Reduction. Information and Software Technology 40, 347–354 (1998)

7. Chevalley, P., Thevenod-Fosse, P.: Automated Generation of Statistical Test Cases from UML State Diagrams. In: 25th Annual International Computer Software and Applications Conference, COMPSAC 2001, October 8-12, pp. 205–214 (2001)
8. Cormen, T.H., Leiserson, C.E., Rivest, R.L., Stein, C.: Introduction to Algorithms, Second edn. MIT Press, Cambridge (2001)
9. Ganter, B., Wille, R.: Formal Concept Analysis: Mathematical Foundations. Springer, Heidelberg (1999)
10. Godin, R., Mili, H.: Building and Maintaining Analysis-Level Class Hierarchies Using Galois Lattices. In: OOPSLA 1993 Conference on Object-oriented Programming Systems, Languages and Applications, pp. 394–410 (1993)
11. Harrold, M.J.: Testing: a Roadmap. In: ICSE - The Future of Software Engineering Track, Limerick, Ireland, June 4-11, pp. 61–72 (2000)
12. Harrold, M.J., Gupta, R., Soffa, M.L.: A Methodology for Controlling the Size of a Test Suite. ACM Transactions on Software Engineering and Methodology 2(3), 270–285 (1993)
13. Hartmann, J., Imoberdorf, C., Meisinger, M.: UML-based Integration Testing. In: ACM Symposium on Software Testing and Analysis, pp. 60–70 (2000)
14. Kim, Y.G., Hong, H.S., Cho, S.M., Bae, D.H., Cha, S.D.: Test Cases Generation from UML State Diagrams. IEEE Software 146(4), 187–192 (1999)
15. Korel, B., Singh, I., Tahat, L., Vaysburg, B.: Slicing of State-based Models. In: International Conference on Software Maintenance, ICSM 2003, pp. 34–43 (2003)
16. Lindig, C.: Fast Concept Analysis. In: Stumme, G. (ed.) Working with Conceptual Structures - Contributions to ICCS 2000. Shaker Verlag, Aachen (2000)
17. Murthy, P.V.R., Anitha, P.C., Mahesh, M., Subramanyan, R.: Test Ready UML Statechart Models. In: 2006 International Workshop on Scenarios and State Machines: Models, Algorithms, and Tools SCESM 2006, pp. 75–82 (2006)
18. Nobe, C.R., Warner, W.E.: Lessons Learned from a Trial Application of Requirements Modeling using Statecharts. In: Second International Conference on Requirements Engineering, April 15-18, pp. 86–93 (1996)
19. Offutt, J., Liu, S., Abdurazik, A., Ammann, P.: Generating Test Data from State-based Specifications. Software Testing, Verification and Reliability 13(1), 25–53 (2003)
20. Rumbaugh, J., Jacobson, I., Booch, G.: The Unified Modeling Language Reference Manual, 2nd edn. Addison-Wesley, Boston (2005)
21. Sampath, S., Mihaylov, V., Souter, A., Pollock, L.: A Scalable Approach to User-Session Based Testing of Web Applications through Concept Analysis. In: Automated Software Engineering, 19th International Conference on (ASE 2004), Linz, Austria (2004)
22. Snelting, G.: Reengineering of Configurations Based on Mathematical Concept Analysis. ACM Transactions on Software Engineering and Methodology 5(2), 146–189 (1996)
23. Tallam, S., Gupta, N.: A Concept Analysis Inspired Greedy Algorithm for Test Suite Minimization. In: 6th ACM SIGPLAN-SIGSOFT Workshop on Program Analysis for Software Tools and Engineering PASTE 2005, vol. 31(1), pp. 35–42 (2005)
24. Utting, M., Legeard, B.: Practical Model-Based Testing: A Tools Approach. Morgan Kaufmann, San Francisco (2007)

# The Prediction Model of Software Reliability Based on Fractals

Yong Cao[1], Qingxin Zhu[1], and Bo Yang[2]

[1] Institute of Computer Science and Engineering, University of Electronic Science and
Technology of China, Chengdu, Sichuan, China
[2] Institute of Computer Science and Engineering, Sichuan University, Chengdu, Sichuan, China
cn_caoyong@126.com

**Abstract.** Software-reliability models are used for the assessment and improvement of reliability in software systems. It is one of the most important
qualities of software, and failure analysis is an important part of the research of
software reliability. An underlying assumption of these models is that software
failures occur randomly in time. This assumption has never been quantitatively
tested. But we try to predict software failures by fractal method. Fractals are
mathematical or natural objects that are made of parts similar to the whole in
certain ways. A fractal has a self-similar structure that occurs at different scales.
In this paper the failure data of software are analyzed, the fractals are discovered in the data, and the method of software failure prediction based on fractals
is proposed. Analyzing the empirical failure data (three data sets including two
of Musa's) validates the validity of the model. It should be noticed that the
analyses and research methods in this paper are differ from the conventional
methods in the past, and a new idea for the research of the software failure
mechanism is presented.

**Keywords:** reliability, fractals, software failure prediction, qualities of software.

## 1 Introduction

As the development of computer science, software has been applied in national economy and national defense widely, and it plays an essential part in the contemporary
information society. Software reliability, namely the capability that a given component or system within a specified environment will operate correctly for a specified
period of time, has been one of the most important qualities [9, 16, 17]. In general, the
probability of correct operation is inversely related to the length of time specified; the
longer a system operates, the greater the chance of failure. The software reliability
model is used not only to estimate reliability, but also to measure and control the
software test. The important problem of the software reliability model is to calculate
and predict the next failure time in advance [10]. It was treated as random and statistical problem in the past, and the modeling methods are usually based on probability
statistics. The famous models are Jelinsky-Moranda based on time measurement,
Littlewood, and Goel -Okumoto etc. Their fundamental essence is to fit the sequence

T.-h. Kim et al. (Eds.): ASEA 2008, CCIS 30, pp. 124–136, 2009.

of failure time according to statistics, and predict the next failure time through conditional distribution. Jelinsky-Moranda model based on maximum likeness estimation [34], and Littlewood model based on Gamma distribution are categorized in exponential model. Goel-Okumoto model is the mutation of Jelinsky-Moranda model based on non-homogeneous Poisson process [15, 34, 36]. An non-homogeneous Poisson process is a counting process $N(t)$ of the form

$$P\{N(t) = k\} = \frac{(m(t))^k}{k!} e^{-m(t)} \tag{1}$$

where $N(t)$ is the number of events observed by time $t$ and $m(t)$ is the mean value function. The non-homogeneous Poisson process is a very common framework for Software-reliability models; development of new non-homogeneous Poisson process models continues to this day, with some recent examples found in [27], [28], [29], and [30].

Software-reliability engineering is based on the collection of reliability growth data only, as opposed to the collection of both reliability growth and life data in hardware reliability. This is due to the logical nature of the software. Life testing is an attempt to estimate the mean and variance of the lifetime of a system in operation, by running many copies until failure under identical conditions. Reliability growth data, on the other hand, consist of the times between successive failures of a system under test; this corresponds with th*e usual debug and test cycle used in software development. Once these data are collected, we can attempt to fit a software-reliability model to the model and thereby obtain the reliability function, failure rate, and mean time to failure for the software system.

A few papers have used time-series analysis in the construction of Software-reliability models, by treating reliability growth data as an auto-regressive process. In [32], a time series of software reliability data was assumed to arise from a power-law process.

$$T_i = \delta_i T_{i-1}^{\theta(i)} \tag{2}$$

where $T_i$ is the time to the ith failure, $\theta(i)$ is an unknown constant, and $\delta_i$ is a random coefficient. By assuming that the $T_i$s and $\delta_i$s are lognormally distributed, we can take the logarithm of both sides and obtain a first-order auto-regressive process. A more complex time-series model based on an auto-regressive integrated moving average process is presented in [31]. This paper also stands out because a small number of software complexity metrics are integrated into the model along with reliability growth data.

The term fractal, which means broken or irregular fragments, was originally coined by Mandelbrot to describe a family of complex shapes that possess an inherent self-similarity or self-affinity in their geometrical structure. It was generally believed by mathematicians and scientists that such complex natural phenomena were almost beyond rigorous description. Despite this general sentiment, Benoit Mandalbrot studied the structures of these objects and succeeded not only in describing them well for the first time, but also in showing that they are all related to one another. The original inspiration for the development of fractal geometry came largely from an in-depth study of the patterns of nature. Fractals are mathematical or natural objects that are made of parts similar to the whole in "some" ways. A fractal has a self-similar structure that occurs at different scales. For example, a small branch of a tree looks like the whole tree due to the existence of branching structures. When the length of a shoreline is measured using the box counting method, the length of any segment can cover the same number of mesh boxes as the whole shoreline if a change of scale is performed. For a detailed explanation of fractals, the reader can refer to Mandelbrot's book Fractal Geometry of Nature [7].

Since the pioneering work of Mandelbrot and others, a wide variety of applications for fractals continue to be found in many branches of science and engineering [1, 2]. Fractals can be applicable in depicting natural complexities, which have been applied to biology, geophysics, solid physics, chemistry, and astronomy etc. It is also well known that fractals have been applied to analyse and prediction of some random affairs like earthquakes. They are also used in random movements like random walk or Brown movement so that we can discover the character of fractional dimension. Can fractals be applied to analyse and prediction of software failures?

In this paper after analyzing data of software failure, we find out the fractal relation between the cumulate time of software failure and the accumulative number of software failure and we alter the tradition method of fractal research and bring forward the software reliability model based on fractals. We will approach software-reliability modeling by investigating three sets of software-reliability data using the methods of nonlinear time-series analysis. Our results do, indeed, indicate that a deterministic process, rather than a stochastic one, is most likely at work in these datasets. Furthermore, there is some evidence of fractal dynamics in these datasets, although this latter is not conclusive.

The outline of this paper is the following: Section 2 introduces fractal power law; Section 3 presents fractal model of software failure prediction and validate the model through analyzing the empirical failure data; Section 4 concludes this paper and describes the future research.

## 2   Power Law

The word Fractal describes a new system of mathematics so powerful that it can actually describe the structure of mountains, coastlines, galaxies, and other such natural phenomena. It was generally believed by mathematicians and scientists that such complex natural phenomena were almost beyond rigorous description. Fractal objects are Self-Similar under some change in scale, either strictly, or statistically. For Strictly Self-Similar Fractals do not change their appearance significantly when viewed under a microscope of arbitrary magnifying power, whereas for Statistically Self-Similar Fractals, when a small portion of it is magnified, results into a Fractal, which is seemingly but not exactly similar to the original Fractal itself. Fractal objects, by definition, contain infinite datail i.e., they contain the same degree of detail in each part as is contained in the entire object, no matter how many times sections of it are enlarged [7].

A power law is a relationship between two scalar variables $x$ and $y$, which can be written as follows:

$$y = Cx^k \tag{3}$$

where C is the constant of proportionality and k is the exponent of the power law. Such a power law relationship shows as a straight line on a log-log plot since, taking logs of both sides, the above equation is equivalent to

$$\log(y) = k\log(x) + \log(C) \tag{4}$$

which has the same form as the equation for a straight line

$$Y = kX + c \tag{5}$$

The equation $f(x) = C \cdot x^k$ has a property that relative scale change $f(sx)/f(x) = s^k$ is independent of $x$. In this sense, $f(x)$ lacks a characteristic scale or is scale invariant. Consequently, $f(x)$ can be related to fractals because of its scale invariance. The $k$ is called Fractal Dimension [7].

For Strictly Self-Similar Fractals, two scalar variables $x$ and $y$ fit power law strictly described as (2); for Statistically Self-Similar Fractals, the $x$ and $y$ fit power law statistically and fractal dimension $k$ is slope of linear regression on a log-log plot described as (2) [7].

## 3   The Software Failure Prediction Based on Fractals

Time series are able to characterize the prediction of software systems. The software failure can be described as the cumulate time of software failure and the accumulative number of software failure. Nonlinear time-series analysis is used to extract invariant features from systems that exhibit deterministic fractals. Table 1 is the first Musa's data set of failure time. In order to analyze the failure time data correctly, we must transform Table 1 into Table 2 for we need analyze the relationship between the cumulate time of software failure and the accumulative number of software failure.

**Table 1.** The Musa's data set 1 of software failure time series, and from left to right time in each cell denotes distance between the i-1th failure and the ith failure, i=1, 2, ...... .  Unit: second.

| 3 | 30 | 113 | 81 | 115 |
|-----|-----|------|-----|------|
| 9 | 2 | 91 | 112 | 15 |
| 138 | 50 | 77 | 24 | 108 |
| 88 | 670 | 120 | 26 | 114 |
| 325 | 55 | 242 | 68 | 422 |
| 180 | 10 | 1146 | 600 | 15 |
| 36 | 4 | 0 | 8 | 227 |
| 65 | 176 | 58 | 457 | 300 |
| 97 | 263 | 452 | 255 | 197 |
| 193 | 6 | 79 | 816 | 1351 |
| 148 | 21 | 233 | 134 | 357 |
| 193 | 236 | 31 | 369 | 748 |
| 0 | 232 | 330 | 365 | 1222 |
| 543 | 10 | 16 | 529 | 379 |

| 44 | 129 | 810 | 290 | 300 |
|------|------|------|------|------|
| 529 | 281 | 160 | 828 | 1011 |
| 445 | 296 | 1755 | 1064 | 1783 |
| 860 | 983 | 707 | 33 | 868 |
| 724 | 2323 | 2930 | 1461 | 843 |
| 12 | 261 | 1800 | 865 | 1435 |
| 30 | 143 | 108 | 0 | 3110 |
| 1247 | 943 | 700 | 875 | 245 |
| 729 | 1897 | 447 | 386 | 446 |
| 122 | 990 | 948 | 1082 | 22 |
| 75 | 482 | 5509 | 100 | 10 |
| 1071 | 371 | 790 | 6150 | 3321 |
| 1045 | 648 | 5485 | 1160 | 1864 |
| 4116 | | | | |

**Table 2.** The Musa's data set 1 of failure time series, and from left to right the time in each cell denotes the cumulate time of the ith software failure, i=1, 2, ...... . Unit: second.

| 3 | 33 | 146 | 227 | 342 |
|------|------|------|------|------|
| 351 | 353 | 444 | 556 | 571 |
| 709 | 759 | 836 | 860 | 968 |
| 1056 | 1726 | 1846 | 1872 | 1986 |
| 2311 | 2366 | 2608 | 2676 | 3098 |
| 3278 | 3288 | 4434 | 5034 | 5049 |
| 5085 | 5089 | 5089 | 5097 | 5324 |
| 5389 | 5565 | 5623 | 6080 | 6380 |
| 6477 | 6740 | 7192 | 7447 | 7644 |
| 7837 | 7843 | 7922 | 8738 | 10089 |
| 10237 | 10258 | 10491 | 10625 | 10982 |
| 11175 | 11411 | 11442 | 11811 | 12559 |
| 12559 | 12791 | 13121 | 13486 | 14708 |
| 15251 | 15261 | 15277 | 15806 | 16185 |
| 16229 | 16358 | 17168 | 17458 | 17758 |
| 18287 | 18568 | 18728 | 19556 | 20567 |
| 21012 | 21308 | 23063 | 24127 | 25910 |
| 26770 | 27753 | 28460 | 28493 | 29361 |
| 30085 | 32408 | 35338 | 36799 | 37642 |
| 37654 | 37915 | 39715 | 40580 | 42015 |
| 42045 | 42188 | 42296 | 42296 | 45406 |
| 46653 | 47596 | 48296 | 49171 | 49416 |
| 50145 | 52042 | 52489 | 52875 | 53321 |
| 53443 | 54433 | 55381 | 56463 | 56485 |
| 56560 | 57042 | 62551 | 62651 | 62661 |
| 63732 | 64103 | 64893 | 71043 | 74364 |
| 75409 | 76057 | 81542 | 82702 | 84566 |
| 88682 | | | | |

Fractals can be characterized by dimensional measures, such as the Hausdorff dimension etc. The fractal dimension is often noninteger and smaller than the embedding topological dimension. Previously we always adopt "scale variation" to analyze fractal dimension of data such as earthquakes etc. We select time section $t$ as scale $\varepsilon$, divide the time section into some time subsections and take count of $N(\varepsilon)$ which is the number of subsections the earthquake happen. Then we change the time section $\varepsilon$ to obtain a new $N(\varepsilon)$ and we repeat the above steps to obtain a series of $\varepsilon - N(\varepsilon)$ pairs. We regard a $\varepsilon - N(\varepsilon)$ pair of the series as a point in log-log coordinate and draw a $\log \varepsilon$-log $N(\varepsilon)$ graph to analyze the data. This method is inapplicable to analyzing the data of software failure time for its key is prediction of next failure time whereas the next failure time is non- determinate. There will make a lot of waste if we adopt "scale variation" to analyze the data of software failure. According to (2), let $y=N(r)$ which is the accumulative number of software failure and $x=r$ which is the cumulate time of software failure. The formula will be describe as:

$$\log r = \frac{1}{k}\log(N(r)) - \frac{1}{k}\log(C) \tag{6}$$

Let $L= r$, $d = \frac{1}{k}$, and $l = N(r)$. The formula (4) can be transformed into:

$$\log L = d \log l - d \log(C) \tag{7}$$

$$L = sl^d \tag{8}$$

where let $s = C^{-d}$. When software failures happen, if there exists fractal relationship between the cumulate time of software failure and the accumulative number of software failure, the time fractal dimension will be computed.

$$d = \frac{\log(t_{i_j}) - \log(t_{i_k})}{\log(i_j) - \log(i_k)} \tag{9}$$

where $i_j$, $i_k$ denote the ordinal number of software failure and $t_{i_j}$, $t_{i_k}$ denote corresponding failure time.

At first, we compute double log coordinates of the cumulate time of software failure and the accumulative number of software failure log t-log N(t) (See Fig.1). Obviously the slope $d$ of each beeline connects point pairs (3, 20), (3, 21), (3, 22), ......, (3 80) is between 1.52-0.07 and 1.52+0.07. All points are almost in a beeline, where $d= \frac{1}{k}$ and k is fractal dimension. It is observed that the there exists fractal relationship between the cumulate time of software failure and the accumulative number of software failure in part. Whether the relationship always exists need further validation.

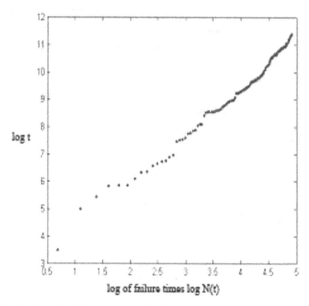

**Fig. 1.** The double log coordinates of the cumulate time of software failure and the accumulative number of software failure log t -log N(t) of Musa's failure data set 1

After software failure happens, maintenance personnel will repair software system, correct mistake and reliability of software will be changed. The fractal dimension $k$ will change and $d$ will also change. We adopt method of slide window to compute.

We suppose there are $m$ points in a slide window, and from point 1 to $m$ we compute the double logarithm of each point and work out parameters according to method linear regression. Then using the parameters we can predict the failure time of point $m+1$. We slide the window to point 2 and there are point 2, 3,......, $m+1$ in the slide window. From point 2 to $m+1$ we compute the double logarithm of each point in slide window and work out parameters according to method linear regression. We can predict the failure time of point $m+2$ again. The rest points may be deduced by analogy and we obtain the all predictions after point $m$. Now we choose slide window $m=7$ and make prediction of Musa's data set 1 of software failure. The comparison between prediction data and practical data is shown as Fig. 2. It is obvious that the prediction data almost fit practical data in Musa's failure data set 1.

When $m=7$, the maximal difference between prediction data and practical data of Musa's data set 1 of software failure is less than 5.6% and commonly the difference is less than 1%. Then we choose $m$ from 8 to 30 and the maximal difference is less than 5.8% and when $m=26$ the difference is less than 2%, which is optimum. Obviously in the slide window the double log coordinates of the cumulate time of software failure and the accumulative number of software failure log t-log N(t) preserve linearity well. Although with the slide of window the slope that we use linear regression to obtain will change, the linearity still exists, namely when window slides, the points in the anterior window and the points in the subsequent window may not be in a beeline

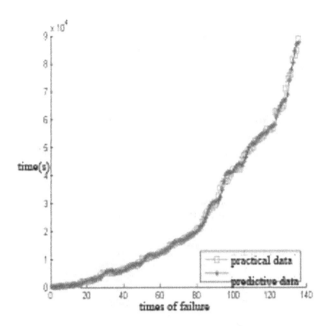

**Fig. 2.** The comparison between prediction data and practical data of Musa's data set 1 of software failure

approximately, the points in same window are sure in a beeline approximately. We can make a relatively exact prediction to next point. The prediction algorithm will be described as follow:

## Algorithm 1

```
Begin
Initialization: suppose the size of slide window m, k=1
and A is a array of the number of failure corresponding
failure time;
Repeat for i=k to m+k-1 {
        B(i)=log(A(i));/*the Alogarithm of practical failure time in the slide
window.*/
        C(i)=log(i);/*the Alogarithm of failure number in the slide window.*/
    }
```

(1)        According to (5) and method of linear regression, compute the slope of linear regression in the slide window $b=d=\dfrac{1}{k}$ and constant $a=\log(s)=-d\log(C)$;

(2)        Make a prediction of next point out of the slide window using the above $a$ and $b$.

(3)             Add the practical failure time of the
               next point to *A*;
               *k*++; /\*the slide window move backwards.\*/
Until test over
End

Then we analyze the Musa's data set 2 (Table 3) and NTDS data set (Table 4) in same method. Their prediction data almost fit practical data in Musa's data set 2 and NTDS data set (see Fig.3, Fig.4 and Table 5). It is observed that the fractal model of prediction is valid.

**Table 3.** The Musa's data set 2 of software failure time series, and from left to right time in each cell denotes distance between the i-1th failure and the ith failure, i=1, 2, ...... . Unit: second.

| | | | |
|---|---|---|---|
| 320 | 1439 | 9000 | 2880 |
| 5700 | 21800 | 26800 | 113540 |
| 112137 | 660 | 2700 | 28493 |
| 2173 | 7263 | 10865 | 4230 |
| 8460 | 14805 | 11844 | 5361 |
| 6553 | 6499 | 3124 | 51323 |
| 17010 | 1890 | 5400 | 62313 |
| 24826 | 26335 | 363 | 13989 |
| 15058 | 32377 | 41632 | 4160 |
| 82040 | 13189 | 3426 | 5833 |
| 640 | 640 | 2880 | 110 |
| 22080 | 60654 | 52163 | 12546 |
| 784 | 10193 | 7841 | 31365 |
| 24313 | 298890 | 1280 | 22099 |
| 19150 | 2611 | 39170 | 55794 |
| 42632 | 267600 | 87074 | 149606 |
| 14400 | 34560 | 39600 | 334395 |
| 296015 | 177395 | 214622 | 156400 |
| 166800 | 10800 | 267000 | |

**Table 4.** The NTDS data set of software failure time series, and from left to right time in each cell denotes distance between the i-1th failure and the ith failure, i=1, 2, ...... . Unit: hour.

| | | | | |
|---|---|---|---|---|
| 9 | 21 | 32 | 36 | 43 |
| 45 | 50 | 58 | 63 | 70 |
| 71 | 77 | 78 | 87 | 91 |
| 92 | 92 | 95 | 98 | 104 |
| 105 | 116 | 149 | 156 | 247 |
| 249 | 250 | 337 | 384 | 396 |
| 405 | 540 | 798 | 814 | 849 |

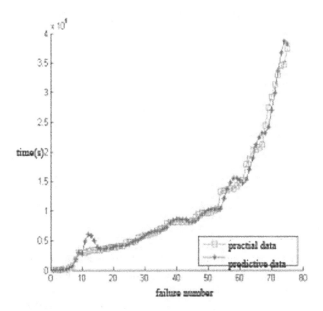

**Fig. 3.** The comparison between prediction data and practical data of Musa's data set 2 of software failure

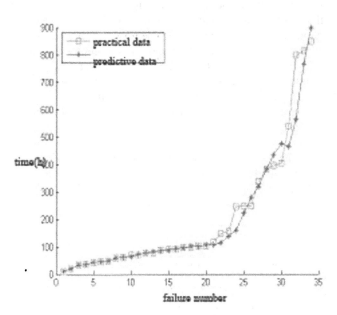

**Fig. 4.** The comparison between prediction data and practical data of NTDS data set 2 of software failure

Table 5. The deviation of Algorithm 1. m stands for the size of slide window.

|  | m(the size of slide window) | Accumulative Deviation | Mean Square Deviation |
|---|---|---|---|
| NTDS | 9 | 2.2972 | 51.7252 |
| Musa 1 | 8 | 5.4717 | 1087.4 |
| Musa 2 | 8 | 6.1718 | 116670 |

## 4  Conclusions

Reliability is one of the most important qualities of software, and failure analysis is an important part of the research of software reliability. The important problem of the software reliability model is to calculate and predict the next failure time in advance. This paper analyzes the empirical failure data, discovers the fractal relationship between the cumulate time of software failure and the accumulative number of software failure, and proposes the software reliability model based on fractals to predict the next software failure time which almost fit the practical failure time. Studying the empirical data (three data sets including two of Musa's) validates the model. It should be noticed that the analyses and research methods in this paper are differ from the conventional methods in the past, and a new idea for the research of the software failure mechanism is provided. In the future we will attempt to replicate our experimental results on high-quality reliability data obtained from a modern software project. Then we will attempt to reconstruct the fault set of a large software system, and determine if this fault set is, in fact, a fractal subset of the system input space. It is well known that random or chaos can give rise to fractals. We will research the mechanism behind fractals further in future work and draw a clear conclusion.

**Acknowledgments.** The work described in this paper was supported by a grant from the National Science Foundation of China (NSFC) (60671033) and the Doctoral Foundation of the National Ministry of Education (2006061405).

## References

1. Mandelbrot, B.B.: Fractal: Form, chance and Dimension. Freeman, San Francisco (1977)
2. Mandelbrot, B.B.: The Fractal Geometry of Nature. Freeman, San Francisco (1982)
3. Feder, J.: Fractals. Plenum Press, New York (1988)
4. Gleick, J.: CHAOS. Viking Penguin Inc., New York (1988)
5. Wolf, A., Swift, B., Swinney, H.L., Vastano, J.A.: Determining Lyapunov Exponents from a Time Series. Physics 16D(1), 285–347 (1985)
6. Musa, J.D.: Software Reliability Data, Technical report available from Data Analysis Center for Software. Rome Air Development Center, New York (1979)

7. Wu, J., Holt, R.C., Hassan, A.E.: Empirical Evidence for SOC Dynamics in Software Evolution. In: ICSM 2007. IEEE CS, Los Alamitos (2007)
8. Grebogi, C., Ott, E., Peliken, S., York, J.A.: Strange attractors that are not chaotic. Physics 13D(1&2), 261–268 (1984)
9. Chen, H_w., Wang, J., Dong, W.: High Confidence Software Engineering Technologies. Acta Electronica Sinica 12 (2003)
10. Cai, K.: Fundamentals of Engineering of Software Reliability. Tsinghua University Press, Beijing (1995)
11. Zhang, J.: Fractals. Tsinghua University Press, Beijing (1995)
12. Chen, S.: Image and Chaos. Defense Industry Press, Beijing (1995)
13. Ge, S., Zhu, H.: Fractals of tribology, vol. 4. China Machine Press, Beijing (2005)
14. Zhan, K., Xiong, Q.: Software Defect Fractal Growing and Mechanism Analysis. Journal of Wuhan University of Technology 1 (2004)
15. Zou, F., Li, C.: A Chaotic Model for Software Reliability. Chinese Journal of computers 3 (2001)
16. Dick, S., Bethel, C.L., Kandel, A.: Software-Reliability Modeling: The Case for Deterministic Behavior. IEEE Transactions On Systems, Man, And Cybernetics—Part A: Systems And Humans 37(1) (January 2007)
17. Lewis, E.E.: Introduction to Reliability Engineering, 2nd edn. Wiley, New York (1996)
18. Brooks, W.D., Motley, R.W.: Analysis of discrete software reliability models. Rome Air Development Center, Rome, NY, Tech. Rep. RADCTR-80-84 (April 1980)
19. Cai, K.-Y., Wen, C.-Y., Zhang, M.-L.: A critical review on software reliability modeling. Reliab. Eng. Syst. Safety 32(3), 357–371 (1991)
20. Dunham, J.R.: Experiments in software reliability: Life-critical applications. IEEE Trans. Softw. Eng. SE-12(1), 110–123 (1986)
21. Dunham, J.R., Finelli, G.B.: Real-time software failure characterization. In: Proc. 5th Annu. Conf. Comput. Assurance, COMPASS, Gaithersburg, MD, June 25–28, pp. 39–45 (1990)
22. Farr, W.: Software reliability modeling survey. In: Lyu, M.R. (ed.) Handbook of Software Reliability Engineering, pp. 71–115. McGraw-Hill, New York (1996)
23. Finelli, G.B.: NASA software failure characterization experiments. Reliab. Eng. Syst. Safety 32(1/2), 155–169 (1991)
24. Friedman, M.A., Voas, J.M.: Software Assessment: Reliability, Safety, Testability. Wiley, New York (1995)
25. Goel, A.L.: Software reliability models: Assumptions, limitations, and applicability. IEEE Trans. Softw. Eng. SE-11(12), 1411–1423 (1985)
26. Kantz, H., Schreiber, T.: Nonlinear Time Series Analysis. Cambridge Univ. Press, NewYork (1997)
27. Huang, C.-Y., Kuo, S.-Y.: Analysis of incorporating logistic testingeffort function into software reliability modeling. IEEE Trans. Rel. 51(3), 261–270 (2002)
28. Huang, C.-Y., Lyu, M.R., Kuo, S.-Y.: A unified scheme of some nonhomogenous Poisson process models for software reliability. IEEE Trans. Softw. Eng. 29(3), 261–269 (2003)
29. Pham, H., Nordmann, L., Zhang, X.: A general imperfect-software debugging model with S-shaped fault-detection rate. IEEE Trans. Rel. 48(2), 169–175 (1999)
30. Zhang, X., Teng, X., Pham, H.: Considering fault removal efficiency in software reliability assessment. IEEE Trans. Syst., Man, Cybern. A, Syst., Humans 33(1), 114–120 (2003)
31. Khoshgoftaar, T.M., Szabo, R.M.: Investigating ARIMA models of software system quality. Softw. Qual. J. 4(1), 33–48 (1995)

32. Singpurwalla, N.D., Soyer, R.: Assessing (software) reliability growth using a random co-efficient autoregressive process and its ramifications. IEEE Trans. Softw. Eng. SE-11(12), 1456–1464 (1985)
33. Iyer, R.K., Rossetti, D.J.: Effect of system workload on operating system reliability: A study on IBM 3081. IEEE Trans. Softw. Eng. SE-11(12), 1438–1448 (1985)
34. Jelinski, Z., Moranda, P.B.: Software reliability research. In: Proc. Statistical Comput. Performance Eval., Providence, RI, November 22–23, pp. 465–484 (1971)
35. Kanoun, K., Laprie, J.-C.: Trend analysis. In: Lyu, M.R. (ed.) Handbook of Software Reliability Engineering, pp. 401–437. McGraw-Hill, New York (1996)
36. Littlewood, B., Verrall, J.L.: A Bayesian reliability model with a stochastically monotone failure rate. IEEE Trans. Rel. R-23(2), 108–114 (1974)
37. Peitgen, H.-O., Henriques, J.M., Penedo, L.F. (eds.): Fractals in the Fundamental and Applied Sciences. North Holland, Amsterdam (1991)
38. Cherepanov, G.P., Balankin, A.S., Ivanova, V.S.: Fractal fracture mechanics. Eng. Fracture Mechan. 51, 997–1033 (1995)
39. Jeng, J.H., Varadan, V.V., Varadan, V.K.: Fractal finite element mesh generation for vibration problems. J. Acous. Soc. Amer. 82, 1829–1833 (1987)
40. Werner, D.H., Haupt, R.L., Werner, P.L.: Fractal antenna engineering: the theory and design of fractal antenna arrays. IEEE Antennas Propagat. Mag. 41, 37–59 (1999)

# New Approach to Information Sharing Using Linguistic Threshold Schemes

Marek R. Ogiela

AGH University of Science and Technology
Institute of Automatics
Al. Mickiewicza 30, PL-30-059 Krakow, Poland
mogiela@agh.edu.pl

**Abstract.** This publication presents a new proposal for extending classical algorithms of secret splitting and threshold secret sharing schemes to include another stage of information coding with the use of the linguistic approach. Such an algorithm would be based on the appropriate context-free grammar allowing shared bit sequences, and more generally blocks of several bits, to be changed into new representations, namely sequences of production numbers of the introduced grammar. This stage can be executed by a trusted arbiter or by a system generating shadows of the secret. Such methods would form an additional stage improving the security of shared data.

**Keywords:** Secret sharing, threshold schemes, intelligent information management.

## 1 Introduction

Modern information management systems use various techniques and methods to acquire data, order it, search for it semantically, classify it as secret, make meaning tables etc. They are designed to simplify the access to and improve the effectiveness of finding information with specific meaning. Cryptographic algorithms for threshold information sharing are among such techniques. They can be used to split important, strategic data and to assign its components to people from an authorised group. Such authorised, selective access to information is used when it is necessary to safely manage strategic information. This information may be military, but also sensitive personal or economic data. This last type of information is gaining increasing importance due to the globalisation of the world economy. Every modern company uses important information about the market situation, its own achievements, development plans, strategic activities, new launches, patents etc. Such data is usually classified and inaccessible to ordinary people. Within the structure of the specific organisation or company, there are individuals at the appropriate management levels who have access rights to the data addressed to them. Such rights are exercised in hierarchic structures, usually connected with the office held. In practice, this means that higher-placed individuals have access to more confidential data, and people at lower levels to less information. Consequently, the flow of information within such structures may require implementing hierarchical threshold

T.-h. Kim et al. (Eds.): ASEA 2008, CCIS 30, pp. 137–146, 2009.

schemes for secret and data splitting, which schemes assign the appropriate level of rights to individuals who want to receive authorised access to secret data at particular levels. Obviously, when talking of information management, we refer to data stored on digital media or in computer databases. For such data, there is a need to intelligently split it between the authorised individuals and then to reconstruct it in secret. Therefore, it is worth turning our attention to the other significant question related to intelligent information management. It is the question of the capacity to ensure secrecy and selective access to such data for the authorised persons. Such a potential of managing strategic information may be acquired thanks to the use of certain mathematical techniques, originating from the fields of cryptography and steganography. In our case, the task comes down to searching for the formulas that allow intelligent sharing of information in a way that would allow its reconstruction to appropriately authorised people. The only condition here is the possibility of splitting the data and later their reconstruction by a group of appropriately authorised people.

The task of this paper is to discuss such techniques. Especially the questions of information management will in this case focus on the development of linguistic extensions for the known threshold schemes of information sharing. The idea of threshold schemes itself was proposed already in the field of cryptography in [6]. This work, however, makes an attempt to enrich such techniques with an additional stage of splitting the linguistic representation, defining the split data in the binary form. To achieve this, a simple, context free grammar is introduced to allow converting a sequence of bits (representing the secret data) into its linguistic representation. This representation will then be subject to sharing with the use of one of the known threshold schemes. To reconstruct the entire secret, however, it will also be necessary to know a number of linguistic rules that will be assigned to one of the participants in the scheme.

## 2  Secret Sharing Algorithms

Algorithms for splitting and sharing information are a young branch of information technology and cryptography. In the most general case, their objective is to generate such parts for the data in question that could be shared by multiple authorised persons. What arises here is the problem of splitting information in a manner allowing its reconstruction by a certain $n$-person group interested in the reconstruction of the split information. Algorithm solutions developed to achieve this objective should at the same time make sure that none of the groups of participants in such a protocol, whose number is lesser than the required $m$ persons, could read the split message. The algorithms for dividing information make it possible to split it into chunks known as shadows that are later distributed among the participants of the protocol so that the shares of certain subsets of users, when combined together, are capable of reconstructing the original information. There are two groups of algorithms for dividing information, namely, *secret splitting* and *secret sharing*.

In the first technique, information is distributed among the participants of the protocol, and all the participants are required to put together their parts to have it reconstructed. A more universal method of splitting information is the latter method, i.e. *secret sharing*. In this case, the message is also distributed among the participants of the protocol, yet to have it reconstructed it is enough to have a certain number of constituent shares defined while building the scheme. The other type of splitting techniques are the methods for information sharing. They are information distribution methods that are somewhat more complex (in the mathematical sense). The algorithms for information sharing are also known as threshold schemes. Using such a scheme allows taking any information and splitting it into $n$ discretional parts known as shadows. In such a manner that any $m$ (where $m \leq n$) from among them may be used to reconstruct the information. This is the so-called $(m, n)$-threshold scheme. Threshold schemes for information sharing were devised independently by A. Shamir[17] and G. Blakley [1], and were thoroughly analysed by G. Simmons [18].

The next subsection describes a method of extending such classical threshold schemes for secret splitting to include an additional linguistic stage at which binary representations of the shared secret are coded into new sequences representing the rules of a formal grammar introduced. It also presents an opportunity to generalise the binary conversion procedure into the linguistic conversion of a larger number of bits. Such stages will introduce additional security against the unauthorised reconstruction of the information and can be executed in two independent versions of protocols for assigning created shadows to protocol participants. The first one is the version involving a trusted arbiter to mediate in the assignment and reconstruction of information. The second is the version without the arbiter (an additional trusted party), but with the assignment of the introduced grammar as a new, additional part of the secret.

## 3   Protocol for Grammar Extension during Shadow Generation

Executing the secret sharing protocol with the use of context-free grammars will lead to generating one additional shadow for the shared information. As already mentioned above, depending on the function of this information element, you can execute an arbitration protocol with a trusted arbiter holding the linguistic component necessary to reconstruct the secret, or a simple protocol without an arbiter. However, in the second case, the person holding the linguistic information (the grammar rule set) will be privileged, as his/her information will always be necessary to reconstruct the original secret. This situation will depend on the scheme executed and will be independent of the selected threshold secret sharing algorithm. This version can be beneficial when executing hierarchical threshold schemes, i.e. schemes with privileged shares. However, if it is necessary to create a fair, equal threshold scheme, the generation rule set of the grammar can be made public and then all shadows will have exactly equal rights.

Further, this work proposes an algorithm for expanding the operation of such schemes and generation of a single additional shadow in the form of linguistic information necessary for the reconstruction of the entirely secret. Main steps of using the grammatical approach to the expansion of threshold systems are presented in Table 1.

Table 1. Methodology of linguistic expansion threshold schemes

| Stage | Function |
|-------|----------|
| 1 | selection of one classical schemes for secret sharing e.g. the algorithms devised by Blakley, Shamir, Tang etc. |
| 2 | transformation of the input data into the form of bit sequence |
| 3 | definition of grammar generating bit positions for the shared data |
| 4 | application of analyser to parse the bit sequence |
| 5 | receiving a sequence of grammar rule numbers, being the result of parsing binary secret representation |
| 6 | splitting the new secret representation (in the form of sequence of production numbers) with the application of selected threshold scheme |
| 7 | distribution of shadows among the participants of the protocol |
| 8 | if the rules of grammar are known only to a trusted arbiter (arbitration protocol), the arbiter must always be included in the reconstruction of the secret |
| 9 | if the rules of grammar are made public, this is a pure threshold scheme |

The section below describes a sample context-free grammar converting bit sequences into linguistic representations.

## 4  Grammar Approach for Information Sharing

Expansion of the threshold scheme by an additional stage of converting the secret recorded in the form of a bit sequence is performed thanks to the application of context-free grammar in the following formula:

$$G_{SECRET}=(N, T, P, STS), \text{ where:}$$

$N = \{SECRET, A, B\}$ – non-terminal symbols,
$T = \{0, 1, \varepsilon\}$ – terminal symbols which define each bit value,
$\varepsilon$ – an empty symbol.
$STS = SECRET$ - grammar start symbol.
A production set P is defined in following way:

1. SECRET $\rightarrow$ A
2. A $\rightarrow$ B A
3. A $\rightarrow$ $\varepsilon$
4. B $\rightarrow$ 0
5. B $\rightarrow$ 1

The grammar presented here is context-free grammar [14], changing the bit sequences in the form of zeros and ones into a sequence of grammar production numbers that allow the generation of the original bit sequence. In practice, this means that the resulting sequence contains the numbers of rules of the grammar (i.e. values from the range 1,.., 6).

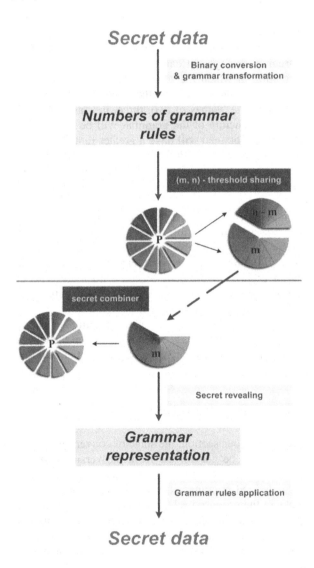

**Fig. 1.** Shadow generation scheme in the expanded threshold algorithm. The expansion concerns the use of grammar at the stage of converting the bit representation into sequences of numbers of linguistic rules in grammar.

The conversion of representation is ensured through syntax analyser (parser) that changes the bit sequence into numbers of linguistic rules of the grammar in square time. The graphic representation of using the grammar expansion in classical threshold schemes is presented in Fig. 1.

After performing such a transformation, any scheme of secret sharing can be applied to distribute the constituents among any number of $n$ participants of the protocol. This means that at this stage, any classical (m, n)-threshold algorithm for secret sharing can be run. However, the secret being split is not a pure bit sequence, but a sequence composed of numbers of syntactic rules of the introduced grammar. Depending on its structure and type, it can contain values of two or more bits. So you can imagine a situation in which the grammar conversion will not consist in transforming single bits (as shown above) but also transforming pairs or greater numbers of bits at the same time (i.e. values of two, three, four and more bits will be considered). In that case, the structure of the grammar will be similar, but the sequence of generation rule numbers obtained will have a greater range of values (i.e. the number of generation rules of the grammar defined for the conversion will increase). At the same time, as the number of generation rules in the grammar increases, the representations of coded bits (now understood as character sequences and not numerical values) grow shorter.

Executing the introduced algorithms provides an additional stage for re-coding the shared secret into a new representation using grammatical rules. The grammar itself can be kept secret or made available to the participants of the entire protocol.

If the allocation of grammatical rules is to remain secret, as mentioned earlier, what we deal with is an arbitration protocol, which – to reconstruct the secret for the authorised group of shadow owners –requires the participation of a trusted arbiter, equipped with information about grammar rules.

Should the grammar be disclosed, the reconstruction of the secret is possible without the participation of the trusted person and only on the basis of the constituent parts of the secret kept by the authorised group of participants in the algorithm of information sharing.

## 5   Grammars for Converting Bit Blocks

As pointed out in the previous section, the stage of converting the bit representation of the shared secret can also be generalised from the version coding single bits to the grammatical coding of bit blocks of various lengths. However, to avoid too many generation rules in the defined grammar, it is worth imposing a restriction on the length of coded bit blocks in the proposed scheme. It seems easy and natural to consider bit clusters no longer than 4-5 bits. Based on information theory, it is then easy to calculate that all representations of values coded with such lengths of machine words will fall within the range of 16 or 32 values, which, when combined with a few additional grammatical rules, allows us to estimate the total number of productions of this grammar as not exceeding 20 for 4-bit words and 40 for 5-bit words.

To illustrate the idea of such a broader linguistic coding, an example of a grammar that converts 3-bit clusters is presented below.

The main steps in executing that extended version are presented in Table 2. Table 2 shows that the version for 3-bit block linguistic transformation is distinguished from the original version converting single bit values only by stages 2 and 3 (in Table 2) which require defining the appropriate grammar and applying it during the transformation to sequences constituting the new representations.

**Table 2.** Extended threshold scheme with a version of three-bit block coding

| Stage | Function |
|-------|----------|
| 1 | selection of one classical schemes for secret sharing |
| 2 | creating a binary representation and grouping it into blocks 3 bits long |
| 3 | defining a grammar generating values with the preset bit length (here: 3 bits) |
| 4 | application of analyser to parse the bit sequence |
| 5 | receiving a sequence of grammar rule numbers, being the result of parsing binary secret representation |
| 6 | splitting the new secret representation with the application of selected threshold scheme |
| 7 | distribution of shadows among the participants of the protocol |

An example of a grammar capable of converting three-bit blocks to a new representation, which constitutes the shared secret at subsequent stages, is presented below. Such a grammar can be defined as follows:

$$G_{3\,BIT}=(\,N,\,T,\,P,\,STS),\text{ where:}$$

$N = \{$SECRET, A, B$\}$ – non-terminal symbols,
$T = \{$000, 001, 010, 011, 100, 101, 110, 111, $\varepsilon\}$ – terminal symbols which define each 3-bit value,
$\varepsilon$ – an empty symbol.
$STS =$ SECRET - grammar start symbol.
A production set P is defined in following way:

1.  SECRET$\rightarrow$ A
2.  A $\rightarrow$ B A
3.  A $\rightarrow \varepsilon$
4.  B $\rightarrow$ 000
5.  B $\rightarrow$ 001
6.  B $\rightarrow$ 010
7.  B $\rightarrow$ 011
8.  B $\rightarrow$ 100

9.   B → 101
10.  B → 110
11.  B → 111

A grammar introduced in this way can support a quicker and briefer re-coding of the input representation of the secret to be shared. Versions for longer bit blocks can be used in the same way. However, this will require introducing a greater number of generation rules. An obvious benefit of grouping bits into larger blocks is that during the following steps of the secret sharing protocol we get shorter representations for the data that is split and then reconstructed. This is particularly visible when executing procedures that use excessive bit representations, i.e. when single-bit or several-bit values are saved and interpreted using codes in 8 or 16-bit representations.

The level of security achieved does not depend on the length of blocks converted using the rules of the introduced grammar.

## 6  Conclusion

This work presents the potential of expanding threshold secret sharing schemes with the linguistic descriptions that allow obtaining additional representations that improve the security of the information being split. Linguistic representations were achieved as a result of using context-free grammars that allow conversion of bit representation (the shared secret) to the form of a series of numbers of grammatical rules that allow the generation of the bit description.

In addition to converting representations in the form of single bits, a methodology of generalising the proposed scheme to a linguistic conversion of larger bit blocks is also presented.

Such a conversion to the linguistic form is possible thanks to the use of a parser of polynominal complexity. The possibility of establishing new types of arbitration protocols is the result of introducing linguistic descriptions to the schemes used. The arbitration protocol operates when the rules of the introduced grammar remain secret and are stored with a trusted arbiter. In this case, however, what is necessary to reconstruct the secret is the participation of the arbiter, who will have to disclose his share (being the rules of grammar). Another solution is developing an extended scheme in the case when the grammar defined is public. In such a case, the secret split has the form of a series of grammar production numbers. Such a presentation is shared by all the participants of the protocol with the same authorisation. The authorised subset of generated shadows allows for the composition of the secret, and the knowledge of the grammatical rules allows for converting this secret into the form of a bit, and later numerical or text, sequence.

The research conducted in this field by the author is focused on the definition of methodology and effective means of using threshold techniques for information sharing for multilevel, intelligent management of strategic data in digital form. The implementation of the method described allows using mathematical techniques for tasks from the realm of intelligent information management in the case of information assigned to large groups of users or employers of institutions and enterprises. As application of such methods allows sharing information in any institution, the subsequent step in our research will be an attempt to define the model structure or flow and assignment of constituent information to individual groups of interested and authorised persons. Such a model may later be implemented practically on the basis of existing information systems (personal, payment and project data, company secrets, etc.).

An important element of the approach presented here is the application of methods of mathematical linguistics. Recently, such methods have been widely used in semantic interpretation of patterns in [14][20]. Author of this work make efforts to create intelligent cognitive schemes used for information sharing tasks that make use of biometric techniques.

**Acknowledgements.** This work has been supported by the AGH University of Science and Technology under Grant No. 10.10.120.783.

# References

1. Asmuth, C.A., Bloom, J.: A modular approach to key safeguarding. IEEE Transactions on Information Theory 29, 208–210 (1983)
2. Ateniese, G., Blundo, C., De Santis, A., Stinson, D.R.: Visual cryptography for general access structures. Information and Computation 129, 86–106 (1996)
3. Ateniese, G., Blundo, C., De Santis, A., Stinson, D.R.: Constructions and bounds for visual cryptography. In: Meyer auf der Heide, F., Monien, B. (eds.) ICALP 1996. LNCS, vol. 1099, pp. 416–428. Springer, Heidelberg (1996)
4. Beguin, P., Cresti, A.: General short computational secret sharing schemes. In: Guillou, L.C., Quisquater, J.-J. (eds.) EUROCRYPT 1995. LNCS, vol. 921, pp. 194–208. Springer, Heidelberg (1995)
5. Beimel, A., Chor, B.: Universally ideal secret sharing schemes. IEEE Transactions on Information Theory 40, 786–794 (1994)
6. Blakley, G.R.: Safeguarding Cryptographic Keys. In: Proceedings of the National Computer Conference, pp. 313–317 (1979)
7. Blakley, G.R.: One-time pads are key safeguarding schemes, not cryptosystems: fast key safeguarding schemes (threshold schemes) exist. In: Proceedings of the 1980 Symposium on Security and Privacy, pp. 108–113. IEEE Press, Los Alamitos (1980)
8. Blakley, B., Blakley, G.R., Chan, A.H., Massey, J.: Threshold schemes with disenrollment. In: Brickell, E.F. (ed.) CRYPTO 1992. LNCS, vol. 740, pp. 540–548. Springer, Heidelberg (1993)
9. Blundo, C., De Santis, A.: Lower bounds for robust secret sharing schemes. Inform. Process. Lett. 63, 317–321 (1997)
10. Charnes, C., Pieprzyk, J.: Generalised cumulative arrays and their application to secret sharing schemes. Australian Computer Science Communications 17, 61–65 (1995)
11. Desmedt, Y., Frankel, Y.: Threshold cryptosystems. In: Brassard, G. (ed.) CRYPTO 1989. LNCS, vol. 435, pp. 307–315. Springer, Heidelberg (1990)
12. van Dijk, M.: On the information rate of perfect secret sharing schemes. Designs, Codes and Cryptography 6, 143–169 (1995)
13. Hang, N., Zhao, W.: Privacy-preserving data mining Systems. Computer 40(4), 52–58 (2007)
14. Jackson, W.-A., Martin, K.M., O'Keefe, C.M.: Ideal secret sharing schemes with multiple secrets. Journal of Cryptology 9, 233–250 (1996)

15. Ogiela, M.R., Tadeusiewicz, R.: Modern Computational Intelligence Methods for the Interpretation of Medical Images. Springer, Heidelberg (2008)
16. Ogiela, M.R., Ogiela, U.: Linguistic Extension for Secret Sharing (m, n)-threshold Schemes. SecTech, 2008-2008, International Conference on Security Technology, Hainan Island, Sanya, China, December 13–15, pp. 125–128 (2008) ISBN: 978-0-7695-3486-2, DOI: 10.1109/SecTech.2008.15
17. Shamir, A.: How to Share a Secret. Communications of the ACM, 612–613 (1979)
18. Simmons, G.J.: An Introduction to Shared Secret and/or Shared Control Schemes and Their Application in Contemporary Cryptology. In: The Science of Information Integrity, pp. 441–497. IEEE Press, Los Alamitos (1992)
19. Tang, S.: Simple Secret Sharing and Threshold RSA Signature Schemes. Journal of Information and Computational Science 1, 259–262 (2004)
20. Tadeusiewicz, R., Ogiela, M.R.: Medical Image Understanding Technology. Springer, Heidelberg (2004)
21. Wu, T.-C., He, W.-H.: A geometric approach for sharing secrets. Computers and Security 14, 135–146 (1995)
22. Zheng, Y., Hardjono, T., Seberry, J.: Reusing shares in secret sharing schemes. The Computer Journal 37, 199–205 (1994)

# An Innovative Approach for Generating Static UML Models from Natural Language Requirements

Deva Kumar Deeptimahanti and Ratna Sanyal

Indian Institute of Information Technology-Allahabad,
Deoghat, Jhalwa, Allahabad-211012, Uttar Pradesh, India
{deva,rsanyal}@iiita.ac.in

**Abstract.** Moving from requirements analysis to design is considered as one of the most complex and difficult activities of software development life cycle. Errors caused in this activity can be quite expensive to fix. Tool support for integrating both requirement analysis and design phases by automating some of the tasks involved in this activity is highly desirable. To this end we proposed a tool, named Static UML Model Generator from Analysis of Requirements (SUGAR), which generates static UML models by emphasizing on natural language requirements. This tool extends previously existing approaches and implemented with the help of efficient natural language processing tools using the modified approach of Rational Unified Process with better accuracy. SUGAR generates all static UML models in Java in conjunction with Rational Rose and provides all functionalities of the system even though the developer is having less domain knowledge.

**Keywords:** Rational Unified Process, Unified Modeling Language, Natural Language Processing, Software Requirement Specification.

## 1 Introduction

Software development life cycle (SDLC) [1] is a conceptual model which represents the various phases involved in software development project from feasibility study through completion. In Waterfall Model of SDLC [2], there is an interaction between the later five phases, in which Unified modeling language (UML) [3] tools like Rational Rose [4] or Visual Paradigm [5] works as interacting tool between design and implementation phases which produces code model from design diagrams using forward engineering technique. A vast number of testing tools have been provided for interacting design and implementation phases with testing phase. System will be made operational after testing phase completes. Supporting manuals, installation procedures, help files and documentation are available for interacting previous phases with operation and maintenance phase, but there are only few tools developed which works semi-automatically to interact requirement analysis phase with design phase.

Static UML Model Generator from Analysis of Requirements (SUGAR) follows Object Oriented Analysis and Design (OOAD) [6] technique for object elicitation from natural language requirements to generate static UML models to assist developer

T.-h. Kim et al. (Eds.): ASEA 2008, CCIS 30, pp. 147–163, 2009.

to move further phases. An "object" is an important concept in object-oriented programming (OOP) [6]. In Object-oriented Programming, classes are identified first and then objects are instantiated from it, but in OOAD, objects are identified first and then classes are abstracted from objects.

Till now tools like Use Case Driven Development Assistant Tool (UCDA) for Class Model Generation [7], Linguistic assistant for Domain Analysis (LIDA) [8] were developed to bridge the gap between the requirement analysis phase and design phase using Natural Language Processing (NLP) techniques. These tools are able to generate UML diagrams semi-automatically. But UCDA just identifies the analysis model of the class and can just visualizes the UML diagrams in Rational Rose [4], which is not convenient for those users who have not installed Rational Rose on their systems. LIDA needs more user interaction while generating diagrams, as it identifies just the list of nouns, verbs and adjectives and the developer has to decide which word goes in classes or attributes or operations. So LIDA depends on knowledge of problem domain, which is familiar to the developer. If the developer is having a less knowledge then this tool will loose the most important functionalities of the system.

SUGAR follows the Rational Unified Process (RUP) [9] to generate static UML models from requirements with the help of efficient natural language processing tools. RUP provided a vast number of methods for iterative software development among which SUGAR uses Use case modeling technique for object elicitation.

In this paper, section 2 describes about the methodology used while developing the tool, section 3 discusses about the features of the tool, its architecture and work flow process, section 4 explains the technique of Use case driven object oriented analysis and design for generating Use-case and Class models, section 5 demonstrates the usage of SUGAR with the help of a case study "Musical Store System", and finally Section 6 gives the conclusions about the paper.

## 2   The Methodology

According to the standard Software Requirement Specification (SRS) format, SRS contains both functional and non-functional requirements. As functional requirements are mostly written in natural language, the various possible grammar related concepts related to natural English language like noun phrases and verb phrases has been discussed in section 2.1. Section 2.2 gives brief details about natural language processing tools used for developing SUGAR. The need for syntactic reconstruction also has been emphasized to increase the accuracy of the tool is given in section 2.3. And section 2.4 describes about the methodology used to generate the static UML models from functional requirements.

### 2.1  Natural Language Requirements:

Many methods have been proposed to identify objects from functional requirements. But the problem occurs with accuracy as requirements are of two types:

1. Requirements in formal language.
2. Requirements in natural language.

Requirements represented in formal languages are used in research areas and are not used in general application developments in industries for which they will use requirements represented in natural language.

While representing natural language requirements, structure of the sentence plays an important role. Mainly English sentences are of three types [10], namely:

1. **Question Sentences:** Sentences which makes user to say answer in return.
   e.g.: What's your name?
2. **Request Sentences:** Sentences which makes user to perform some work.
   e.g.: Hurry up!
3. **Statement Sentences:** Sentences which notifies messages to the user.
   e.g.: User withdraws cash from his account.

Among these sentences, syntax of natural language requirements and statement sentences are similar. Each statement sentence consists of two parts namely subject and predicate. Some other statement sentences also contain subject, predicate and object. Mostly, subject will be commonly the noun phrase and predicate will be the verb phrase.

### Nouns and Noun Phrases

Noun phrase (denoted as NP) is a phrase which contains noun and based on a noun. Certain words called determiners (denoted as DET), acts as markers of nouns or noun phrases like the, a, an, these, this. In a noun phrase only a particular noun can be acted as a head noun. All others like determiners, adjectives and prepositional phrase are part of noun phrase. Recursion occurs in natural language requirements structures also, i.e., a noun phrase can in turn consist of another one or more noun phrase [10].

### Verbs and Verb Phrases

Verb phrase which are denoted as VP can also consists of another verb phrase just like noun phrase. Each verb phrase should contain a verb denoted as VBZ. VP's are very important category which has various types of form when compared to other categories. Requirement structure mainly depends on the verb phrase type. Different types of verb phrase structure are as follows [10]:

1. **Transitive Verbs:** Verb group (VBZ) followed by a single noun phrase (NP) is treated as a transitive verb structure. An example for transitive verb is as shown in Fig. 1:

**Fig. 1.** Structure of Transitive verb structure

2. **Intransitive Verbs:** In a predicate, if a verb group (VBZ) alone exists is treated as intransitive verbs. An example for intransitive verbs is as shown in Fig. 2:

**Fig. 2.** Structure of Intransitive verb structure

**3. Ditransitive:** A verb group (VBZ) followed by a noun phrase (NP) and a prepositional phrase (PP) is called as ditransitive structure which is as shown in Fig. 3. The prepositional phrase in turn may contain a preposition (IN) and a noun phrase (NP).

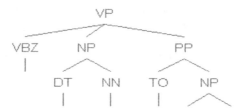

**Fig. 3.** Structure of Ditransitive verb structure (An example)

**4. Prepositional:** The verb group (VBZ) followed by the prepositional group (PP) is called prepositional verb structure which is as shown in Fig. 4:

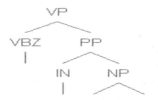

**Fig. 4.** Structure of Prepositional verb structure (An example)

**5. Intensive:** The verb group (VBZ) followed by a single noun phrase (NP), or adjective phrase (ADJP) or a prepositional phrase (PP) is called intensive verb structure which is as shown in Fig. 5:

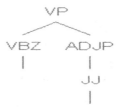

**Fig. 5.** Structure of Intensive verb structure (An example)

6. **Complex Transitive:** The verb group (VBZ) followed by a noun phrase (NP) this which in turn contains a noun phrase (NP) or prepositional phrase (PP) or a adjective phrase (ADJP) is treated as complex transitive verb structure which is as shown in Fig. 6:

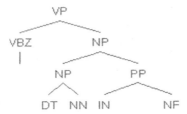

**Fig. 6.** Structure of Complex Transitive verb structure (An example)

7. **Non-finite:** In non-finite verb structure, the verb group (VBZ) is followed by a non-finite verb group which is as shown in example Fig. 7:

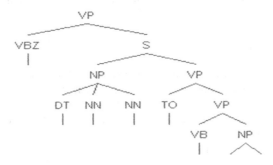

**Fig. 7.** Structure of Non-finite verb structure (An example)

## 2.2 Features of Natural Language Processing Tools Used for Developing SUGAR:

Following are the list of natural language processing tools used for developing SUGAR:

1. **Stanford Parser:** Stanford Parser [12] is a highly optimized PCFG probabilistic natural language parser implemented in java, is used to generate parse tree for each sentence. This parser helps in avoiding various other NLP tools like using tokenization, sentence splitting and part-of-speech (POS) tagging tools.
2. **WordNet2.1:** WordNet2.1 [13] is a large lexical database of English in which nouns, verbs, and adjectives are grouped into cognitive synonyms (Synsets), is used to perform morphological analysis which converts plural word into singular form.

Various rules have been implemented to handle plural form for compound words where WordNet feature fails. The problem occurs at situation when an object name which is a combination of two words occurs like "Musical Stores", then for such words WordNet [13] will strip off the suffix and return just the word "Musical" which looses exact information. To accommodate such cases, various rules have been implemented for converting plural nouns, verbs and adjectives into their corresponding singular forms.

3. **Stanford Named Entity Recognizer 1.0 (NER):** Sanford Named Entity Recognizer 1.0 (NER) [14] is a linear chain Conditional Random Field (CRF) Classifier implemented in Java which labels sequences of words in a text into person, organization, and location.

   Main usage of NER is to combine adjacent names together to reduce the number of objects. When a word of the form "Sachin Tendulkar" occurs, NER identifies it as two different names, but can be merged as a single name with a small modification to NER.

4. **JavaRAP:** JavaRAP [15] is a tool for pronoun resolution is an implementation of the classic Resolution of Anaphora Procedure (RAP) algorithm given by Lappin and Leass, resolves up to third person pronouns. It is used to replace all the possible pronouns with its correct noun form, which is quite helpful while analyzing large documents.

## 2.3 Syntactic Reconstruction

As requirements are expressed in natural language, there is a need to have syntactic reconstruction tools to decompose complex requirements to simple requirements. But till now no perfect automatic tool is available to split complex sentence structure to simple sentence. So some manual rules are proposed and implemented to increase the accuracy of information extraction from requirement document. Some basic rules for syntactic reconstruction are as follows:

1. Discard prepositional phrase (PP), adjective phrase (ADJP), determiner (DT) or adjective (JJ), if they precedes the subject of the sentence.
2. If NP and VP is preceded by "No", then convert it into "NP not VP".
3. Noun phrases (NP) which are separated by connectives like "and, or" are taken as individual sentences.
4. If {{NP1}{VP1{ VBZ NP2,NP3 and NP4}}} then convert it into {{NP1}{VP1 { VBZ NP2 }}}, {{NP1}{VP1{ VBZ NP3}}}, {{NP1}{VP1{ VBZ NP4}}}.
5. Sentences which are connected by connectives like "and, or, but, yet" are spitted at their connectives and created at two individual sentences.
6. If sentence1 and/or sentence2, then convert it into two sentences {sentence1} {sentence2}.
7. If a sentence has no verbs (VP) then discard that sentence.
8. If a sentence is of the form {{NP1} {VP1 {NP2} {VP2 {NP3}}}}, then convert it into two sentences like {{NP1} {VP1 {NP2}}} and {{NP2} {VP2 {NP3}}}.
9. In the Sentences which are having a semicolon, treat the sentence after the semicolon as extra information for the preceding sentence and so discard sentence after semicolon.

10. If a sentence is in passive voice, ask user to convert it into active voice. Normally passive voice sentences will contain word "be" which gives the sense as passive voice form. This needs some user interference to decide which sentence acts as passive voice.

*Mostly the requirements will be in simple sentence format or in the above specified rule format, so if any other complex sentence appears which violates these rules, an option is given to the user to change it to simple sentence.*

## 2.4  Rational Unified Approach

This approach [9] was proposed by Booch, Rambaugh, and Jacobson and their attempt to unify modeling efforts was proven successful in system development tool. The main motivation of RUP is to combine the best practices of previous methodologies by these three members, and guidelines along with UML notations and diagrams for better understanding object-oriented concepts and system development. RUP [9] consists of various processes like

1. Use-case driven object-oriented analysis
2. Object-oriented design
3. Incremental development and prototyping and
4. Continuous testing.

In this paper both Use-case driven object-oriented analysis and Object-oriented design are used for static UML model generation.

### 2.4.1  Use Case Driven Object-Oriented Analysis and Design
Functional requirements can be extracted by using the Use case modeling technique [11]. This technique provides both graphical and textual notations of how actors behave with the system [11]. A use-case acts as an interaction between system and users, where it identifies the user goals and system responsibilities to its users. This use-case model shows the sequence of events performed in the system, also discover classes from them. Then object-oriented design helps in identifying attributes, methods of each object and relationships that exists between objects.

### 2.4.2  Glossary
Glossary is an important artifact of RUP [9]. The glossary plays an important role in any software development, as a number of system analysts may be working on a system and each will use their own terminology depending on their domain knowledge. So there may be a chance of conflicting in terminology. A common vocabulary should be used among the team to avoid communication gap and to have unambiguous requirements.

# 3   Static UML Model Generator from Analysis of Requirements (SUGAR)

Static UML Model Generator from Analysis of Requirements is a tool aimed at assisting the developer in generating static UML diagrams namely; Use-case diagram and Class diagram from natural language requirements. SUGAR has been developed using most sophisticated Natural Language Processing tools [12-15].

## 3.1  Overview

SUGAR has the following salient features:

- The tools takes stakeholder requests as input and splits a complex sentence into simple sentences using rules for syntactic reconstruction, so that each sentence should have only one set of subject (NP) and predicate (VP).
- Each sentence should be expressed in active voice.
- The resulting document is parsed by using the Stanford Parser [12] which generates parse tree for each sentence, through which subject and predicate can be identified.
- "WordNet2.1" [13] is used to perform morphological analysis to convert plural forms to singular forms, where class name 'Customers' and 'Customer' both refer to same class name.
- "Stanford Named Entity Recognizer 1.0" [14] is used to combine the adjacent names together. For example, the tokens 'ATM' and 'card', which are identified as two nouns, can be combined to 'ATM card' to make it a single token.
- Using "JavaRAP" [15] a tool for Pronoun Resolution which resolves up to third person pronouns developed by National University of Singapore is used to replace all the possible pronouns with its correct noun form.
- Actors and its associated use cases can easily be extracted from the parsed tree.
- Class models are generated by extracting attributes and operations from the parsed document.
- Use case diagram and class diagram are built using the Java technology which is convenient for the users who have no UML tool installed on their machines.

## 3.2  Architecture

SUGAR is aimed at generating the two static UML diagrams, in which class model is developed from Use-case model. The architecture, which is of linear shape, is as shown in Fig. 8.

Stakeholder requests, which are basically the functional requirements for the system, are analyzed first to identify actors. This is done using "Stanford Parser" [12] by identifying the subjects of each sentence. The use cases associated with the actors are identified by extracting the predicates of each requirement. From this Use-case model is generated with proper association among use-cases. Using the use case model and the requirements, noun phrases are identified which will be the candidate objects of the system. The next step is to use the RUP approach to refine the identified objects. Then the methods and attributes of each object are identified by recognizing the verb phases and adjectives. The relationship among objects is identified using the RUP approach, which finally generates the both analysis and design class models [16] [17] of the system.

The work flow for SUGAR is as shown in Fig. 9.

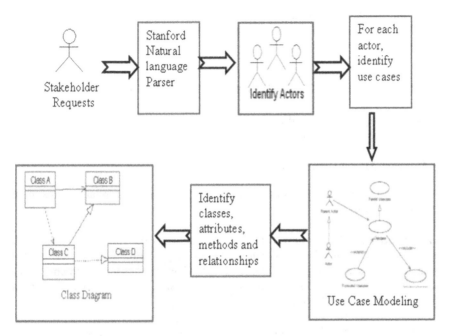

**Fig. 8.** Architecture of SUGAR

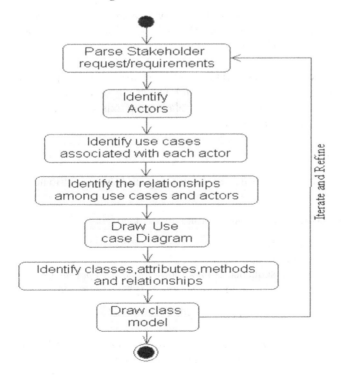

**Fig. 9.** Workflow for SUGAR

This is an iterative procedure where the accuracy increases after refining the stakeholder requests. This iteration continues till the sentence becomes simple and expressed in active voice form.

# 4 Use Case Driven Object Oriented Analysis and Design

This section explains about the process of generating Use-case model and Class model using Rational Unified Approach (RUP) [9].

## 4.1 Use-case Model Generator

This consists of identifying actors, its associated use cases and relationships among actors and use cases.

**4.1.1 Identifying the Actors:** Term 'actor' represents the role a user plays in the system [18]. Candidates for actors can be identified by examining who is using the system or who is affecting the system or for whom the system is intended. This process is an iterative process and can't be done in a single step [9]. Actors mostly are subjects (Noun Phrases (NP)) of a sentence.

**4.1.2 Identifying the Use-Cases:** Use-cases explain how events flow in the system. As actors represent the way in which they interact with the given system so the process of identifying use-case is related with actors [11] [18]. So use cases are mostly the predicates (verb phrases (VP)) in the sentence which will follow the subject of the sentence. (NP: VP).

**4.1.3 Relationships between Actors and Use Cases:** If in the predicate of sentence is in turn having both use case and actor which are separated by prepositions like "from, to, about, with, in etc"., then a relationship exists between that use case and actor. (Verb + Preposition + Noun).

## 4.2 Class Model Generator

Class model generator consists of identifying classes, its attributes, methods and relationships among classes.

According to RUP, there are four alternatives in identifying classes namely [19][20]:

1. Noun-phrase approach
2. Common class patterns approach
3. The use-case driven, sequence/collaboration modeling approach
4. The classes, responsibilities and collaborators (CRC) approach.

SUGAR uses the noun phrase approach for Class model generation.

**4.2.1 Noun-Phrase Approach:** This approach was proposed by Rebecca Wirfs-Brock, Brian Walkerson, and Lauren Wiener [19][20]. In this approach, the requirements are used for identifying the nouns which are considered as classes and verbs are treated as methods of classes. A list of nouns are collected and divided into three categories, namely relevant classes, fuzzy classes and irrelevant classes. Irrelevant classes are eliminated as they won't have any purpose which can be decided from experience.

Following rules are followed in identifying classes from relevant and fuzzy categories:

1. **Redundant Classes**: Remove a class if two classes reveal same information. This type of classes can be eliminated with the help of glossary maintained with each project.

   e.g.: Client, Bank Client= Bank client
   
           ATM card, card= ATM card

2. **Adjective Classes:** If a noun-phrase contains an adjective, it is treated as an adjective class. If this adjective object represented by noun behaves differently from adjective, then make it as a new class.

   e.g.: Musical Store, Overdue Notice

3. **Attribute Classes:** Some objects which take only values are taken as attributes of a class but not as a class.

   e.g.: Account Balance, Amount, Money, PIN code.

4. **Irrelevant Classes:** Every class should have a specific purpose and should be necessary in system, otherwise eliminate that class.

   e.g.: Four Digits, Step

### 4.2.2  Relationships among Objects.

Three types of relationships [16][17] exist among objects, namely association, inheritance and aggregation.

1. **Association:** Represents physical connection between two or more objects, normally exists when one object has responsibility of telling some thing to other object.

   Normally a prepositional phrase represents an association between objects like "has, next to, part of, works for, contained in, talk to, order to" or "verb phrases which is a collection of two verbs" like savings-checking etc. Search for these phrases in requirement document and identify the noun phrases associated with it.

2. **Inheritance (Super-Sub Relationships):** Search for objects having similar attributes or methods and group similar things to an abstract class.

   e.g.: Checking Account and Savings Account objects both are type of Account object. So these two objects can be specializations of Account class.

3. **Aggregation:** In this relationship look for the objects which are collective nouns and then decide to which other object this is associated with. This class of relationship is purely conceptual and taken from general knowledge or experience.

## 5  SUGAR- Case Study

This section describes about usage of tool with the help of an example named "Musical Store System (MSS)". This requirement document is a slight modification of the case study taken while identifying the class model in LIDA [8] and discriminates the benefits of using SUGAR when compared to other tools.

Requirement document for "Musical Store System (MSS)" is as follows:

*"The musical store receives tape requests from customers. The musical store receives new tapes from the Main office. Musical store sends overdue notice to customers. Store assistant takes care of tape requests. Store assistant update the rental list. Store management submits the price changes. Store management submits new tapes. Store administration produces rental reports. Main office sends overdue notices for tapes. Customer request for a tape. Store assistant checks the availability of requested tape. Store assistant searches for the available tape. Store assistant searches for the rental price of available tape. Store assistant checks status of the tape to be returned by customer. Customer can borrow if there is no delay with return of other tapes. Store assistant records rental by updating the rental list. Store assistant asks customer for his address."*

As a first step, the whole requirements are made into simple sentences, breaking complex sentences so that each sentence should have only one subject and predicate by using syntactic reconstructing rules.

Then the simplified document is parsed using JavaRAP tool [15] to replace pronouns by its suitable nouns.

Glossary has to be maintained to develop an unambiguous system.

Determiners like "a, an, the etc.," have to be removed from the text to have perfect document which is able to identify all the functionalities of the system.

Stanford Parser [12] parses each simple requirement statement into subject and predicate form. This also displays the parse tree for each sentence which helps in extracting required information from each requirement.

## 5.1 Use Case Model Generation

Actor which is commonly a noun phrase (NP) is someone who is interacting with the system or playing some role (work) in the system, which means the noun phrase, is followed by a verb phrase (VP).

e.g., {{musical store [NP]} {receives tape requests from customers [VP]}}.

So extract all the noun phrases which represent actors and immediately following verbs phrases which represent use-cases of the system.

Association among use cases and actors is identified by searching prepositions like "from, to, about, with, in etc.," and then checks the predicate of each sentence is in the sequence of Verb: Preposition: Noun form.

Use-case diagram for the Musical Store System is generated with the help of Java graphics as shown in Fig.10. It has the feature to show the association relationship between actors and use- cases. The whole image drawn on the panel has been saved to a "Usecase_Diag.jpg" file for later references. By using SUGAR almost all the actors and use-cases are identified which have the better accuracy than the previous tools.

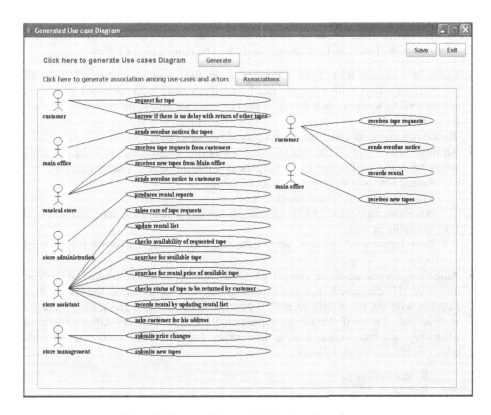

**Fig. 10.** Use-case Diagram for Musical Store System

## 5.2 Class Model Generation

Class objects are usually the nouns of the system, which can be recursively identified by identifying nouns of the system. The attributes are adjectives and methods are the verbs of each class object. Associating attributes and methods to exact class is the main feature of SUGAR.

Using "Word Net 2.1" [13], SUGAR converts plural form of the word to singular form, and by using the glossary SUGAR removes the redundant classes.

Using the "Stanford Named Entity Recognizer 1.0" [14], SUGAR combines relevant adjacent nouns together; otherwise it results in increase in number of objects which will be difficult to identify the attributes and operations of such objects.

For "Musical Store System", SUGAR has obtained a total of thirteen objects where as LIDA has identified more than twenty objects for the same case study.
The Possible objects are as follows:

Customer, Store Assistant, Musical Store, Store Administration, tape, Store Management, rental, rental list, available tape, rental report, price change, new tape, main office.

For the possible identified objects, Rational Unified Approach (RUP) is applied to refine the objects which are to be used in the system. After applying RUP, redundant classes, attribute classes and adjective classes will be eliminated as follows:

- Redundant classes have been identified from the glossary where a list of all possible meanings will be maintained and if an unambiguous word comes its corresponding meaning will be replaced. For this case study, the redundant classes are as follows:

  Rental report=rental (As 'report' is a part of  rental class)
- Attribute classes are eliminated by using a text file which contains a list of words which takes values. For this case study the possible attribute classes are as follows:

  Rental list (As 'list' represents set of values)

  Price change (As 'price' takes value)

  Available tape=tape (As 'available' shows the status of the tape whether it si available or not)

  New tape=tape (As 'new' shows the status of the tape whether it is new or not)
- Adjective classes are those classes which are having adjective phrase (ADJP) or adjective (JJ) contained in a noun phrase and then entered into the list if they matches with the previously identified possible classes. These classes are included in finalized classes if the object represented by noun behaves differently from adjective, and then make it as a new class. For this case study the possible adjective classes are as follows:

  Rental list

  Rental

  Musical store

  Main office

  Among these adjective classes, rental list is also an attribute. So remove this class from the remaining classes list. Other three classes, rental, musical store and main office are included in remaining classes list.
- Irrelevant Classes are those classes won't have a specific purpose and is unnecessary for the current system, so eliminate such classes. For the present case study, tape and rental (rental report is same as rental) are mostly treated as attributes and so considered as irrelevant classes in current scenario, so remove these two classes from the remaining classes list.

Finally remaining classes list is as follows: Customer, Store Assistant, Musical Store, Store Administration, Store Management, Main office.

For each parsed sentence, SUGAR identifies the noun phrases in it and associated adjectives and verbs to it. Operations are the verbs of a requirement which can be related to the class name with the help of Stanford Parser [12].

**Relationships among Objects:**

Three types of relationships are as follows:

1. **Association among Objects:** As association represents the physical connection between two or more objects, SUGAR searches for the prepositional phrases or

verb phrases between identified objects. For this case study association exists between "Customer-Musical Store", "Main office-Musical Store", "Customer-Store Assistant".

2. **Inheritance among Objects:** As inheritance exists among objects which have common attributes or methods, in this current situation inheritance exist between "Main office and Musical Store" as they both share a common method "sends".

3. **Aggregation among Objects:** This class of relationship is purely conceptual and taken from general knowledge or experience. Search for collective nouns and then decide to which other object this is associated with.

Class model for the MSS is generated with the help of Java graphics as shown in Fig.11 which shows classes along with their attributes and operations and also has the feature to show the association relationship between classes. The whole image drawn on the panel has been saved to a "Class_Diag.jpg" file for later references.

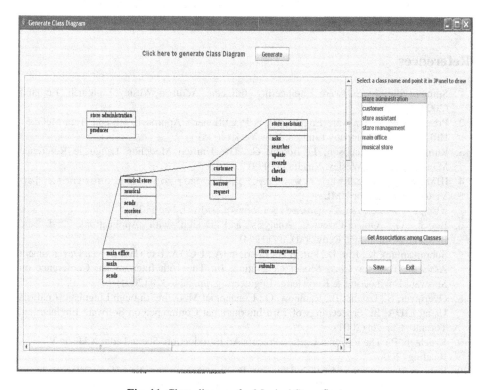

**Fig. 11.** Class diagram for Musical Store System

# 6   Conclusions

In this paper, RUP approach is used to automate the static UML model generation from stakeholder requests. SUGAR has successfully overcome the problem of handling the domain knowledge of system which is a problem in other tools by using efficient NLP tools of Stanford NLP Group like Stanford Parser, Stanford Named Entity Recognizer, WordNet2.1 and JavaRAP. This paper has shown the results derived by taking the slightly modified case study of "Musical Store System" taken while illustrating LIDA tool and obtained better results than LIDA [8]. SUGAR is able to visualize UML diagrams without any additional tool support. SUGAR has automated the whole process of generating static UML diagrams except at the situation, where SUGAR needs very less human interaction at the time of eliminating irrelevant classes. The work can be extended to other dynamic UML diagrams like collaboration diagram and state chart diagram to test the class model without the need generating code.

## Acknowledgments

The authors gratefully acknowledge Indian Institute of Information Technology-Allahabad, India.

## References

1. Sommerville, I.: Software Engineering, 6th edn. Addison Wesley Longman, England (2000)
2. Pressman, R.S.: Software Engineering-A Practitioner's Approach, 6th edn. Tata McGraw Hill Publishing Company Limited, New York (2005)
3. Rumbaugh, J., Jacobson, I., Booch, G.: The Unified Modeling Language Reference Manual. Addison-Wesley, Reading (1999)
4. IBM Rational Rose, http://www.rational.com/products/rose/index.jsp
5. Visual Paradigm for UML,
   http://www.visual-paradigm.com/product/vpuml
6. Booch, G.: Object-Oriented Analysis and Design with Applications, 2nd edn. Benjamin/Cummings, Redwood City (1994)
7. Subramaniam, K., Liu, D., Far, B.H., Eberlein, A.: UCDA: Use Case Driven Development Assistant Tool for Class Model Generation. In: The 16th International Conference on Software Engineering & Knowledge Engineering, pp. 324–329 (2004)
8. Overmyer, S., Lavoie, B., Rambow, O.: Conceptual Modeling through Linguistic Analysis Using LIDA. In: Proceedings of 23rd International Conference on Software Engineering, Toronto, Canada (2001)
9. Kruchten, P.: The Rational Unified Process An Introduction, Second edn. Addison Wesley, Reading (2000)
10. Roberts, P.: Patterns of English. Harcourt, Brace and Company, New York (1956)
11. Leffingwell, D., Widrig, D.: Managing Software Requirements: A Use Case Approach, Second edn. Addison-Wesley, Reading (2003)
12. The Stanford Natural Language Processing Group, Stanford Parser 1.6,
    http://nlp.stanford.edu/software/lex-parser.shtml
13. Cognitive Science Laboratory, Princeton University, WordNet2.1,
    http://wordnet.princeton.edu/obtain
14. The Stanford Natural Language Processing Group, Stanford Named Entity Recognizer 1.0,
    http://nlp.stanford.edu/software/CRF-NER.shtml

15. Qiu, L., Kan, M.-Y., Chua, T.-S.: A Public Reference Implementation of the RAP Anaphora Resolution Algorithm. In: Proceedings of the Fourth International Conference on Language Resources and Evaluation (LREC), vol. I, pp. 291–294 (2004)
16. Booch, G.: Object Oriented Design with Applications. The Benjamin Cummings Publishing Company, New York (1991)
17. Jacobson, I.: Object oriented development in an industrial environment. In: Proceedings of Object-Oriented Programming, Systems, Languages, and Applications, pp. 183–191. ACM, New York (1987)
18. Cockburn, A.: Writing Effective Use Cases. Addison-Wesley, Reading (2000)
19. Wirfs-Brock, R.: Object Design: Roles, Responsibilities, and Collaborations. Addisson Wesley, London (2002)
20. Wirfs-Brock, R., Walkerson, B., Wiener, L.: Designing Object-Oriented Software. Prentice-Hall, Englewood Cliffs (1990)

# A Hybrid Approach for Designing an Adaptive User Interface: IDSS and BDI Agents

Noria Taghezout[1], Abdelkader Adla[1,2], and Pascale Zaraté[2]

[1] Computer Science Department, University of  Es-Senia Oran,  BP 1524, El-M' Naouer,
31000, Oran, Algeria
taghezoutnour@yahoo.fr
[2] IRIT – INPT – ENSIACET, 118 route de Narbonne 31062 Toulouse Cedex 9, France
{adla,Zarate}@irit.fr

**Abstract.** Adaptive user interfaces (AUI) are designed to support users in performing their tasks by adapting to their individual characteristics. AUIs can facilitate user performance, make the interaction more efficient, improve ease of use and assist the user in overcoming information overflow and help them use complex systems. Utilizing these advancements, we present an approach for the design of complex adaptive interface. This latter uses Intelligent Agents based on a Belief, Desire, and Intention (BDI) architecture to achieve problem resolution in a typical boiler combustion management system (GLZ). The proposed architecture separates generic knowledge base about adaptive user interface from application specific knowledge in order to provide an IDSS. Integrating BDI agents into an IDSS can improve the ability of human operators and decision makers to perform their duties in a better way and provide useful enhancements to existing systems. The study reports the basic design principles of the user interface as well as details of the application.

**Keywords:** Adaptive user interfaces (AUI), BDI agents, Decision Support System (DSS), Adaptive Model, Multi-agent system (MAS) and IDSS.

## 1 Introduction

Adaptive interfaces are a promising attempt to overcome contemporary problems due to the increasing complexity of human-computer interaction. They are designed to tailor a system's interactive behavior with consideration of both individual needs of human users and altering conditions within an application environment. Increasing differences in skill level, culture, language, and goals have resulted in a significant trend towards adaptive and customizable interfaces, which use modeling and reasoning about the domain, the task, and the user, in order to extract and represent the user's knowledge, skills, and goals, to better serve the users with their tasks.

This new class of interfaces promises knowledge or agent-based dialog, in which the interface gracefully handles errors and interruptions, and dynamically adapts to the current context and situation, the needs of the task performed, and the user model. This interactive process is believed to have great potential for improving the effectiveness of human computer interaction [20].

T.-h. Kim et al. (Eds.): ASEA 2008, CCIS 30, pp. 164–182, 2009.
© Springer-Verlag Berlin Heidelberg 2009

A grand challenge of adaptive interfaces is, therefore, to represent, reason, and exploit various models to more effectively process input, generate output, and manage the dialog and interaction between human and machine so that to maximize the efficiency, effectiveness, and naturalness, if not joy, of interaction [23].

However, some research studies found gaps on the methods and techniques for designing interface, For example, Lopez et al. stated in [18] that the lack of general techniques, methods and tools for adaptation design produces systems where the support for adaptation is rather inflexible, and the knowledge injected into the adaptation engine is very hard to be reused. Then a software architecture is required able to cope with requirements such as: (i) supporting adaptivity in a flexible manner; ( ii) integrating knowledge with the  user interface design method and (iii) providing the required formalism to build UIs in a systematic way.

This paper presents a user interface of the boiler combustion management system, which employs adaptivity technique, in order to provide high-quality interaction to users (operators).

More precisely, BDI agents are integrated in an IDSS to achieve a final goal: adaptation. The global system is able to cope with the adaptation process in a flexible manner.

The proposed approach uses Intelligent Agents based on a Belief, Desire, and Intention (BDI) architecture to achieve problem resolution in a typical boiler combustion management system (GLZ). In our approach, MAS is used in order to coordinate an adaptive interface with a distributed decision and distributed information architecture.

We consider that the BDI framework is a useful starting point for modelling human operators. It provides goal-directed behaviour, whereby an agent's actions are motivated by a hierarchy of goals rather than being purely reactive. The notion of intentions is also useful; this prevents complicated reasoning at every time step. Another feature of the BDI architecture is the structure of knowledge within an agent (beliefs, goals and plans) which can simplify communication between the programmers and the domain experts. Integrating BDI agents into an IDSS can improve the ability of human operators and decision makers to better perform their duties and provide useful enhancements to existing systems.

BDI theory is thus of interest in at least four areas of research: in modeling human behavior (Particularly human practical reasoning); in developing and improving BDI theory and therefore its implementations; in building complex and robust agent applications; and as a candidate for logical specification, leading to the possibility of automatic verification and compilation. In section 5, we explore why BDI became one of the building blocks of agent technology.

## 1.1  Motivation

We identify the following gaps for our review of prior work on adaptive user interface: (1) Most of the work related to the adaptation of UI(s), has led to solutions where the adaptation (s) were hardcoded with the system, making it very difficult to modify the way adaptations are made, or to reuse the solution from one application to another [19]. And (2) that an adaptive interface does not exist in isolation, but rather is designed to interact with a human user. Moreover, for the system to be adaptive, it must improve its interaction with that user, and simple memorization of such interactions does not suffice. Rather, improvement should result from generalization over past experiences and carry over to new user interactions. For instance, many control rooms use graphic user interfaces GUIs, so there could be many usability problems that might lead to serious safety accidents or malfunctions unless careful considerations are made in the design of the user interface, as discussed by Han et al. in [12].

The envisaged objectives of adaptive user interface in such systems are: to adapt the interface to best suit the current task/problem/operator; to ease the task of the operator, and reinforce effectiveness during system disturbances; to filter information according to criteria such as urgency and operator condition; and to help diagnose correctly the problems.

This paper is concerned with the user interface (called interface subsystem). The presented work deals with the interactive and adaptive aspects concerning the utilization and technology of DSS in the context of manufacturing system. We describe in the following a simple case for a boiler combustion management system.

The management system of the boiler combustion is one of the most critical systems for the good functioning of the plant and has a high impact on the methods of cogitation and apprehension of various problems related to maintenance. The exploiting staff is often confronted with situations that impose a quick reaction of decision-making. This requires consequent human and material resources and adapted skills.

We experiment our system on a case of boiler breakdown to detect a functioning defect of the boiler (GLZ: Gas Liquefying Zone) (for more details see [1]), to diagnose the defect and to suggest one or several appropriate cure actions. If a breakdown occurs, this can be:

1. Automatically signposted to the operator by means of a triggered off alarm, the flag (the reference given to every alarm) is pointed out on the board (control room). It acquaints with a particular alarm and allows the operator to locate the defect from the database. Once the defect identified, diagnosis and actions of cure are automatically generated by the system and validated by the user, or
2. Intercepted by the operator (case of defectiveness of the sensor where no alarm is triggered off but the boiler does not work), the operator must explore a large research space of potential defects with a series of tests. Here the system also plays an important role to optimize the action plan to be carried out. Before starting to solve this problem (diagnosis and actions of cure), the operator updates user model which meets his competences (a set of tasks and methods that his able to carry out), and initializes the cooperation mode (e.g.: decision and critic roles for the operator, aid and execution roles for the system).

Thus, **the Interface Sub system (IS)** (described in Fig.4) continuously receives data from the process – e.g. alarm messages about unusual events and status information about the process components. From this information, the IS periodically produces a snapshot which describes the entire system state at the current instant in time. It also performs a preliminary analysis on the data it receives from the process to determine whether there may be a fault. Interface agents have the following knowledge: User models and knowledge of what must be displayed to the user and in what way. User models could be interactively updated.

The main motivation of this work is to discuss how an hybrid approach based on BDI agents and an intelligent decision support system is able to provide an efficient user interface design method where system decisions about adaptation should be grounded in the UI model developed at the design time and generic knowledge base about adaptive user interface is completely separated from application specific knowledge in order to provide the IDSS. The total system intelligence will therefore be the result of the collective intelligence and communication capacities of the agents.

The proposed approach might choose the appropriate interaction techniques taking into account the input and output capabilities of the devices and the user preferences.

The rest of the paper is organized as follows. In Section 2 we give a short introduction in state-of-the art of adaptive user interface. Section 3 surveys DSS and IDSS and examines the potential integration of agent technology into a framework of IDSS. Section 4 describes the application area. The section 5 introduces the multi-agent systems with a particular attention to the BDI agents. Following that, the methodology used to design the UI is outlined, and the adaptivity mechanism developed is presented in section 6. Finally, some concluding remarks and future work are reported in Section 7.

## 2   Related Research

There have been several studies investigating the numerous dimensions of adaptation in interactive software systems (for a review see Dieterich et al, in [8]), namely, what constitutes an adaptation constituent, the level and timing of adaptation, the controlling agent, the type of knowledge that is required to arrive at meaningful adaptations, etc. Nevertheless, despite the substantial contributions of these efforts to the study of adaptation, there are still several issues that need attention, if user interface adaptation is to be adequately served by designers and developers of interactive software applications.

Adaptive graphical user interfaces have the potential to improve the user's experience by personalizing the interface to better suit his or her needs. If adaptation is present, it is often focusing on adapting the UI (User Interface) to a given platform as part of a code/UI generation process. There are three main approaches for adaptive UIs, taking a model-based approach more or less into account. The first approach is to handle adaptation at design time [11] [28] [30]. This is the most common way of handling adaptation in model-based UI development environments. The UIs are adapted to different platforms as part of a UI generation process. A second approach is to provide some kind of transformation mechanism at run time [22], e.g., a mechanism that transforms a UI designed for one platform to fit to a different one. The effect is thus similar to the first approach, only using different means. A third approach is to provide adaptation mechanisms in the UI itself [26], i.e., it is considered part of the functionality of a UI and it is the responsibility of the UI itself both finding out what kind of changes to perform, and performing the changes when needed.

In our work, we consider that, the adaptation is managed and handled by independent, generic mechanisms, grouped together to an adaptation middleware. By using this model, the adaptation middleware is both responsible for finding out when to perform an adaptation and for doing the actual adaptation. Our proposal is a model-based approach for describing the variants of a UI.

In addition to the above research efforts towards adaptation process, a number of systems have been developed to investigate the complementary objective of adaptive user interface. The state of the art in adaptive user interface includes AIDA [6], UIDE [32] as well as the other projects. In fact, software agents have already proved useful in the interaction between the user and the UI in some projects such as [18]. In their work, Lopez et al. [18] consider that a multi-agent system is an alternative to design the adaptation capabilities required to cope with the problem in a natural manner.

Another advantage found in multi-agent systems is the natural distribution of computation, which supports the integration of the implemented multi-agent system with existing services easily. Indeed, multi-agent systems (MAS) enhance overall system performance, in particular along such dimensions as computational efficiency, reliability, extensibility, responsiveness, reuse, maintainability, and flexibility.

The MAS does not require a restriction to a single task. The major concerns in these systems include coordinating intelligent behaviour among a collection of autonomous intelligent agents, and how they can integrate their knowledge, goals, skills, and plans jointly to take action or to solve problems. Although an agent here can also be a special task performer, it has an open interface, which is accessible to everyone (using the right standard). The agents may not only be working toward a single goal, but also toward separate individual goals.

Different reasoning models have been proposed so far: rule based systems, neural networks, Bayesian networks, etc. However, a great interest has appeared for software agents [19] as a means to represent reasoning capabilities in an abstract manner similar to human reasoning. Most of them use the BDI model (Beliefs, Desires, Intentions), which is inspired by human reasoning theories. Beliefs represent the view the agent has of itself and the world where it is immersed. Desires describe the goals that the agent is trying to achieve. Finally, Intentions are the plans the agent is executing to achieve the goals it pursues.

[35] has developed an adaptive interface framework for industrial applications. The research project, called AMEBICA (Auto-adaptive Multimedia Environment Based on Intelligent Agents Collaborating Agents), has many features, the two most important ones; (i) In AMEBICA, adaptation of the presentation have two possible initiatives: the process and the operator, and (ii) presentation of a composition of three models. In [7] author adopts a distributed architecture named Godart. This latter is applied to the mix of image from a television program and showing the sound recording of this show. The work presented in [15] uses an environment (GOLIATH) based on models and agents, for user interfaces design. The main objective of this work is to offer a possibility to describe easily the relation between the functional core and the presentation module. Indeed, this aspect is completely far from traditional programming languages and visual construction tools. The objective of this work has first allowed to offer a solution in order to precisely describe these relations, and secondly to help the designer in the construction of this description. In [15], his work is based on the principle that the design and implementation should involve explicit knowledge of expert designers. The set of knowledge used in the system is supported by a multi-agent system. The designer can get a complete interface from a partial description, and correct the result until the final interface.

We propose to develop an agent-based architecture for an IDSS. Agents can assist all the efforts in the design of the interface by executing actions such as anticipating the needed information, using the internet to collect data, assisting the user in analysis and treatment. The main feature of the proposed approach is to present the Operator with the most salient information in a timely fashion.

We got inspired by the generic framework of a DSS, proposed by [13], the so-called BHW model, is quite general and can accommodate the recent technologies and architectural solutions. It is based on four essential components: language subsystem, presentation subsystem, knowledge subsystem, and problem processing subsystem. Holsapple et al. showed [13] that the BHW model can accommodate, as a particular case, the largely utilized D/IDM (Dialogue/interface, Data, and Models) paradigm of Simon (see Fig. 1).

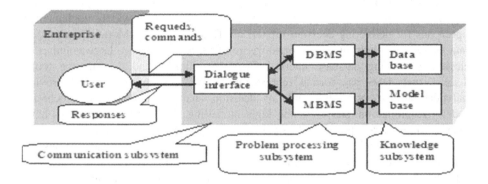

**Fig. 1.** The correspondence between BHW model and D/IDM paradigm

## 3 Decision Support Systems

### 3.1 Literature Survey

Decision support systems (DSS) are designed to actively interact with an individual decision maker in order to assist him to make better decisions based on information obtained [16] [31]. According to Turban and Aronson [33], the central purpose for a DSS is to support and improve decision making. Simon [29] defines DSS as a "model-based set of procedures for processing data and judgements to assist a manager in his decision making". She argues that to be successful such a system needs to be adaptive, easy to use, robust and complete on important issues. These features are desired but not required in a DSS. Holtzman [14] defines a DSS as a computer-based system consisting of three interacting components: a language system, a knowledge system and a problem processing system. This definition covers both old and new DSS designs, as the problem processing system could be a model-base or an ES or an agent-based system or some other system providing problem manipulation capabilities.

However, despite their impressive functionalities, DSS are focused on supporting, not replacing, a human decision maker for important decision tasks, as many of the problem situations faced by managers are unstructured in nature and require the use of reasoning and human judgement. Therefore, as articulated by Lévine and Pomerol [17], "the DSS and the decision maker form a united problem solver". In DSS, the user is defined by physical and purposeful interaction with the system. Therefore, a system might have one, or many users, each interacting with the system in different ways, for different purposes, and with varying frequencies.

Classic standalone DSS tool design comprises components for: (1) database management capabilities with access to internal and external data, information and knowledge; (2) powerful modelling function accessed by a model management system; and (3) user interface design that enable interactive queries, reporting and graphic functions.

A number of frameworks or typologies have been proposed for organizing our knowledge about decision support systems [25]. The two most widely implemented approaches for delivering decision-support are Data-Driven and Model-Driven DSS. Data-Driven DSS help managers organize, retrieve, and synthesize large volumes of relevant data using database queries, OLAP techniques, and data mining tools. Model-Driven DSS use formal representations of decision models and provide analytical support using the tools of decision analysis, optimisation, stochastic modelling, simulation, statistics, and logic modelling. Three other approaches have become more wide spread and sophisticated because of collaboration and web technologies: Knowledge-Driven DSS can suggest or recommend actions to managers, Document-Driven DSS integrate a variety of storage and processing technologies to provide managers document retrieval and analysis, and Communication-Driven DSS rely on electronic communication technologies to link multiple decision makers who might be separated in space or time, or to link decision makers with relevant information and tools.

Some other advantages proposed by Marakas [21] give the advantages of using intelligent components with DSS as opposed to plain DSS as increased timeliness in making decisions, improved consistency in decisions, improved explanations and justifications for specific recommendations, improved management of uncertainty, and formalisation of organisational knowledge. The most useful of these advantages is the improved explanations and justifications which is an extremely useful feature particularly in the fields like medicine, etc. where it helps if the real expert can validate the machine reasoning.

Decision aid and decision making have greatly changed with the emergence of information and communication technology (ICT). Decision makers are now far less statically located; on the contrary they play the role in a distributed way. This fundamental methodological change creates a new set of requirements: Distributed decisions are necessarily based on incomplete data. "Distributed decision" means that several entities (humans and machines) cooperate to reach an acceptable decision, and that these entities are distributed and possibly mobile along networks. Distributed decision making must be possible at any moment. It might be necessary to interrupt a decision process and to provide another, more viable decision.

## 3.2  Intelligent Decision Support System (IDSS)

Recently, many improvements have been witnessed in the DSS field, with the inclusion of artificial intelligence techniques and methods, as for example: knowledge bases, fuzzy logic, multi-agent systems, natural language, genetic algorithms, neural networks and so forth. The inclusion of AI technologies in DSS is an effort to develop computer based systems that mimic human qualities, such as approximate, reasoning, intuition, and just plain common sense. The new common denomination is: Intelligent Decision Support Systems (IDSS) [27].

Intelligent decision support systems (DSS) are interactive computer-based systems that use data, expert knowledge and models for supporting decision makers in organizations to solve complex, imprecise and ill-structured problems by incorporating artificial intelligence techniques [27]. They draw on ideas from diverse disciplines such decision analysis, artificial intelligence, knowledge-based systems and systems engineering. The usage of IDSS is intended to improve the ability of operators and decision makers to better perform their duties and work together.

There may be different ways to make a DSS more intelligent; the most frequently suggested method is to integrate a DSS with an ES. Turban and Watson [33] suggested two fundamental ES/DSS integration models: (1) ES are integrated into DSS components, the incorporation of ES aims to enhance the function of particular components in a DSS; for example, integrating an ES into the Data Base Management System (DBMS) of a DSS, which adds reasoning capability to data manipulation. This particular integration enables users to perform higher-level queries. According to Turban, the integration of ES in DSS components could be applied independently. (2) ES is integrated as a separate component in the DSS; an ES is an add-on to the original DSS. We argue that an IDSS is able to capture the domain knowledge and provide intelligent guidance during the process. While the data and model manipulations are done through the DSS, decision makers can focus solely on the process issues.

As shown in Fig. 2, the IDSS has inputs that include the database(s) needed for the decision problem and a model base that includes, for example, the statistical techniques needed for the analysis [5] [34].

Agents may be used to interact with the user or to learn what types of data are needed and assemble them. The processing component permits analysis of the data, including what-if scenarios that the user may desire. During processing, agents may acquire the needed models or consult with the user. The feedback loop indicates interaction between the processing and input components such as real-time updating or user requirements for additional information. The output component provides the result of the analysis to the user and possibly recommendations about the decision. In this component agents may, for example, personalise the output to particular user so that it is presented in a desired way or so that drill-down information is available. The decision maker and the computer technology are components of the overall system and are recognised explicitly in the diagram. The decision maker is usually a human user, although robotic applications increasingly utilize automated decisions that may be implemented with agents [24].

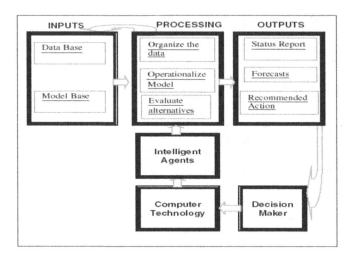

**Fig. 2.** Components of an IDSS [34]

### 3.3 Agent Integration in DSS

The main ideas resumed in the table described in [10] were very interesting for our study (see table 1). It defines how the capability of an agent may be utilised in a DSS application, and also identifies alternative agent design architectures suitable to underpin this. As a constituent part of problem-solving in the domain, an agent may choose particular sources of information to use. Data Gathering may be a function within an agent (sensing), or a dedicated activity of a specialised information agent if the task is complex. The goal is to maintain an accurate model of the domain for the purpose of the class of tasks to be performed. Once created, alternatives can be arbitrated among either by the agent itself, or alternatively through communication with another agent or with the user who makes the final selection choice.

**Table 1.** Mapping DSS functions to agent capabilities

| DSS Function | Agent Function |
|---|---|
| Data collection | Knowledge acquisition and assimilation |
| Model creation | Perception and knowledge representation |
| Alternatives case creation | Planning and reactivity |
| Choice | Action selection |
| Implementation | Action execution |

## 4  The Boiler Combustion Management System

Usually, in a situation of contingency (breakdown of a boiler), the exploiting engineer (the process administrator and the direct operator), tent to identify the breakdown, to analyze and diagnose it on the local site, to make contact with other exploiting engineers of the parent company and send for the technicians of the boilers constructor company, in general located abroad. This type of situation, compels the plant to work in degraded functioning if not to stop the process (case of shutdown alarm) waiting for the problem solving, The analysis of the problem related to a boiler defect results in the hierarchy of tasks, sub-tasks and associated methods partially presented in Fig. 3.

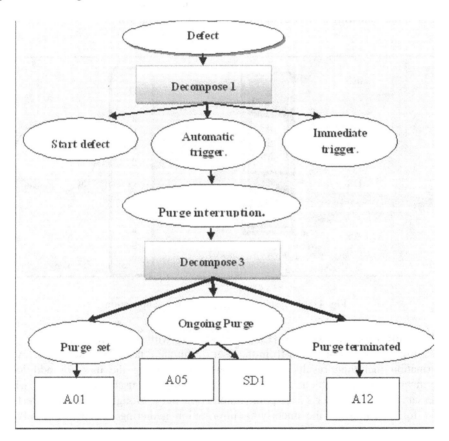

**Fig. 3.** A partial hierarchy of tasks and methods of the application
( A01, A05, SD1 and A12: feasible methods; Decompose1, 2 : Decomposition methods)

Different sensors are set up to detect anomalies at different stages of the process. Breakdown can be automatically signposted by means of an alarm or intercepted by the exploiting engineers (case of defectiveness of the sensor where no alarm is triggered off but the boiler does not work). If there is a defect, an alarm will be triggered off. In case an alarm is signposted to the operator: the flag (the reference given to every alarm) is pointed out on the board (control room). It acquaints with an alarm and locates the defect. To solve this problem, diagnosis and actions of cure are generated by the system.

Otherwise, a breakdown is directly raised by the operator (not triggered off alarm). This scenario occurs when a sensor defect doesn't allow to automatically signpost the breakdown. In this case, the operator must explore a large research space of potential defects with a series of tests. In both cases, the operator tries to solve the problem. Managing this process is a complex activity which involves a number of different sub-tasks: monitoring the process, diagnosing faults, and planning and carrying out maintenance when faults occur.

The boiler combustion management system comprises six modules or sub-systems, here is in the following a brief description (as shown in Fig. 4.):

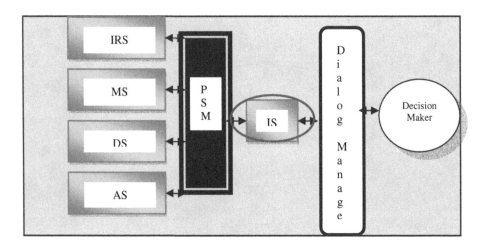

**Fig. 4.** Sub-System Architecture for the application

**The Interface Sub-system (IS)** is concerned with some functions like: 1) collecting relevant information from the user to initiate a task, 2) presenting relevant information including results and explanations, 3) asking the user for additional information during problem solving, and 4) asking for user confirmation, when necessary. From the user's viewpoint, interacting only through a relevant interface agent for a task hides the underlying information gathering and problem solving complexity.

**Problem Solving Module (PSM)** performs most of the autonomous problem solving: (1) receives user delegated task specifications from an IS, (2) interprets the specifications and extracts problem solving goals, (3) forms plans to satisfy these goals, (4) identifies information seeking sub-goals that are present in its plans, (5) decomposes the plans and coordinates with appropriate sub-systems for plan execution, monitoring, and results composition. PSM has the following knowledge: 1) knowledge for performing the task (e.g. query decomposition, sequencing of task steps), 2) information gathering needs associated with the task model, 3) knowledge about relevant information, modelling, diagnosis, and action components that it must coordinate with in support of its particular task, 4) coordination rules that enable coordination with the other relevant agents.

**An Information Retrieval Sub-system** (**IRS**) primarily provides intelligent information services. The simpler of these services is a shot retrieval of information in response to a query: A more enhanced information service is constant monitoring of available database for the occurrence of predefined information patterns.

**A Modelling Sub-system** (**MS**) anticipates the occurrence of contingencies using mathematical and computational models. It integrates data from different sources with mathematical and computational models that model the contingency in order to predict its behaviour and consequences.

**A Diagnosis Sub-system** (**DS**) is activated by the receipt of information from PSM which indicates that there might be a fault. It uses IS snapshot information and knowledge to update its knowledge model of the process on which its diagnosis is based. It pinpoints the approximate region of the fault then it generates and verifies the cause of the fault in the process.

**The Action Sub-system** (**AS**) generates a plan of action which can be used to repair the process once the cause and location of the fault have been determined.

## 5   Basic Notions in BDI Architectures in MAS

Agents have a set of characteristics, such as autonomy, reasoning, reactivity, social abilities, pro-activity, mobility, organization, etc. which allow them to cover several needs for highly dynamic environments. Agent and multi-agent systems have been successfully applied to several scenarios, such as education, culture, entertainment, medicine, robotics, etc. The characteristics of the agents make them appropriate for developing dynamic and distributed systems, as they possess the capability of adapting themselves to the users and environmental characteristics. Most of the agents are based on the deliberative Belief, Desire, Intention (BDI) model [36], where the agents' internal structure and capabilities are based on mental aptitudes, using beliefs, desires and intentions [3]. Nevertheless, complex systems need higher adaptation, learning and autonomy levels than pure BDI model. This is achieved by modelling the agents' characteristics to provide them with mechanisms that allow solving complex problems and autonomous learning.

The functional units thus presented of the highest level correspond to the main parts of a typical BDI architecture given in Fig.5. The diagram shows with bold lines the corresponding data bases, and with thinner the functions of revising the plans (brf), for options generation (options generator), for filtering the intentions (desires filter) and action selection (action selection), as well as the sensor input (sensor input), the action output (action output) and the transition edges.

The beliefs of an agent are its view of the world, which is not necessarily the same as the state of the world, because the sensors may be imperfect. The information supplied can be both incomplete and noisy.

Rather than the desires of an agent we refer to its goals. These give the state of the world in which the agent wishes to be, and must be consistent. Its intentions are the plans that it is currently executing.

A plan is a "recipe" to achieve a particular goal. It is a sequence of actions and/or sub-goals to achieve. One of the features of a BDI system is that when a plan fails, the agent will recover (if possible). It will try to find another way of achieving the goal, taking into account the fact that the world (and hence the agent's beliefs) is changing. The agent goes through a continuous cycle of:

1. sensing the environment
2. reasoning about beliefs, goals and intentions
3. performing one or more actions

During the reasoning stage of the cycle, the agent must reason about beliefs (if and how they should change), goals (changes in beliefs may affect feasibility of goals), and intentions (changes in goals may cause the agent to drop some intentions and/or form new ones). The agent must also decide which action (or actions) to perform next, from the current intentions. In practical implementations of BDI architectures, such as JACK [2] each plan is designed to handle a particular goal in a particular context.

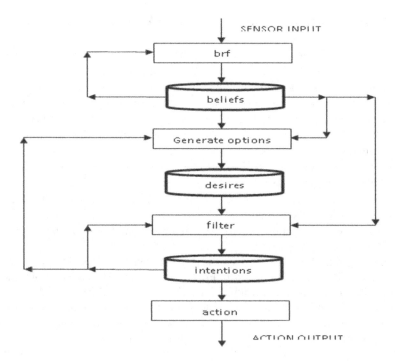

**Fig. 5.** BDI architecture

# 6  Proposed Approach

## 6.1  Architecture of the Adaptive User Interface Sub-system (IS)

We present agent based architecture for an adaptive Interface, it comprises the following items, as it is shown in Fig.6:

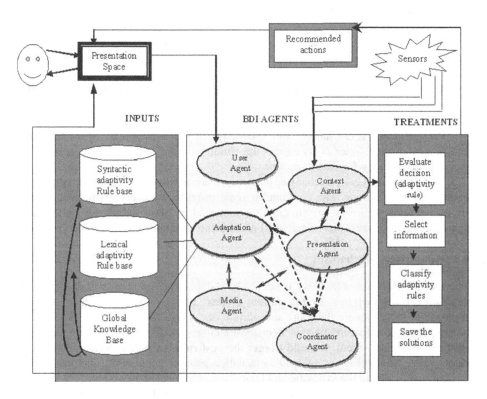

**Fig. 6.** The adaptive interface model

**The Presentation Space** allows the user to interact with the system to achieve the task.

**The input component** comprises:

- **The Syntactic Adaptivity Rule Base** holds the task and style-related rules, referring to dynamic user characteristics and situations

- **The Lexical Adaptivity Rule Base** retains the lexical element-related rules, referring to dynamic user characteristics and situations.

- **Global Knowledge Base (GKB)** possesses knowledge on "static" and dynamic user characteristics and preferences.

**The Treatment Component** represents at the same time the organization and the structuring of a problem of decision, determining all possible resolutions so that the user or the decision-maker can choose the best resolution.

**BDI Agents.** The main functionalities in the system are managed by deliberative BDI agents, including decision making inferred by the IDSS. The user interface system structure has six different deliberative agents based on the BDI model (BDI Agents), each one with specific roles and capabilities:

- **User Agent** manages the users' personal data and behavior (monitoring, location, daily tasks, and anomalies).

- **Context Agent** is responsible for detecting context of user's changes and notices those changes by means of sensors.

- **Adaptation Agent** aims to retaining and applying adativity rules that concern syntactic and lexical adaptivity at the level of UI. Furthermore, it contributes to maintain the GKB in which static user information and dynamically inferred user states and interaction situations are held.

- The main role of **Media Agent** is to associate information with submitting the output media (screen, speaker ...). This is by taking into account the chosen modality and the media availability.

- **Presentation Agent** has the full knowledge of the current state of the interface and presentation. It intends to ensure the fluidity of the user interface in order to increase the capacity for data collection.

- **Coordinator Agent** exchanges plan information with task agents to help them coordinate their actions. The coordinator agent provides two services to task agents: (i) it computes summary information for hierarchical plans submitted by the task agents, and, (ii) coordinates hierarchical plans using summary information.

## 6.2 Adaptivity Mechanism

The user initiates the adaptivity process, the Adaptation Agent proposes the set of adaptation rules that best fit the current context of use. The adapt agent is then responsible for choosing the most appropriate one. (Fig. 7.: (1)). Later, IDSS's role begins; the main feature of this decision-making process is to increase the user confidence in the system. It could trigger the best rules or rather those that the user wants. (Fig. 7.: (3))(Fig. 7.: (4)). The evaluation process begins by triggering the re-evaluation of rules in the syntactic and lexical adaptivity rule bases. (Fig. 7. :( 2))

Hence, all the rules, depending on the modified knowledge, are evaluated. The decisions as for the styles that could be used are evaluated by the IDSS and the notification sent to the presentation agent. (Fig. 7. :( decision-part1))

When the Presentation Agent receives the notification from the decision mechanism, it activates the corresponding behaviour. (Fig. 7.: (5)). In parallel, the same work is done with the lexical adaptivity rule base. In this case, the decision is concerned with some attributes of the user interface. (Fig. 7. :( decision-part2)).

## 6.3 Implementing the UI Architecture

The dynamic changes in system properties that result from adaptivity may have differential effects in different situations, while performing different tasks and on different users. For instance, adaptivity may be more beneficial for complex tasks. The evaluation might consider properties of the user.

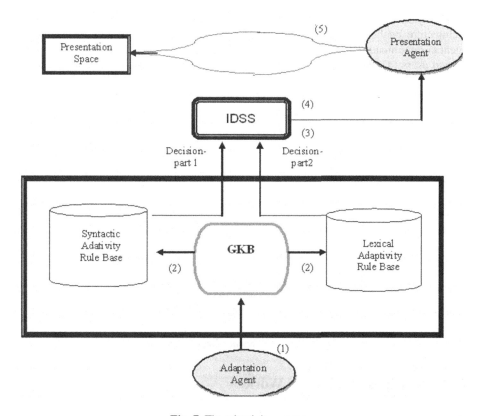

**Fig. 7.** The adaptivity process

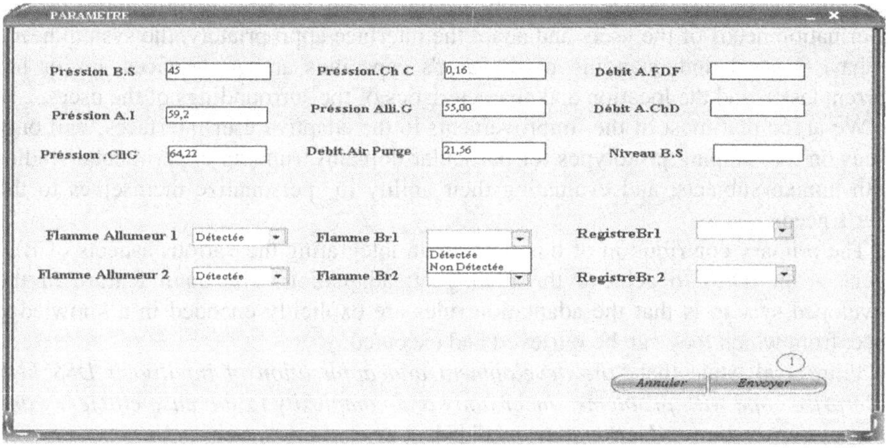

**Fig. 8.** Task and method definition

The system is built upon Java Agent Development (JADE) Platform. The JADE architecture enables agent communication through message exchange based on the agent communication language (ACL). The Adaptive UI is currently under evaluation by end users [4], the print screens given in the Fig.8 and Fig.9 describe some of the graphical interface details.

**Fig. 9.** Parameter acquisition print-screen

# 7   Conclusions and Future Work

Adaptive interfaces have the potential to improve overall human–machine system performance if properly designed; they also have a very real potential to degrade performance if they are not properly designed. To be able to anticipate on the information needs of the users and adapt the interface appropriately, the system needs to have a good understanding of the user's capacities and preferences, his or her current tasks, and the location and characteristics of the surroundings of the user.

We argue that most of the  improvements to the adaptive user interfaces, will only focus on  developing prototypes for particular domains, running experimental studies with human subjects, and evaluating their ability to  personalize themselves to the user's needs.

The primary contribution of this paper is in integrating the various aspects of BDI agent in an IDSS to achieve the final goal: adaptation. The main feature of the developed system is that the adaptation rules are explicitly encoded in a knowledge base, from which they can be retrieved and executed.

Filip et al. state that "*the development and application of intelligent DSS help enterprise cope with problems, uncertainty and complexity to increase efficiency and competitiveness in production networks*" [9].

Based on this, and considering that communication capabilities play an essential role in IDSS. Further work based on coordination protocols between agents needs to be done. A coordinator agent has been incorporated in the agent architecture and a new relationship defined according to the BDI paradigm is defined.

Finally, our future work on the interface will focus on taking into account a user model with learning capabilities, enabling a better match with the personality and habits of each user. Although the usability problems of the prototypes were found and fixed in the usability testing and evaluation phase, a series of field-testing is still necessary to make sure no unexpected usability problems occur.

# References

1. Adla, A., Soubie, J.-L., Zarate, P.: A Co-operative Intelligent Decision Support System for Boilers Combustion Management based on a Distributed Architecture. J. Decision Systems 16, 241–263 (2007)
2. Agent oriented software pty. Ltd. JACK Intelligent Agents, http://agent-software.com.au/JACK.html
3. Bratman, M.E.: Intention, Plans, and Practical Reason. Harvard University Press, Cambridge (1987)
4. Busetta, P., Ronnquist, R., Hodgson, A., Lucas, A.: Jack intelligent agents - components for intelligent agents in java. AgentLink News Letter (January 1999), http://www.agent-software.com
5. Cheung, W.: An Intelligent decision support system for service network planning. J. Decision Support Systems 39, 415–428 (2005)
6. Cote-Munoz, A.,, H.: AIDA: An Adaptive System for Interactive Drafting and CAD Application. In: Schneider-Hufschmidt, M., Kuhme, T., Mallinowski, U. (eds.) Adaptive User Interfaces, pp. 225–240. Elsevier Science Publishers B.V, North-Holland, Amsterdam (1993)
7. Crampes, M.: Composition Multimédia dans un Contexte Narratif. PhD thesis, University of Montpelllier II - Sciences et Techniques du Languedoc (2005)
8. Dieterich, H., Malinowski, U., Kühme, T., Schneider-Hufschmidt, M.: State of the Art in Adaptive User Interfaces. In: Schneider-Hufschmidt, M., Khüme, T., Malinowski, U. (eds.) Adaptive User Interfaces: Principle and Practice. North Holland, Amsterdam (1993)
9. Filip, F.G.: Decision support and control for large-scale complex systems. Annu Rev Control (2008) doi:10.1016/j.arcontrol.2008.03.002
10. Forth, J., Statis, K., Toni, F.: Decision Making with a KGP Agent System. J. Decision Systems 15, 241–266 (2006)
11. Furtado, E.: KnowiXML: a knowledge-based system generating multiple abstract user interfaces in USIXML. In: Proc. Of TAMODIA 2004 (2004)
12. Han, S., Yang, H., Im, D.-G.: Designing a human–computer interface for a process control room: A case study of a steel manufacturing company. International Journal of Industrial Ergonomics 37, 383–393 (2007)
13. Holsapple, C.W., Whinston, A.B.: Decision support systems: A knowledge-based approach. West Publishing Co, Mineapolis (1996)
14. Holtzman, S.: Intelligent decision systems. Addison Wesley, Reading (1989)
15. Julien, D.: GOLIATH: un environnement a base de modèles et agents pour la conception d'interfaces utilisateur. Thesis University of Paris 6 (2004)
16. Keen, P., Scott-Morton, M.: Decision Support Systems: an organizational perspective. Addison-Wesley Publishing, Reading (1978)
17. Lévine, P., Pomerol, J.-C.: The role of decision maker in DSSs and representation levels. In: Proc. of Hawaii International Conference on System sciences, pp. 42–51 (1995)

18. López-Jaquero, V., Montero, F., Molina, J.P., González, P., Fernandez-Caballero, A.: A Multi-Agent System Architecture for the Adaptation of User Interfaces. In: Pěchouček, M., Petta, P., Varga, L.Z. (eds.) CEEMAS 2005. LNCS (LNAI), vol. 3690, pp. 583–586. Springer, Heidelberg (2005)

19. López-Jaquero, V., Vanderdonck, J., Montero, F., González, P.: Towards an Extended Model of User Interface Adaptation: The ISATINE Framework. In: Gulliksen, J., Harning, M.B., Palanque, P., van der Veer, G.C., Wesson, J. (eds.) EIS 2007. LNCS, vol. 4940, pp. 374–392. Springer, Heidelberg (2008)

20. Maybury, M.: Intelligent Multimedia Interfaces. AAAI/MIT Press, Cambridge (1993)

21. Marakas, G.: Decision support systems in the 21st century. Prentice Hall, Englewood Cliffs (2003)

22. Nilsson, G.E., Jacqueline, F.: Model-based user interface adaptation. J. Computer & Graphics, 692–701 (2006)

23. Pantic, M., Sebe, N., Cohn, J., Huang, T.S.: Affective multimodal human-computer interaction. ACM Multimedia (2005)

24. Phillips-Wren, G., Forgionne, G.: Advanced decision-making support using intelligent agent technology. J. Decision Systems 11(2), 165–184 (2002)

25. Power, D.J.: Supporting Decision-Makers: An Expanded Framework (2000)

26. Repo, P.: Middleware support for implementing contextaware multimodal user interfaces. In: Proc. of the third international conference on mobile and ubiquitous multimedia (2004)

27. Ribeiro, R.: Intelligent Decision Support Tool for Prioritizing Equipment Repairs in Critical/Disaster Situations. In: Proc. of Euro Working On Group Decision Support Systems Workshop, London, England (2006)

28. Seffah, A., Forbrig, P.: Multiple user interfaces: towards a task-driven and patterns-oriented design model. In: Proc. of DSV-IS (2002)

29. Simon, H.A.: Administrative behaviour: a study of Decision-Making process in administrative Organizations. Free Press, New York (1997)

30. Souchon, N., et al.: Task modelling in multiple contexts of us. In: Proc. of DSV-IS (2002)

31. Sprague, R., Carlson, D.: Building Effective Decision Support Systems. Prentice-Hall, Inc., Englewood Cliffs (1982)

32. Sukaviriya, P., Foley, J.: Supporting Adaptive Interfaces in a knowledge-based user Interface Environment. In: Gray, W.D., Hefley, W.E., Murray, V. (eds.) The International Workshop on Intelligent User Interfaces, Orlando, FL, pp. 377–392. ACM Press, New York (1993)

33. Turban, E., Aronson, J.: Decision support systems and intelligent systems. Prentice-Hall International, Englewood Cliffs (2001)

34. Tweedale, J., Ichalkaranje, N., Sioutis, C., Jarvis, B., Consoli, A., Phillips-Wrenc, G.: Innovations in multi-agent systems. J. Network and Computer Applications 30, 1089–1115 (2007)

35. Vaudry, C.: Composition dynamique d'informations dans la communication homme-machine. La problématique de la Pertinence dans la CHM. Thesis. University of Montpellier II Sciences et Techniques du Languedoc (2002)

36. Wooldridge, M., Jennings, N.R.: Intelligent Agents: Theory and Practice. The Knowledge Engineering Review 10(2), 115–152 (1995)

# Rough Kohonen Neural Network for Overlapping Data Detection

E. Mohebi[1] and M.N.M. Sap[2]

[1,2] Faculty of Computer Science and Information Systems, University Technology Malaysia
mehsan3@siswa.utm.my
mohdnoor@utm.my

**Abstract.** The Kohonen self organizing map is an excellent tool in exploratory phase of data mining and pattern recognition. The SOM is a popular tool that maps high dimensional space into a small number of dimensions by placing similar elements close together, forming clusters. Recently researchers found that to capture the uncertainty involved in cluster analysis, it is not necessary to have crisp boundaries in some clustering operations. In this paper to overcome the uncertainty, a two-level clustering algorithm based on SOM which employs the rough set theory is proposed. The two-level stage Rough SOM (first using SOM to produce the prototypes that are then clustered in the second stage) is found to perform well and more accurate compared with the proposed crisp clustering method (Incremental SOM) and reduces the errors.

**Keywords:** Clustering, Rough set, SOM, Uncertainty, Incremental.

## 1 Introduction

The self organizing map (SOM) proposed by Kohonen [1], has been widely used in industrial applications such as pattern recognition, biological modeling, data compression, signal processing and data mining [2]. It is an unsupervised and nonparametric neural network approach. The success of the SOM algorithm lies in its simplicity that makes it easy to understand, simulate and be used in many applications. The basic SOM consists of neurons usually arranged in a two-dimensional structure such that there are neighborhood relations among the neurons. After completion of training, each neuron is attached to a feature vector of the same dimension as input space. By assigning each input vector to the neuron with nearest feature vectors, the SOM is able to divide the input space into regions (clusters) with common nearest feature vectors. This process can be considered as performing vector quantization (VQ) [3].

Also, because of the neighborhood relation contributed by the inter-connections among neurons, the SOM exhibits another important property of topology preservation. In other words, if two feature vectors are near to each other in the input space, the corresponding neurons will also be close in the output space, and vice versa. Usually the output neurons are arranged in 2D grids. Therefore, the SOM is suitable for visualization purpose.

Clustering algorithms attempt to organize unlabeled input vectors into clusters such that points within the cluster are more similar to each other than vectors belonging to

T.-h. Kim et al. (Eds.): ASEA 2008, CCIS 30, pp. 183–196, 2009.

different clusters [4]. Clustering has been used in exploratory pattern analysis, grouping, decision-making, and machine learning situations, including data mining, document retrieval, image segmentation, and pattern classification. The clustering methods are of five types: hierarchical clustering, partitioning clustering, density-based clustering, grid-based clustering and model-based clustering [5].

The rough set theory employs two upper and lower thresholds in the clustering process which result in a rough clusters appearance. This technique also could be defined in incremental order i.e. the number of clusters is not predefined by users. In the Incremental clustering algorithm, first of all, the first data item will be assigned to cluster, then the next data item is considered. Either assigns this item to one of the existing clusters or assigns it to a new cluster. This assignment will be done based on some criterion, i.e., the distance between the new item and the existing cluster centroids. In the rough set clustering the lower approximation contains all the patterns that definitely belong to the cluster and the upper approximation permits overlapped.

In this paper, a new two-level clustering algorithm is proposed. The idea is that the first level is to train the data by the SOM neural network and the clustering at the second level is a rough set based incremental clustering approach [6], which will be applied on the output of SOM and requires only a single neurons scan. The optimal number of clusters can be found by rough set theory which groups the given neurons into a set of overlapping clusters (clusters the mapped data respectively). In this case, the existing overlapped data is efficiently detected by the proposed Rough-SOM.

This paper is organized as following; in section 2 the basics of SOM algorithm are outlined. The basic of incremental clustering and rough set based approach are described in section 3. In section 4 the proposed algorithm is presented. Section 5 is dedicated to experiment results and section 6 provides brief conclusion and future works.

## 2   Self Organizing Map

The Self Organizing Map, Originated by Kohonen [1], is an unsupervised, competitive learning algorithm that maps high dimensional data onto a discrete network structure of lower dimensions. Since the mapping of data from a high dimensional space to a two or three-dimensional grid makes the inter-relation among the data points perceptible, it provides a better insight into the data structure and clustering tendency. This mapping retrains the relationship between input data as faithfully as possible, thus describing a topology-preserving representation of input similarities in terms of distances in the output space. It is then possible to visually identify clusters on the map. This feature capability has made the SOM an important tool in a wide range of applications such as data mining, and more generally, pattern recognition and knowledge acquisition.

Competitive learning is an adaptive process in which the neurons in a neural network gradually become sensitive to different input categories, sets of samples in a specific domain of the input space. A division of neural nodes emerges in the network to represent different patterns of the inputs after training.

The division is enforced by competition among the neurons: when an input $x$ arrives, the neuron that is best able to represent it wins the competition and is allowed to learn it even better. If there exist an ordering between the neurons, i.e. the neurons are located on a discrete lattice, the competitive learning algorithm can be generalized. Not only the winning neuron but also its neighboring neurons on the lattice are allowed to learn, the whole effect is that the final map becomes an ordered map in the input space. This is the essence of the SOM algorithm. The SOM consist of $m$ neurons located on a regular low-dimensional grid, usually one or two dimensional. The lattice of the grid is either hexagonal or rectangular.

The basic SOM algorithm is iterative. Each neuron $i$ has a $d$-dimensional feature vector $w_i = [w_{i1}, ..., w_{id}]$. At each training step $t$, a sample data vector $x(t)$ is randomly chosen for the training set. Distance between $x(t)$ and all feature vectors are computed. The winning neuron, denoted by $c$, is the neuron with the feature vector closest to $x(t)$:

$$c = \arg \min_i \| x(t) - w_i \|, \qquad i \in \{1, ..., m\} \tag{1}$$

A set of neighboring nodes of the winning node is denoted as $N_c$. We define $h_{ic}(t)$ as the neighborhood kernel function around the winning neuron $c$ at time $t$. The neighborhood kernel function is a non-increasing function of time and of the distance of neuron $i$ from the winning neuron $c$. The kernel can be taken as a Gaussian function:

$$h_{ic}(t) = e^{-\frac{\| Pos_i - Pos_c \|^2}{2\sigma(t)^2}} \tag{2}$$

where $Pos_i$ is the coordinates of neuron $i$ on the output grid and $\sigma(t)$ is kernel width. The weight update rule in the sequential SOM algorithm can be written as:

$$w_i(t+1) = \begin{cases} w_i(t) + \varepsilon(t) h_{ic}(t)\big(x(t) - w_i(t)\big) \forall i \in N_c \\ w_i(t) \qquad\qquad\qquad\qquad\qquad ow \end{cases} \tag{3}$$

Both learning rate $\varepsilon(t)$ and neighborhood $\sigma(t)$ decrease monotonically with time. In particular the learning rate should start at an initial value $\varepsilon_0$, and then decrease gradually with increasing $t$ time. It is shown by

$$\varepsilon(t) = \varepsilon_0 e^{-\frac{t}{\tau_0}}, \quad t = 0,1,2,... \tag{4}$$

where $\tau_0$ is another time constant of the SOM algorithm.

During training, the SOM behaves like a flexible net that folds onto a cloud formed by training data. Because of the neighborhood relations, neighboring neurons are pulled to the same direction, and thus feature vectors of neighboring neurons resemble each other. There are many variants of the SOM [7], [8]. However, these variants are not considered in this paper because the proposed algorithm is based on SOM, but not a new variant of SOM.

The 2D map can be easily visualized and thus give people useful information about the input data. The usual way to display the cluster structure of the data is to use a distance matrix, such as U-matrix [9]. U-matrix method displays the SOM grid according to neighboring neurons. Clusters can be identified in low inter-neuron distances and borders are identified in high inter-neuron distances. Another method of visualizing cluster structure is to assign the input data to their nearest neurons. Some neurons then have no input data assigned to them. These neurons can be used as the border of clusters [10].

## 3    Rough Set Incremental Clustering

### 3.1    Incremental Clustering

Incremental clustering [11] is based on the assumption that it is possible to consider data points one at a time and assign them to existing clusters. Thus, a new data item is assigned to a cluster without looking at previously seen patterns. Hence the algorithm scales well with size of data set.

It employs a user-specified threshold and one of the patterns as the starting leader (cluster's leader). At any step, the algorithm assigns the current pattern to the most similar cluster (if the distance between pattern and the cluster's leader is less or equal than threshold) or the pattern itself may get added as a new leader if its similarity with the current set of leaders does not qualify it to get added to any of the existing clusters. The set of leaders found acts as the prototype set representing the clusters and is used for further decision making. A high level description of a typical incremental algorithm is as following pseudo code [12].

```
Incremental_Clustering (Data, Thr){
  Cluster_Leader = d1;
  While (there is unlabeled data){
    For (i = 2 to  N)
      If (distance(Cluster_Leader, di) <= Thr)
        Put di in the same cluster as Cluster_Leader;
      Else
        Cluster_Leader = di; // new Cluster
  }//end of while
}
```

An incremental clustering algorithm for dynamic information processing was presented in [13]. The motivation behind this work is that, in dynamic databases, items might get added and deleted over time. These changes should be reflected in the partition generated without significantly affecting the current clusters. This algorithm was used to cluster incrementally a database of 12,684 documents.

The quality of a conventional clustering scheme is determined using within-group-error [14] $\Delta$ given by:

$$\Delta = \sum_{i=1}^{m} \sum_{u_h,u_k \in C_i} distance(u_h, u_k) \qquad u_h, u_k \text{ are objects in the same cluster } C_i. \tag{5}$$

where $u_h$ and $u_k$ are objects in the same cluster. The function *distance* provides the distance between two objects.

Most of the incremental algorithms are *order-dependent*. This property is illustrated in Figure 1, where there are 6 two dimensional objects labeled 1 to 6. If we present these patterns to the Leader Incremental algorithm in the order 2,1,3,5,4,6 then the two clusters obtained are shown by ellipse. If the order is 1,2,6,4,5,3 then we get a two partition as shown by triangles.

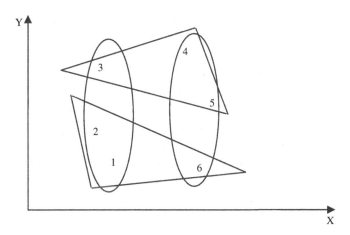

**Fig. 1.** The Leader Incremental algorithm is order-dependent

## 3.2 Rough Set Incremental Clustering

Rough set theory [15] is a relatively new mathematical and AI technique introduced by Z. Pawlak in the early 1980s. This area has remained unknown to most of the computing community recently. Rough set theory is particularly useful for discovering relationships in data. This process is commonly called knowledge discovery or data mining. In the theory of rough set for any subsets $X, Y \subseteq U$ in the universe, the following properties hold:

(1) $\underline{A}(X \cap Y) = \underline{A}(X) \cap \underline{A}(Y)$
(2) $\underline{A}(X \cup Y) \supseteq \underline{A}(X) \cup \underline{A}(Y)$
(3) $\overline{A}(X \cap Y) \subseteq \overline{A}(X) \cap \overline{A}(Y)$
(4) $\overline{A}(X \cup Y) = \overline{A}(X) \cup \overline{A}(Y)$
(5) $\underline{A}(\neg X) = \neg \overline{A}(X), \ \overline{A}(\neg X) = \neg \underline{A}(X)$
(6) $X \supseteq Y \Rightarrow (\underline{A}(X) \supseteq \underline{A}(Y), \ \overline{A}(X) \supseteq \overline{A}(Y))$
(7) $\underline{A}(U) = \overline{A}(U) = U$
(8) $\underline{A}(\emptyset) = \overline{A}(\emptyset) = \emptyset$

In the above properties, let $R \subseteq U \times U$ be an equivalence relation on $U$. The pair $A = (U, R)$ is called an approximation space.

The proposed Rough SOM adopted algorithm is a soft clustering method employing rough set theory. It groups the given data set into a set of overlapping clusters. Each cluster is represented by a lower approximation and an upper approximation $(\underline{A}(C), \overline{A}(C))$ for every cluster $C \subseteq U$. Here $U$ is a set of all objects under exploration. However, the lower and upper approximations of $C_i \in U$ are required to follow some of the basic rough set properties such as:

(1)  $\emptyset \subseteq \underline{A}(C_i) \subseteq \overline{A}(C_i) \subseteq U$
(2)  $\underline{A}(C_i) \cap \underline{A}(C_j) = \emptyset, \ i \neq j$
(3)  $\underline{A}(C_i) \cap \overline{A}(C_j) = \emptyset, \ i \neq j$
(4)  *If an object $u_k \in U$ is not part of any lower approximation, then it must belong to two or more upper approximations.*

Note that (1)-(4) are not independent. However enumerating them will be helpful in understanding the basic of rough set theory.

The lower approximation $\underline{A}(C)$ contains all the patterns that definitely belong to the cluster $C$ and the upper approximation $\overline{A}(C)$ permits overlap. Since the upper approximation permits overlaps, each set of data points that are shared by a group of clusters define indiscernible set. Thus, the ambiguity in assigning a pattern to a cluster is captured using the upper approximation. Employing rough set theory, the proposed clustering scheme generates soft clusters (clusters with permitted overlap in upper approximation) see Fig. 2.

A high level description of a rough incremental algorithm is as following pseudo code [16].

```
Rough_Incremental (Data, upper_Thr, lower_Thr){
  Cluster_Leader = d1;
  While (there is unlabeled data){
    For (i = 2 to   N)
      If (distance(Cluster_Leader, di) <= lower_Thr)
        Put di in the lower approx of Cluster_Leader;
      Else If (distance(Cluster_Leader, di) <= upper_Thr)
        Put di in all existing clusters (j=1 to k)that
        distance(Cluster_Leaderj, di) <= upper_Thr ;
      Else
        Cluster_Leader = di; // new Cluster
  }//end of while
}
```

For a rough set clustering scheme and given two objects $u_h, u_k \in U$ we have three distinct possibilities:

1.  Both $u_k$ and $u_h$ are in the same lower approximation $\underline{A}(C)$.
2.  Object $u_k$ is in lower approximation $\underline{A}(C)$ and $u_h$ is in the corresponding upper approximation $\overline{A}(C)$, and case 1 is not applicable.
3.  Both $u_k$ and $u_h$ are in the same upper approximation $\overline{A}(C)$, and case 1 and 2 are not applicable.

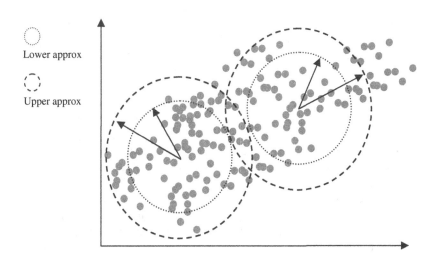

Lower approx

Upper approx

**Fig. 2.** Rough set incremental clustering

For these possibilities, three types of equation (5) could be defined as following:

$$\Delta_1 = \sum_{i=1}^{m} \sum_{u_h, u_k \in \underline{A}(X_i)} distance(u_h, u_k)$$

$$\Delta_2 = \sum_{i=1}^{m} \sum_{u_h \in \underline{A}(X_i) \ and \ u_k \in \overline{A}(X_i)} distance(u_h, u_k) \tag{6}$$

$$\Delta_3 = \sum_{i=1}^{m} \sum_{u_h, u_k \in \overline{A}(X_i)} distance(u_h, u_k)$$

The total error of rough set clustering will then be a weighted sum of these errors:

$$\Delta_{total} = w_1 \times \Delta_1 + w_2 \times \Delta_2 + w_3 \times \Delta_3 \qquad where \quad w_1 > w_2 > w_3. \tag{7}$$

Since $\Delta_1$ corresponds to situations where both objects definitely belong to the same cluster, the weight $w_1$ should have the highest value. On the other hand, $\Delta_3$ corresponds to the situation where both objects may or may not belong to the same class. Hence, $w_3$ should have the lowest value. In other words, $w_1 > w_2 > w_3$. There are many possibel ways of developing an error measure for tough set clustering. The measure $\Delta_{total}$ is perhaps one of the simplest possibilities.More sophistocated alternative may be used for different applications.

## 4   Rough Set Clustering of the Self Organizing Map

In the first level, we use the SOM to form a 2D feature map. The number of output neurons is significantly more than the desired number of clusters. This requires more neurons to represent a cluster, rather than a single neuron to represent a cluster. Then in the second level the output neurons are clustered such that the neurons on the map are divided into as many different regions as the desired number of clusters. Each input data point can be assigned to a cluster according to their nearest output neuron (see Fig. 3).

In the classical agglomerative hierarchical clustering a pair of cluster to be merged has the minimum inter-cluster distance. The widely measure of inter-cluster distance are listed in Table 1 ( $m_i$ is the mean for cluster $C_i$ and $n_i$ is the number of points in $C_i$ ). All of these distance measures yield the same clustering results if the clusters are compact and well separated. The single-linkage clustering (which is used in the proposed method) with distance measure $d_{\min}$ may have "*chaining-effect*" a few points located so as to from a bridge between two cluster cause points across the clusters to be grouped into a single cluster.

In this paper rectangular grid is used for the SOM. Before training process begins, the input data will be normalized. This will prevent one attribute from overpowering in clustering criterion. The normalization of the new pattern $X_i = \{x_{i1},...,x_{id}\}$ for $i = 1,2,...,N$ is as following:

$$X_i = \frac{X_i}{\|X_i\|}.$$

(8)

Once the training phase of the SOM neural network completed, the output grid of neurons which is now stable to network iteration, will be clustered by applying rough set algorithm as described in the previous section. The similarity measure used for rough set clustering of neurons is Euclidean distance (the same used for training the SOM). In this proposed method (see Fig. 4) some neurons, those never mapped any data are excluded from being processed by rough set algorithm.

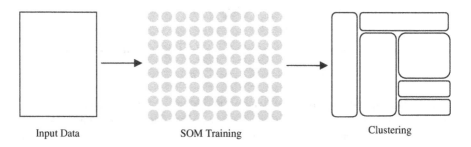

Input Data            SOM Training                    Clustering

**Fig. 3.** The proposed tow-level clustering algorithm

From the rough set algorithm it can be observed that if two neurons are defined as indiscernible (those neurons in the upper approximation of two or more clusters), there is a certain level of similarity they have with respect to the clusters they belong to and that similarity relation has to be symmetric. Thus, the similarity measure must be symmetric.

**Table 1.** Four types of definition of inter-cluster distance

| Definition | Inter-cluster distance |
|---|---|
| Single-linkage | $d_{\min}(C_i, C_j) = \min\limits_{p \in C_i, p' \in C_j} \lVert p - p' \rVert$ |
| Complete-Linkage | $d_{\max}(C_i, C_j) = \max\limits_{p \in C_i, p' \in C_j} \lVert p - p' \rVert$ |
| Centroid-linkage | $d_{mean}(C_i, C_j) = \lVert m_i - m_j \rVert$ |
| Average-linkage | $d_{\min}(C_i, C_j) = 1/(n_i n_j) \sum\limits_{p \in C_i,} \sum\limits_{p' \in C_j} \lVert p - p' \rVert$ |

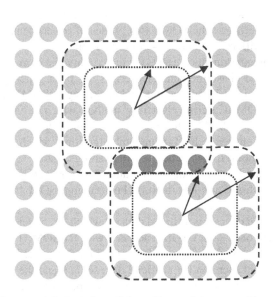

**Fig. 4.** Rough set incremental clustering of the self organizing map. The overlapped neurons have been highlighted (the overlapped data is mapped with these neurons).

According to the rough set clustering of SOM, overlapped neurons and respectively overlapped data (those data in the upper approximation) are detected. In the experiments, to calculate errors and uncertainty, the previous (6) and (7) will be applied to the results of SOM (clustered and overlapped data). The overall proposed algorithm is summarized as follows:

1. Prepare the input data by (8).
2. Train the input data by the SOM.

3.  Cluster SOM by rough set theory approximations. The lower approximation contains the data which are definitely belonging to the cluster. The upper approximation permits overlapped.
4.  Find the overlapped data based on upper approximation and errors by (6) and (7).

The aim of the proposed approach is making the rough set clustering of the SOM to be as precise as possible. Therefore, a precision measure needs to be used for evaluating the quality of the proposed approach. A possible precision measure can be defined as the following equation [15]:

$$certainty = \frac{\text{Number of objects in lower approximation}}{\text{Total number of objects}} \tag{9}$$

## 5   Experimentation and Results

To demonstrate the effectiveness of the proposed clustering algorithm RI-SOM (Rough set Incremental clustering of the SOM), two phases of experiments has been done on two data sets, one artificial and one real-world data set.

The first phase of experiments presents the uncertainty that comes from the both data sets and in the second phase the generated errors has been generated. The results of RI-SOM are compared to I-SOM (Incremental clustering of SOM), which described in section 3.1. The I-SOM is a crisp clustering method which is based on Incremental clustering of the output of SOM. After the SOM is trained by the input dataset then the output neurons are clustered by Incremental algorithm which employs only one approximation (threshold) to assign neurons to existing clusters.

In Out experiments first of all the input data are normalized such that the value of each datum in each dimension lies in [0,1]. For training, SOM $10 \times 10$ with 100-500 epochs on the input data is used.

The first predefined data set is artificial data set which has 569 data of 30 dimensions and is trained twice, once with I-SOM and once with RI-SOM. The generated uncertainty (see Fig. 5) is gained by the (9). From the Fig. 5 it could be observed that the number of predicted clusters on the artificial data set is 6 and the uncertainty-level in clustering prediction of RI-SOM has less error compared to I-SOM (see Table 2).

$$uncertainty = 1 - \frac{\text{Number of objects in lower approximation}}{\text{Total number of objects}} \tag{10}$$

The second data set is Iris data set [17] has been widely used in pattern classification. It has 150 data points of four dimensions. The data are divided into three classes with 50 points each. The first class of Iris plant is linearly separable from the other two. The other two classes are overlapped to some extent.

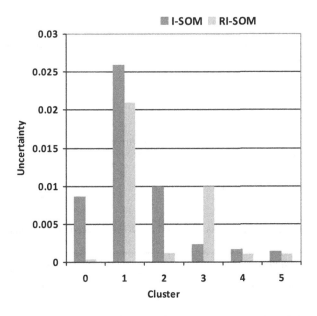

**Fig. 5.** Comparison of the error of RI-SOM and I-SOM on the artificial data set

**Table 2.** The generated error of I-SOM and RI-SOM on the artificial set

| Cluster | 1 | 2 | 3 | 4 | 5 | 6 |
|---------|------|------|------|------|------|------|
| **I-SOM** | 0.0078 | 0.026 | 0.01 | 0.0023 | 0.0017 | 0.0014 |
| **RI-SOM** | 0.0035 | 0.021 | 0.0012 | 0.01 | 0.001 | 0.001 |

Fig. 4 shows the certainty generated from epoch 100 to 500 by the (8). From the gained certainty it's obvious that the RI-SOM could efficiently detect the overlapped data that have been mapped by overlapped neurons (Table 3).

**Table 3.** The certainty-level of I-SOM and RI-SOM on the Iris data set from epoch 100 to 500

| Epoch | 100 | 200 | 300 | 400 | 500 |
|-------|-------|-------|-------|-------|-------|
| **I-SOM** | 33.33 | 65.23 | 76.01 | 89.47 | 92.01 |
| **RI-SOM** | 67.07 | 73.02 | 81.98 | 91.23 | **97.33** |

In the second phase, the same initialization for the SOM has been used. The errors that come from both data sets, according to the equations (6) and (7) have been generated by our proposed algorithms (Table 4). The weighted sum equation (7) has been configured as following:

$$\sum_{i=1}^{3} w_i = 1$$

*and for each $w_i$ we have :*    (11)

$$w_i = \frac{1}{6} \times (4 - i).$$

**Table 4.** Comparative generated errors of I-SOM and RI-SOM according to equations (5) and (6)

| | Method | $\Delta_1$ | $\Delta_2$ | $\Delta_3$ | $\Delta_{total}$ |
|---|---|---|---|---|---|
| Artificial Data set | **RI-SOM** | 0.6 | 0.88 | 0.04 | **1.4** |
| | **I-SOM** | | | | 1.8 |
| Iris Data set | **RI-SOM** | 1.05 | 0.85 | 0.043 | **1.94** |
| | **I-SOM** | | | | 2.8 |

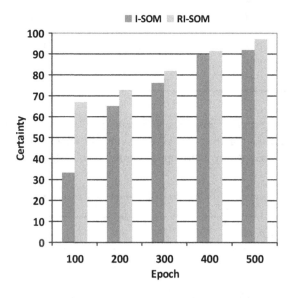

**Fig. 6.** Comparison of the certainty-level of RI-SOM and I-SOM on the Iris data set

# 6 Conclusion and Future Work

In this paper a two-level based clustering approach (RI-SOM), has been proposed to predict clusters of high dimensional data and to detect the uncertainty that comes from the overlapping data. The approach is based on the rough set theory that employs a soft clustering by assigning two variation of threshold for each cluster.

The process results in a soft clustering algorithm which employs upper and lower approximation. The lower approximation contains all the patterns that definitely belong to the cluster and the upper approximation permits overlapped. In this case the proposed Rough SOM could detect overlapped data from the data set and makes clustering as precise as possible. The results of the both phases indicate that RI-SOM more accurate and generates less errors as compare to crisp clustering (I-SOM).

The proposed algorithm detects accurate overlapping clusters in clustering operations. As the future work, the overlapped data could be assigned correctly to true clusters they belong to, by assigning *fuzzy membership value* to the indiscernible set of data. Also a weight can be assigned to the data's dimension to improve the overall accuracy.

## Acknowledgments

This research was supported by the Research Management Centre, University Technology Malaysia (UTM) and the Malaysian Ministry of Science, Technology and Innovation (MOSTI) under vote number 79224.

## References

1. Kohonen, T.: Self-organized formation of topologically correct feature maps. Biol. Cybern. 43, 59–69 (1982)
2. Kohonen, T.: Self-Organizing Maps. Springer, Berlin (1997)
3. Gray, R.M.: Vector quantization. IEEE Acoust. Speech, Signal Process. Mag. 1(2), 4–29 (1984)
4. Pal, N.R., Bezdek, J.C., Tsao, E.C.K.: Generalized clustering networks and Kohonen's self-organizing scheme. IEEE Trans. Neural Networks (4), 549–557 (1993)
5. Han, J., Kamber, M.: Data mining: concepts and techniques. Morgan Kaufman, San Francisco (2000)
6. Asharaf, S., Narasimha Murty, M., Shevade, S.K.: Rough set based incremental clustering of interval data. Pattern Recognition Letters (27), 515–519 (2006)
7. Yan, Yaoguang: Research and application of SOM neural network which based on kernel function. In: Proceeding of ICNN&B 2005 (1), pp. 509–511 (2005)
8. Sap, M.N.M., Mohebi, E.: Outlier Detection Methodologies: A Review. Journal of Information Technology, UTM 20(1), 87–105 (2008)
9. Ultsch, A., Siemon, H.P.: Kohonen's self organizing feature maps for exploratory data analysis. In: Proceedings of the International Neural Network Conference, Dordrecht, Netherlands, pp. 305–308 (1990)

10. Zhang, X., Li, Y.: Self-organizing map as a new method for clustering and data analysis. In: Proceedings of the International Joint Conference on Neural Networks, Nagoya, Japan, pp. 2448–2451 (1993)
11. Jain, A.K., Murty, M.N., Flynn, P.J.: Data Clustering: A Review. ACM Computing Surveys 31(3), 264–323 (1999)
12. Stahl, H.: Cluster analysis of large data sets. In: Gaul, W., Schader, M. (eds.) Classification as a Tool of Research, pp. 423–430. Elsevier North-Holland, Inc., New York (1986)
13. Can, F.: Incremental Clustering for dynamic information peocessing. ACM Trans. Inf. System 11(2), 143–164 (1993)
14. Sharma, S.C., Werner, A.: Improved method of grouping provincewide permanent traffic counters. Transaction Research Report 815, 13–18 (1981)
15. Pawlak, Z.: Rough sets. Internat. J. Computer Inf. Sci. (11), 341–356 (1982)
16. Lingras, P.J., West, C.: Interval set clustering of web users with rough K-means. J. Intelligent Inf. Syst. 23(1), 5–16 (2004)
17. UCI Machine Learning Repository,
    http://www.ics.uci.edu/mlearn/MLRepository.html

# Design and Implementation of a PC-Cluster Based Video-On-Demand Server

Liang-Teh Lee[1], Hung-Yuan Chang[1,2], Der-Fu Tao[2], and Siang-Lin Yang[1]

[1] Dept. of Computer Science and Engineering, Tatung University, Taipei, Taiwan
[2] Dept. of Electronic Engineering, Technology and Science Institute of
Northern Taiwan, Taipei, Taiwan
ltlee@ttu.edu.tw, {hychang,tftao}@tsint.edu.tw,
g9506031@ms.ttu.edu.tw

**Abstract.** The video-on-demand (VOD) is one of the most potential services of internet applications. In this paper, a load balanced PC-Cluster for implementing the VOD server has been proposed to offer the video-information to users efficiently. In the proposed scheme, two-Tier model has been adopted in the systematic architecture. The PC-Cluster is used to be the storage system of the VOD server and the load balancing mechanism in the proposed system is based on the Least-Connection-First algorithm. For enhancing the sharing and balancing of the system load among video servers in the cluster, a video placement strategy has also been proposed. Accompany with the dynamically adjusted files in each video level, a dynamical cyclical video replacement mechanism is applied to replicate and allocate video files for improving the load balance of the system. From the experimental results, we can see that a better load balance of the system can be achieved by applying the proposed scheme.

**Keywords:** Video-on-demand (VOD), PC-Cluster, Load balance.

## 1 Introduction

Because of dynamically audio-visual information in the developed process of multimedia, the information is usually transported with huge amount of data, such as, video data [1], [2]. But according to the factor of network bandwidth, it restricts by development. Then, we integrate multiple mechanisms into load balanced PC-cluster server system which can share the load of incoming requests by an equitably distributed scheme. We adopt Two-Tier model in the systematic structure, and use the PC-cluster to be the storage system of the VOD server in order to reach a better scalability. The load balancing mechanism is based on the Least-Connection-First algorithm. We propose a video placement strategy to share and balance the loads among video servers in the cluster. In video level algorithm, videos are classified into three categories according to the popularity of the video. In video placement mechanism, video files are replicated to different amount of copies according to their levels, and these replicas are distributed to other video servers by the duplicated mechanism of Chained-Declustering [3], [4]. In this paper, a dynamically cyclical video replacement mechanism has been proposed to replicate and allocate video files

T.-h. Kim et al. (Eds.): ASEA 2008, CCIS 30, pp. 197–209, 2009.

for improving load balancing of the system so as to obtain a better performance of the load balanced system.

The rest of the paper is organized as follows. Section 2 will describe some background knowledge of techniques about the PC-cluster system, overview of streaming server, load balancing method, and video duplicated mechanism. We present our approach of adopting the architecture of PC-cluster as VOD server and proposing a video placement strategy in section 3. In section 4, we will introduce the environment of the experiment to set up and show the experimental results. Finally, section 5 is the conclusions and future works.

## 2   Related Works

PC-cluster system built in 1994; Beowulf is a class of computer clusters similar to the original NASA system [3], [5]. The systems belong to high-performance parallel cluster computers that are composed of cheap personal computers. Originally developed by Thomas Sterling and Donald Becker at NASA, Beowulf systems are now deployed worldwide, chiefly in support of scientific computing. A Beowulf cluster is networked into 16 DX4 processor and have libraries and programs installed which allow processing to be shared among them. The PC-cluster system is composed of some cheap hardware and software. For example: PC, SMP, Ethernet, Gigabit, Myrinet, Windows, Linux, Solaris, etc. The PC-cluster system has some important properties and advantages as described follows [9]:

1. High availability (HA): The purpose of the high availability cluster is implemented for improving the availability of services. So, operating by having redundant nodes.
2. Scalability: Appropriately adjusting number of machines according to users' demand.
3. Load Balancing: Operating by distributing a workload evenly over multiple back end nodes. Typically, the cluster will be configured with multiple redundant load balancing front ends.

A complete video streaming service is based on player of client, video data, streaming server and internet. The player is used to supporting playing way of streaming. A MP4 file format is as an audio-video code to be appropriate compression. Streaming server is based on three protocols which are called RTSP (Real-Time Streaming Protocol), RTP (Real-Time Transport Protocol), RTCP (RTP Control Protocol) to control and transport video data [1], [10]. When video is demanded by user, the player sends RTSP packets to streaming server with communication.

According to different types and contents of streaming server, the player informs streaming server about video on demand. Streaming server issues VCR-like commands such as "play", "pause", and "teardown" and allowing time-based access to files on a server. The sending of streaming data itself is not part of the RTSP protocol. Most RTSP servers use the standards-based RTP as the transport protocol for the actual audio-video data, acting somewhat as a metadata channel.

In the course of video play, the player can regularly send RTCP packets inform streaming server about received cases of video data. The RTSP is a network communication protocol. It is used to control audio-video data and initializes the audio-video data, analyzes streaming data, and controls VCR-like commands. There are several functions in the RTSP, including DESCRIBE, SETUP, PLAY, PAUSE, TEARDOWN. All RTSP packets are formed of Request-Response Pair.

The real-time multimedia transfers by RTP and RTCP over the internet. The RTP defines a standardized packet format for delivering audio-video information. RTP can also be used in conjunction with RTSP protocol which enhances the field of multimedia applications. RTCP provides out-of-band control information for an RTP flow. RTCP partners RTP in the delivery and packaging of multimedia data. RTCP is used periodically to transmit control packets to participants in a streaming multimedia session. The primary function of RTCP is to provide feedback on the quality of service being provided by RTP.

Besides, we adopt MPEG-4 compression standard and stored format of media data by MP4 file format [2]. A MP4 file format is based on object and consists of Atoms. The relationship of Atom is form of tree and exists on parallel or covering with other Atoms. If the media data is sent by streaming, the media data must be with extra hint track to be encapsulated special packet and sent in the internet. In streaming service, the very important role is hint track that also includes Session Description Protocol. Streaming server responds by the demand SDP of RTSP DESCRIBE-Request to informs client for the information as type of data flow, length of video, and compression way. Streaming server captures the corresponding media data of data flow according to the allocation of hint track and encapsulates appropriately packet-sized for client.

The load balancing in the network is the use of devices external to the processing servers in a cluster to distribute workload or network traffic load across the PC-cluster [6]. The servers must be connected directly or indirectly to the balancing server. The load in the PC-cluster is distributed somewhat evenly across multiple servers, allowing for faster responses and less likelihood of a server over loading. Load Balancing is achieved by having at least one load balancing server and at least two Back-End servers. The live load balancing server receives incoming requests, monitors the load and available system resources on the Back-End servers, and redirects requests to the most appropriate server. The Back-End servers are all live and all handling requests. There are two algorithms in Load balancing, including static and dynamic balancing. Static algorithm is based on a regular schedule for the order and the systemic operation of current state doesn't be considered. In contrast, dynamic algorithm is based on server to be considered in the systemic operation of load state, and current minimum load of server will be allocated to users' demand. The common used balancing methods in PC-cluster system are described below:

1. Round-Robin algorithm: Assigning the next incoming requests to the next video server in order and rotates through the order continuously for further requests. It is suitable to systemic environment with the same computing capability and resources in cluster.
2. Weight algorithm: Calculating a weight value by current workload and condition of video server. Load balancing server distributes workload to each video server according to the priority value or weight of that video server.
3. Least-Connection-First algorithm: Load balancing server keeps track of all currently active connections assigned to each video server in the PC-cluster and assigns the next new incoming connection request to the video server that currently is the least connections.

The video duplicated mechanism is to copy the same file in different number of replicas that are stored in different disks. The system does not quickly drop off the utilization of video servers if the same file is connected with high frequency. Video duplicated mechanism averagely distributes requests among video servers in order to reach better load balance in the system. Two different video duplicated mechanisms are introduced below:

1. Mirroring: The file of disk is completely copied and directly allocated to the corresponding disk.
2. Chained-Declustering: The duplicated file is allocated by the displacement-linked way, as shown in Fig. 1.

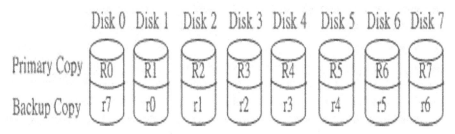

**Fig. 1.** Chained-Declustering

## 3  System Architecture and Video Strategy

The Two-Tier model of the proposed scheme is shown in Figure 2 [7], [8]. This architecture is divided into two parts: one is front-end server and the other is back-end server. Front-End server is a load balancing server that is used for controlling and distributing systemic workloads. Back-End servers are video servers to store videos and deal with requests requested from the Front-End server. All of servers in the system use real IP to connect the Ethernet, but the system only provides IP address of load balancing server as a unified communication channel. Therefore, to users, the IP addresses of video servers are hidden. Servers are responsible for the work as described below:

1. Load balancing server:
   - Responsible for sending and receiving RTSP packets between client and video servers, but the packets are not be analyzed [9], [10].
   - Responsible for load balancing method.
   - Include video information database with serving video states in each video server and connecting load information database with currently load states in each video server.
2. Video servers:
   - Sending video information with serving video states in each video server to load balancing server and stored video files.
   - Analyzing RTSP packets of client. According to the analyzed information, video server sends RTSP responded packets.
   - Stored video files
   - Analyzing video information and video data is encapsulated to RTP packets by directly transporting to the client.

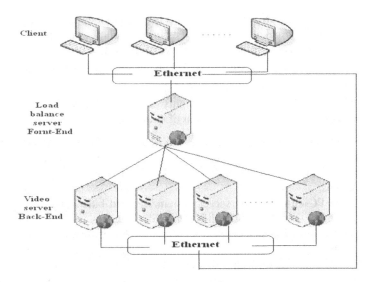

**Fig. 2.** Two-tier architecture

The load balancing algorithm adopted in the proposed PC-cluster VOD system is combining Least-Connection-First algorithm with Round-Robin algorithm. In order to achieve a better load balance, the load balancing server will choose the video server with minimum connections from the video servers with the requested video files. Thus, the selected video servers will not lead to high workloads, and the system can support higher video connections for serving more users' demands. The load balancing server keeps track of connected number of video servers and updates load information database for deciding the next video service. If more than two video servers have the same connected numbers, Round-Robin algorithm determines the next service.

Since the videos are always increased and removed in the PC-cluster VOD system, the Chained-Declustering is applied to allocate duplicated video files. A series of the video placement strategies is applied in the proposed system, that is, video level algorithm, video placement mechanism, and video replacement mechanism. Figure 3 is the flow chart of video placement strategy. First, according to the video level algorithm, videos are classified into three categories, hot video, normal video, and low video. Then, according to different level of videos, the system copies different number of video files to video servers. When video files are completely allocated, videos are connected to play by users' demands. As video levels in the system are altered for the click numbers, they will be dynamically adjusted. Moreover, level videos are dynamically allocated in each cycle. There are three video replacement modes that include as follow:

1. Hot to low mode: The mode replaces the hot video level to low video level.
2. Normal to hot mode: The mode replaces the normal video level to hot video level.
3. Low to normal mode: The mode replaces the low video level to normal video level.

There's video categories are adjusted dynamically.

According to different probability of connections and video categories, video files are allocated. The system keeps statistical records of click numbers in the system. According to click rates of videos, different video levels will have different probability of connections. The click rates of video levels are defined as follows:

1. Hot videos: The front twenty percent of click rate.
2. Normal videos: The front twenty to eighty percent click rate.
3. Low videos: The lastly twenty percent of click rate.

The video level algorithm applies the above different click rates to distinct different video levels. The click rates of videos are sorted by descending order, and different click rates are divided into three categories. The load balancing server handles the data of click rates.

By using the PC-cluster VOD server system for load balancing, we assume that each video file is stored in two different video servers. Table 1 presents the parameters used for video placement mechanism. The parameters include average video size, video rate about hot, normal and low, total number of video, hard disk occupied in each video server. Suppose the system is constructed by six video servers with 75G hard disk size of each video server, averagely each video size is 1GB, and total hard disk size is 450G. Thus, the system should consist of 450 video files. If each video is stored in two different video servers, total number of video files will be 225. According to the video level algorithm, the number of files in each video level of the proposed system will be:

1. Hot video number is calculated by 225 * 20% = 45.
2. Normal video number is calculated by 225 * 60% = 135.
3. Low video number is calculated by 225 * 20% = 45.

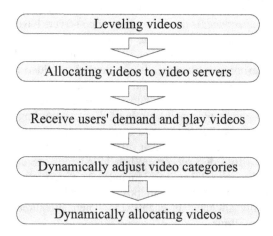

**Fig. 3.** The flow chart of video placement strategy

Duplicated number of level video files is described as follow:

- Hot video: The hot videos have the high click rate in the PC-cluster server systems. The number of duplication is defined as $BS/2=3$.

● Normal video: The number of normal video files duplicated is calculated by considering the total number of video files expected, including replicas, and the hard disk space occupied by hot and low video files.

**Table 1.** The parameters used for video placement mechanism

| Parameters | Names |
|---|---|
| Average Video Size | $V_S$ |
| High_Videos Rate | $HV_R$ |
| Low_Videos Rate | $LV_R$ |
| Normal_Videos Rate | $NV_R$ |
| Number of Video Server (Back-End) | $B_N$ |
| Total Number of Videos in the System | $V_{TN}$ |
| Total Number of High Videos in the System | $HV_{TN}$ |
| Total Number of Low Videos in the System | $LV_{TN}$ |
| Total Number of Normal Videos in the System | $NV_{TN}$ |
| Hard Disk Size of Each Video Server (Back-End) | $B_S$ |
| High_Videos of Hard Disk Occupied in Each Video Server | $HV_{SR}$ |
| Low_Videos of Hard Disk Occupied in Each Video Server | $LV_{SR}$ |
| Normal_Videos of Hard Disk Occupied in Each Video Server | $NV_{SR}$ |

Total number of normal video files, including replicas, in all video servers can be calculated as

$$MV_{TN}=B_S*NV_{SR}/V_S*B_N$$

Since original number of normal video files in all video servers is $VTN*NV_R$

The number of duplicated normal video files can be expressed as: $\lfloor MV_{TN}/V_{TN} * NV_R \rfloor$

The percentage of hard disk occupied by three level video files in each video server is assumed as follow:

> ➢ The $HVR$ is set to 20 %.
> ➢ The $HVSR$ is set to 30 %.
> ➢ The $NVSR$ of normal videos is set to 60 %.
> ➢ The $LVR$ is 20 %.
> ➢ The LVSR is set to 10 %.

Consequently, according to the above analysis and assumptions, the number of duplicated normal video files can be calculated as

$$\lfloor 75*0.6/1*6/225*0.6 \rfloor = 2 \,.$$

● Low video: The number of duplicated videos can be calculated as

$$\lfloor 75*0.1/1*6/225*0.2 \rfloor = 1 \,.$$

Original and total number of files in each video level is shown in Table 2. The sum of original number files is 225. The hot video assigns 45 files. The normal video assigns 135 files. The low video assigns 45 files.

The total number of files in each video level is 450 files. The hot video for total number is 135 files that include original and duplicate video files. As same as the hot video for total number in each video level, there are 270 files in the normal video, and there are 45 files in the low video.

Accompany with the dynamically adjusted files in each video level, a dynamically cyclical video replacement mechanism has been proposed to replicate and allocate video files. There are three video replacement modes in the proposed scheme, such as low to normal, hot to low and normal to hot.

**Table 2.** Original and total number of files in each video level

| video　　　　　number | Original number | Total number |
|---|---|---|
| Hot video | 45 | 135 |
| Normal video | 135 | 270 |
| Low video | 45 | 45 |
| Sum | 225 | 450 |

The modes of operational process are described as following:

1. Hot to low: First, if originally hot video is adjusted to low video, it will be modified video category for low. Then, newly modified video is stored in the originally low video allocation. The originally low video is stored in the originally hot video allocation and is copied two video files to video server of the corresponding originally hot video. The originally low video is modified video category for hot after.
2. Normal to hot: First, if originally normal video is adjusted to hot video, it will be modified video category for hot. Then, newly modified video is stored in the originally hot video allocation and is copied two video files to video server of the corresponding originally hot video.
3. Low to normal: First, if originally low video is adjusted to normal, it will be modified video category for normal. Then, newly modified video is stored in the originally normal video allocation and is copied one video file to video server of the corresponding originally normal video.

Figure 4 is the operational process of video replacement mechanism. For example, there are twelve video files in below system. The operational process in step by step is described as follows:

1. Sort the click number of all original videos by decreasing order.
2. Sort the click number of all newly videos by decreasing order.
3. Compare with allocation of sorted order. If the allocation of original video is not equal to newly video, they will be swapped allocation by themselves.
4. They are modified their categories and copied appropriate video files to store in the corresponding video server.

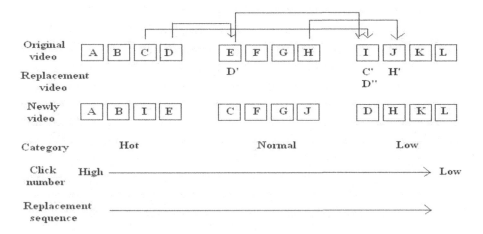

**Fig. 4.** The operational process of video placement mechanism

## 4  Experimental Results

The proposed video placement strategy is applied to allocate video files, and users' connections and click number of videos are simulated. Table 3 shows the tested video information. Fast Ethernet with the highest bandwidth is 100Mb/s. In the simulation, the bandwidth of the internet is considered as 80Mb/s. Thus, the maximum of each video connection is $\lfloor 80*1024/1553 \rfloor = 52$.

The proposed system, Least-Connection-First with Chained-Declustering, is comparing with three other systems, i.e., Round-Robin with Mirroring, Round-Robin with Chained-Declustering, and Least-Connection-First with Mirroring. The connection probabilities of different video categories used in the experiments are listed in Table 4.

Figure 5 shows the comparison of the maximum number of video connections among the proposed system and three other systems. As the result, the proposed system can support more than two times of the maximum number of video connections in comparing with three other systems. Figure 6 is the comparison of utilization of each video server among the proposed system and three other systems when each system is overloaded. It can be seen that the proposed mechanism can maintain the utilization of each video server almost constant.

Because levels of video files are dynamically adjusted, a dynamically cyclical video replacement mechanism has been proposed to replicate and allocate video files for enhancing load balance of the system. As mention before, the connected probabilities of different video categories used in the experiments are listed in Table 4.

**Table 3.** The tested video information

| Length (minute) | Resolution | File size (GB) | Average bit rate (Kb/s) |
|---|---|---|---|
| 90 | 640*480 | 1 | 1533 |

**Table 4.** The connection probabilities of different video categories

| Video category | Connection probability | Connected number/Cycle | | Video number |
|---|---|---|---|---|
| High | 5/9 | 5 | 3 | 1~23 |
| | | | 2 | 24~25 |
| Normal | 3/9 | 3 | 2 | 1~68 |
| | | | 1 | 69~135 |
| Low | 1/9 | 1 | 1 | 1~45 |

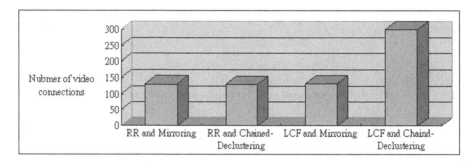

**Fig. 5.** The maximum number of video connections

We assume the levels of video files are adjusted as follows:

1. Hot to Low: Twenty hot videos are selected randomly to be adjusted to low videos.
2. Normal to Hot: The front twenty normal videos are adjusted to hot videos.
3. Low to Normal: The front twenty low videos are adjusted to normal videos.

Because the front twenty hot videos are more frequently visited than that of other level videos. We assume that if a video in the front twenty hot videos is requested, then that video will be requested two more times. For evaluating the effectiveness of the proposed replacement mechanism, the utilization of all video servers and maximum number of video connections are measured without and with applying video replacement mechanism in the pc-cluster VOD system. Figure 7 is the comparison of the maximum number of video connections for the pc-cluster VOD system without and with applying replacement mechanism. Figure 8 is the comparison of the utilization of total video connections and total video files used for the pc-cluster VOD system without and with applying replacement mechanism. For comparing the maximum number of video connections, the system with applying replacement mechanism will be slightly better than that of the system without applying replacement mechanism. However, the proposed system with applying replacement mechanism is much better than without applying replacement mechanism according to total video files used.

In the proposed system, video file levels are adjusted dynamically and a dynamically cyclical video replacement algorithm is applying to replicate and allocate video files for supporting more connections for all video files. Thus, the system with applying replacement mechanism will maintain almost constant utilization of video servers and maximum number of video connections, even if the connection probabilities of some specific hot videos are higher than other videos. On the contrary, the system without applying replacement mechanism will not adjust the number of video files in different video levels, thus, the system cannot be utilized effectively. The experimental results show that an efficient load balanced PC-cluster VOD system can be achieved by applying the proposed scheme.

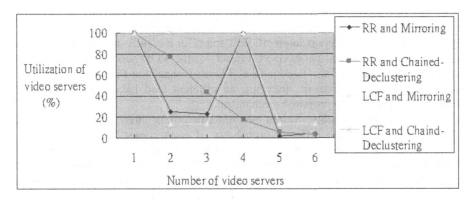

**Fig. 6.** Utilization of each video server

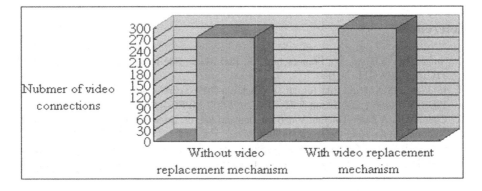

**Fig. 7.** Comparison of the maximum number of video connections for the proposed system without and with applying the replacement mechanism

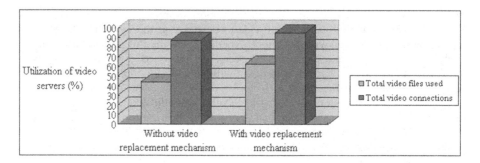

**Fig. 8.** Comparison of the utilization of total video connections and total video files used for the proposed system without and with applying replacement mechanism

## 5 Conclusions

With the development of broadband network and the continuously advance of multimedia technology, in the future, the VOD system is more important for business and home. In order to support more efficient and offer the video-information services to numerous users, a load balanced PC-cluster for the VOD server system has been proposed. According to Two-Tier model and Least-Connection-First algorithm with a series of the video placement strategies, an efficient load balance system can be achieved by applying the proposed mechanism.

In video level algorithm, videos are classified into three categories because different level videos are different probability of connections. In video placement mechanism, the popularity of the video are replicated to more copies than unpopular video and these replicas are distributed to other video servers. Accompany with the dynamically adjusted files in each video level, a dynamically cyclical video replacement mechanism has been proposed to replicate and allocate video files for improving load balance of the system. The experimental results show that a load balanced PC-cluster VOD system can be achieved by applying the proposed scheme.

## References

1. Singer, D., Belknap, W., Franceschini, G.: ISO Media File format specification. ISO/IEC JTC1/SC29/WG11 (2001)
2. ISO/IEC: ISO Media File format specification-MP4 Technology under consideration for ISO/IEC 14496-1:2001/Amd 3. JTC1/SC29/WG11 MPEG01/N4270-1 (2001)
3. Chen, Y.P.: A Fault-Tolerant Video-on-Demand Server. Department of Computer Science, National Chiao-Tung University (1998)
4. Hung, W.S.: An Effective Data Placement Scheme for Supporting Fault-Tolerance in Distributed Video Server Environment, Department of Computer Science, National Chiao-Tung University (1999)
5. Aversa, L., Bestavros, A.: Load balancing a cluster of web servers: using distributed packet rewriting. In: Proceedings of the IEEE International Conference on Performance, Computer, and Communications, pp. 24–29 (2000)

6. Bunt, R.B., Eager, D.L., Oster, G.M., Williamson, C.L.: Achieving Load Balance and Effective Caching in Clustered Web Servers, University of Saskatchewan (1999)
7. Tewari, R., Mukherjee, R., Dias, D.M., Vin, H.M.: Design and Performance Tradeoffs in Clustered Video Servers. In: Proceedings of the International Conference on Multimedia Computing and Systems (1996)
8. Jin, H., Tan, G., Wu, S.: Clustered Multimedia Servers: Architecture and Storage System. Internet and Cluster Computing Center (2003)
9. Schukzrinne, H., Rao, A., Lanphier, R.: Real Time Streaming Protocol (RTSP), RFC2326 (1998)
10. Schukzrinne, H., Casner, S., Frederick, R., Jacobson, V.: RTP: A Transport Protocol for Real-Time Applications, RFC3550-RTP (2003)

# Using WordNet in Conceptual Query Expansion

Jiuling Zhang, Chuan Shi, Beixing Deng, and Xing Li

Dept. Electronic Engineering, Tsinghua University, Beijing, 100084, China
zhang-jl07@mails.tsinghua.edu.cn

**Abstract.** Query expansion is a widely studied technique for improving information retrieval effectiveness. In this paper we proposed a new query expansion technique using the comprehensive thesaurus WordNet and its semantic relatedness measure modules. Word sense disambiguation is performed on original query sentence, yielding the concept of each term in the query. Based on those recovered concepts, expanded query terms are generated from WordNet lexical database. The proposed method has been evaluated in document retrieval on the Web using query sentence. Our extensive experimental results demonstrate a 7% precision improvement over retrieval methods not employing query expansion techniques.

## 1 Introduction

Query expansion has been widely studied as a technique that can deal with the query term incompleteness or term mismatch in information retrieval. Frequently, users may provide incomplete queries as they are not fully aware of the retrieval effectiveness of precise queries. Meanwhile, syntax or spelling errors occur to queries occasionally. Thus it is imperative to construct robust queries, one way to solve this problem is to expand the queries. Many previous expansion methods expand queries by adding terms that are generated either from the statistical result of term co-occurrence in the collections or from the lexical aids such as thesaurus, word books and the like. However, using statistical relations to expand queries has been proved to be unable to improve retrieval effectiveness when used apart from relevance data though it is easy to be accomplished [1].

Faced with the defects of traditional query expansion methods by choosing similar terms to query terms based on some criterion, a query expansion method based on concepts is proposed by Qiu et al. [4], in which terms with a common sense are chosen as one of the term's expanded candidates. While in another work queries were expanded using the well-defined synonymous set in WordNet [2]. But in this work query terms are deemed independent to each other, only synonyms are selected as term candidates for expansion. Smeaton tried to perform query expansion using various strategies of weighting expansion terms, along with manual and automatic word sense disambiguation techniques, but it proved not able to improve the performance of retrieval [7].

Hoeber manually constructed a concept network based on which terms are selected to perform conceptual query expansion [6]. But the performance of this conceptual query expansion depends highly on the quality of the concept network. In contrast to

T.-h. Kim et al. (Eds.): ASEA 2008, CCIS 30, pp. 210–218, 2009.

Hoeber's manually constructing concept network, Liu et al. proposed automatically generating expanded query terms by WordNet [5]. Once original query terms' concepts are determined, their synonyms, hyponyms and the like are considered to be the expanded terms. But in their work, queries to be expanded are confined to noun phrases [5]. The main drawback of query expansion techniques mentioned above is that they haven't take term relationships into consideration.

In another paper, an expansion method employing the local and global document analysis is introduced [13], the method using corpus to extract word relationships and analyzing documents by the initial query is focused. While Fonseca et. al. proposed in interactive query expansion that the a directed graph is built from query relations, from which a cycle is identified [14].

There also exists research on conceptual query expansion using corpus analysis techniques to automatically discover synonym words from the contents of databases rather than by the help of NLP techniques [15]. Term relationship may also be used to expand query model instead of the document model, and the query expansion may be automatically performed [16].

In our work word sense disambiguation is utilized to recover the sense of a word in the given query context. Based on the extracted concepts we can choose similar terms in the corresponding synset in WordNet. Then through combining the newly chosen terms the candidate expanded query set are generated from which final expanded queries are selected. The remainder of this paper is organized as follows: Section 2 introduces the basic components of our concept based query expansion method, that is WordNet and its modules. The procedure of conceptual query expansion is illustrated in section 3. Experiment result is reported in section 4. Finally a conclusion regarding the idea is made in section 5.

# 2   WordNet and WordNet::SenseRelate

In this section, we will firstly introduce WordNet which serves as our thesaurus of the terms and concepts mentioned in our work. Then, a pivotal word sense disambiguation module basing on WordNet is referred to, that is the WordNet::SenseRelate.

## 1.2   Introduction to WordNet

WordNet is a large manually constructed comprehensive thesaurus developed at Princeton University that can be used as the lexical reference aid, it attempts to model the lexical knowledge of English language. WordNet is organized into a network of synonym sets (synset) that each represent one underlying lexical concept and are interconnected with a variety of relations by semantic relations within the open-class categories of noun, adjective, verb and adverb [9]. For nouns the semantic relationships include synonymy, hyponymy, meronymy, troponymy and their corresponding counterparts [10]. A synset in WordNet is a group of words or phrases that are similar in the sense that they can be substituted with each other without changing the meaning of the statement under the given contexts. All synsets in

WordNet are strictly organized by the lexical relations defined on them, they differ from each other by part of speech (POS) and the number of sense associating with the same POS (POS_num).

A concept of a word is represented by three elements that is the word, the POS and the POS_num, we denote it as a triple $< word, POS, POS\_num >$. For example, the term *good* has four concepts when it is used as a noun, as shown in Fig. 1.

```
wn good -synsn
Sense 1
good      => advantage, vantage
Sense 2
good, goodness      => morality
Sense 3
good, goodness      => quality
Sense 4
commodity, trade good, good      => artifact, artifact
```

**Fig. 1.** Four concepts of noun *good*

WordNet is the huge thesaurus that has the potential to perform the task of concept recovery. Using WordNet, one can obtain all the possible concepts of a certain word, its synonyms, antonyms and other semantic relations. Similarly, given a synset one can obtain all of its possible expression words. Thus WordNet is one of the most desirable thesauri. Though comprehensive, WordNet is overall a thesaurus that can only give concepts of a word or give word of a concept. It is not capable to demonstrate which specific concept a word represent given the word's context, and neither it would provide a specific word given a concept.

## 2.2 About WordNet::SenseRelate Modules

For the purpose of recovering the hidden concept of a term given its position in a query, the word sense disambiguation procedure (WSD) which can disambiguate a word's sense given its context is proposed. Word sense disambiguation techniques generally include supervised WSD and unsupervised WSD. Supervised word sense disambiguation relies on sense-tagged corpus and uses information from the corpus to perform sense clarifications, while the unsupervised algorithm relies on a machine readable thesaurus instead of sense-tagged corpus [12].

Semantic relatedness has a very broad notion, generally it measures how strongly two concepts are semantically related. For example, the two concepts 'car' and 'bus' is related, with a score higher than that between 'car' and 'truck'. We use the adapted Lesk measure in WordNet::SenseRelate as the semantic relatedness measure. Adapted Lesk measures the relatedness by counting the number of overlaps not only of glosses of synonymy but also of glosses of other related synsets, hyponymy, meronymy, troponymy e.g. The adapted Lesk is a better similarity measure than other relatedness measures in WordNet::SenseRelate::AllWords module [8]. Word sense disambiguation algorithm calculates scores of each sense of the target word based on its relatedness with its neighbor words. After scores are available, the sense with the highest score is chosen.

# 3   Conceptual Query Expansion

Previous to performing the conceptual query expansion, the concept sequence hidden behind the term sequence should be recovered. The concept recovery process is implemented by the word sense disambiguation algorithms accompanying with WordNet. The expansion procedure first combine all the possible terms of the recovered concepts to be query sentences, then apply the word sense disambiguation to each of them. The sentence has the same concept sequence with the original query are selected as the expanded query. Thus the concept recovering process is illustrated in part 1 firstly, and then we will go into the issues about how to select the good ones from all the expanded queries.

## 3.1   Concept Recovery Process

In conceptual theories, a concept is expressed by words occurred to a person when he was to express his feeling or idea. There is a one-to-many mapping between the set of concepts and the set of words in WordNet. Even there may not be unique mappings between words and concepts in different expressing process, some mappings must be similar to some other with regard to the vocabulary used in order for communication to occur [11].

In sentence queries, the sense of words are not only determined by its definitions, but also determined by the relationships with other words in the sentence [6]. Firstly queries with punctuations are split into sentences by punctuations; sentences with quotation marks are handled to their original form. Thence, sentence queries with punctuations are transformed to the combination of several individual sentences in which each sub-sentence being a completely "clean" sentence with no punctuations in them so that each sentence can be handled further in the later word sense disambiguation procedure.

Since the sentences are clean, they are read by the WordNet::SenseRelate module. Each sentence is processed separately, and the term sequence in which each word's concept represented by a triple $< word, POS, POS\_num >$ is output, which means that the hidden concepts are generated. But for the simplicity of further query generation, the triple $< word, POS, POS\_num >$ is transferred to its corresponding synset in WordNet, which is comprised of a list of words or short phrases that has the same meaning in the given context. Each synset derived from the query terms can be represented by an array of terms that have the same meaning. The elements of the array are terms can be substituted by each other. For simplicity, we construct a two dimensional array, one row of the array represent one synset, while elements in a row comes are of the same synset.

Though the array may have not a definite number of columns since the synsets don't necessarily have the same number of terms, we would still store it as a two array for simplicity. After the array is constructed, we can then perform the expansion in the following part.

## 3.2  Query Expansion Process

Since each sense can be represented by a set of terms which could substitute each other in a certain context as illustrated in the previous part, in the following we would perform query expansion using terms in previously obtained array.

Expanded queries can be generated by the following ways: first, each row of the array is required to provide a term for an expanded query. Each time the generated query should be different from others. We assume that we have N terms in the original query, and then we have N corresponding synsets. The two dimensional array thence has N rows, each of which contains an individual number of terms. If we assume the first synset has $M_1$ terms, the second synset has $M_2$ terms, and the N$th$ synset has $M_N$ terms, the total number of the combinations of terms would be

$$M_1 \times M_2 \times \cdots \times M_N = \prod_{i=1}^{N} M_i.$$

Then, the selected terms are combined to sentences that are the form of expanded query. But the amount of combination is so huge that it will almost be impossible to obtain one retrieved document for each expanded query. More importantly, an arbitrary combination of the terms may lead to very strange term series which cannot be taken as sentence, that is to say not all of them are suitable to act as expanded queries. Thus, we need further to filter out solecistic query sentences.

The filtering process is similar to some degree with the process of concept recovery. Given a series of query terms generated in the expansion step, the concept of each word is extracted with a triple $< word, POS, POS\_num >$ as the output. By employing the Lingua::WordNet module, the triple $< word, POS, POS\_num >$ is transformed to a synset array, which contains all the words of a synset. We apply the same procedure to all terms in the expanded query, and obtain a two-dimensional array.

After the corresponding array of the expanded query is obtained, a comparison is made between the newly generated two-dimensional array and the original two-dimensional concept array. If the two-dimensional arrays are the same to each other, then we say that the expanded query has the same concept sequence with the original query, and they are two equivalent expression of the same concept sequence.

Just as we have mentioned, though the using all combinations of terms in the concept array may lead to a higher recall theoretically, especially when query terms are independent with each other or when the query resist the word sense disambiguation procedure, many documents irrelevant to the original query may also be retrieved as they are relevant to the expanded queries, the result of which is the low precision. Thus, we'd rather make a conservative query expansion, that is to say only queries have the same two-dimensional concept array with that of the original query terms are adopted as the expanded queries.

This is more pertinent to our idea that using the query terms' hidden concept to perform query expansion. The procedure can be summarized as Fig. 2, the flow chart described by dashed lines generate all candidate queries, while the flow chart described by solid lines provide the final desired queries. Here we assume that there are N terms in the original query, and the $i$-th term's corresponding synset has $M_i$ words.

After expanded queries are acquired, they are further submitted to information retrieval system in which the comparison are made between results of not expanded and expanded queries.

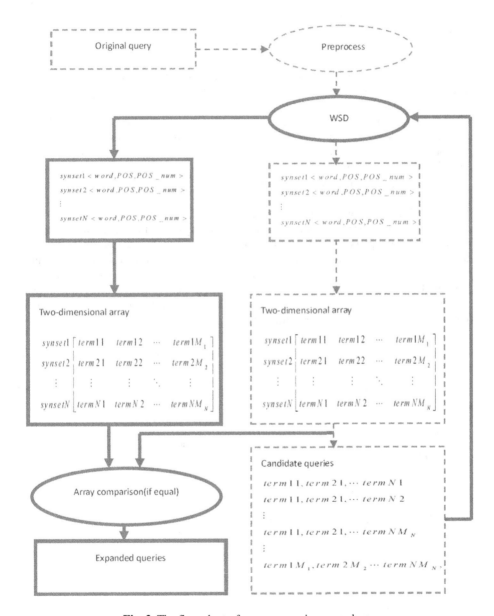

**Fig. 2.** The flow chart of query expansion procedure

## 4  Experiment

Expanded queries generated in section 3 are provided to a web information retrieval system Google. Returned documents from Google are used to evaluate our scheme's effectiveness. For simplicity we only count the precision at 10, that is the percentage of relevant result in the top 10 results. Recall ratio generally would improve through employing the query expansion. However due to the large size of the dataset, recall is difficult to be computed.

Shorter queries are avoided due to the fact that they are not suitable to be getting through the process of word sense disambiguation. In our experiments, Sentence queries are selected from the CACM query collection. Using the query expansion procedures demonstrated in section 3, a set of queries is obtained as the original query's expansions. The set may contain one or more queries depending on whether the concept series of original query can be expressed in a variety of queries without changing the meaning of the query sentence.

After the expanded queries are obtained, each of them is submitted to the Google search engine, retrieved documents are provided by Google [3]. Google is utilized here for that in so doing we may concentrate on the concept based query expansion rather than a design or implementation of a retrieval system. If there is only one query in the expanded query set, the returned top 10 documents are our final retrieved documents, under this situation, the effectiveness is not improved. If there are more than one queries (we assume N here) in the expanded query set, then the N queries are submitted to Google respectively, we utilize the each top 10/N of returned documents as our final retrieved documents. The reason of each query having the same weight is that they are the equivalent expressions of the same conceptual sequence.

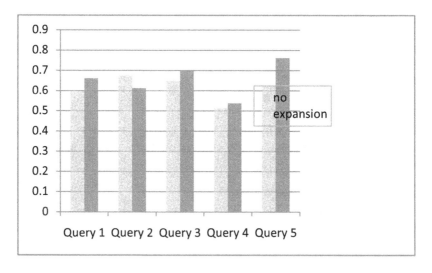

**Fig. 3.** Evaluation Result

Five sentence queries are chosen from the CACM test collection, retrieved documents are obtained and given to 10 people to make blind evaluations. That is to say our evaluators don't know which retrieved documents are of the expanded queries. Their evaluation results are summarized in Fig. 3.

Fig. 3 indicates that we can get a higher precision at 10 using the concept based query expansion than not using it. The average improvement is 7 percent over not employing the expansion method. Though promising, our results still saw some degradation, this is due to that the word sense disambiguation procedure is not able to provide higher precision. Apart from that, the test queries in CACM query collection are domain specific whereas word sense disambiguation is more applicable to ad hoc retrievals. Another drawback of the expansion system using word sense disambiguation is that it is time consuming to recover the correct sense of given words. Thus, by incorporating other techniques such as Markov language model to modify our expanded query is part of future works, improving the word sense disambiguation precision is also imperative.

# 5 Conclusion

In this paper, we presented a new conceptual query expansion mechanism using WordNet and its modules. Experimental results indicate that our new scheme can lead to better retrieval effectiveness with the average precision@10 improvement being 7%. Based on this observation, we demonstrated that expanded queries using concepts which are extracted from the original query can be further used as queries for improving the performance of retrievals on the Web. Future work includes finding or designing a faster and more precise word sense disambiguation method to perform concept extraction of original query sentence and the candidate query sentences, trying more other similarity semantic measures to make a more progressive concept based query expansion, and measuring the performance of concept based query expansion using test collections such as the TREC Web Track collections.

## Acknowledgement

This work is supported by a grant from the Major State Basic Research Development Program of China (973 Program) (No. 2007CB310806).

## References

1. Voorhees, E.M.: Query expansion using lexical-semantic relations. In: Proceedings of the 17th Annual International ACM SIGIR Conference on Research and development in information retrieval, Dublin, Ireland, pp. 61–69 (1994)
2. Varelas, G., Voutsakis, E., Raftopoulou, P.: Semantic Similarity Methods in WordNet and their Application to Information Retrieval on the Web. In: 7th ACM International Workshop on Web Information and Data Management, Bremen, Germany (2005)
3. Palleti, P., Karnick, H., Mitra, P.: Personalized Web Search using Probabilistic Query Expansion. In: IEEE/WIC/ACM International Conferences on Web Intelligence and Intelligent Agent Technology (2007)

4. Qiu, Y., Frei, H.-P.: Concept based query expansion. In: Proceedings of the 16th annual international ACM SIGIR conference on Research and development in information retrieval, pp. 160–169. ACM Press, Pittsburgh (1993)

5. Liu, S., Liu, F., Meng, C.Y.W.: An Effective Approach to Document Retrieval via Utilizing WordNet and Recognizing Phrases. In: Proceedings of the 27th Annual International ACM/SIGIR Conference on Research and development in information retrieval, Sheffield, Yorkshire, UK (2004)

6. Hoeber, O., Yang, X.-D., Yao, Y.: Conceptual query expansion. In: Proceedings of the Atlantic Web Intelligence Conference (2005)

7. Richardson, R., Smeaton, A.F.: Using WordNet in a Knowledge-Based Approach to Information Retrieval. In: Proceedings of the BCS-IRSG Colloquium, Crewe (1995)

8. Patwardhan, S., Banerjee, S., Pedersen, T.: UMND1: Unsupervised Word Sense Disambiguation Using Contextual Semantic Relatedness. In: The Proceedings of SemEval-2007: 4th International Workshop on Semantic Evaluations, pp. 390–393 (2007)

9. Miller, G.A., Leacock, C., Tengi, R., Bunker, R.T.: A Semantic Concordance. In: Proceedings of the 3rd DARPA Workshop on Human Language Technology (1993)

10. Miller, G., Beckwith, R., Fellbaum, C., Gross, D., Miller, K.: Five papers on WordNet. CSL Report 43, Cognitive Science Laboratory, Princeton University (1990)

11. Goddard, C.: Semantic Analysis: A Pratical Introduction. Oxford University Press, Oxford (1998)

12. Ng, H.T., Zelle, J.: Corpus-Based Approaches to Semantic Interpretation in Natural Language Processing. AI Magazine 18(4), 45–64 (1997)

13. Qiu, Y., Frei, H.P.: Proceedings of the 16th annual international ACM SIGIR conference on Research and development in information retrieval. ACM Press, Pittsburgh (1993)

14. Fonseca, B.M., Golgher, P., Pôssas, B., et al.: Concept-based interactive query expansion. In: Proceedings of the 14th ACM International Conference on Information and Knowledge Management (CIKM), Bremen, Germany (November 2005)

15. Gauch, S., Wang, J.: A corpus analysis approach for automatic query expansion. In: Proc. 6th conf. on Information and Knowledge Management (CIKM), pp. 278–284 (1997)

16. Bai, J., Song, D., Bruza, P., Nie, J.Y., Cao, G.: Query Expansion Using Term Relationships in Language Models for Information Retrieval. In: Proceedings of the ACM 14th Conference on Information and Knowledge Management (CIKM), Bremen, Germany (November 2005)

# Pre-processing and Step-Size Adaptation for Performance Improvement in ADM

B.K. Sujatha[1], P.S. Satyanarayana[2], FIETE, and K.N. Haribhat[3]

[1] M S Ramaiah Institute of Technology, Bangalore
[2] B M S College of Engineering, Bangalore
[3] Nagarjuna College of Engineering and Technology, Bangalore
bksujatha08@gmail.com, pssvittala@yahoo.com,
knhari.bhat@gmail.com

**Abstract.** Delta modulation plays a key role in data communication; the problem encountered in delta modulation is the slope over load error, which is inherent in the system. In order for the signal to have good fidelity, the slope-overload error need to be as small as possible. Adaptive delta modulation reduces the slope over load error to a greater extent. ADM attempts to increase the dynamic range and the tracking capabilities of fixed step-size delta modulation. The adaptive algorithms adjust the step size (from a range of step sizes) to the power level of the signal and thus enhance the dynamic range of the coding system appreciably. This paper suggests a novel 1-bit Adaptive Delta Modulation technique for improving the signal-to-noise ratio (SNR) of Adaptive Delta Modulators (ADM). Various step-size algorithms are discussed and also their performance comparison is made. A new technique has also been discussed with a suitable pre-filer used for improving the SNR.

**Keywords:** Adaptive Delta Modulation, Delta Modulation, A/D conversion, Pre-processing, Speech processing.

## 1 Introduction

Non-adaptive delta modulation is known by the name of Linear Delta Modulation (LDM). Linear Delta Modulation uses a constant step size for all the signal levels. In designing a linear delta modulator, the step size and sampling rate are the main concern. The signal-to-granular noise ratio must be minimized so that the low level signal can be encoded. The signal-to-slope-overload distortion ratio must be minimized to encode the highest level signals. Minimizing these optimizes the performance of a linear delta modulator. The LDM suffers from a very limited dynamic range due to two types of errors, namely, the slope-overload noise and the granular noise as shown in Fig 1. Slope-overload occurs when the step size S is too small for the staircase approximation of the input x(n) to follow the steep segments of input waveform. In other words, slope-overload occurs when the rate of change of input exceeds the maximum rate of change in the feedback loop. Granular noise occurs when the step size is too large relative to slope characteristic of input waveform, thereby causing the

T.-h. Kim et al. (Eds.): ASEA 2008, CCIS 30, pp. 219–230, 2009.

staircase waveform to hunt around a relatively flat segment of the input waveform. Smaller the step size, smaller is the granular noise, but small step size increases the likely hood of slope-overload.

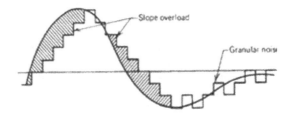

**Fig. 1.** LDM and its characteristics

Analysis of LDM quantization noise have been carried out by several researchers. Important among them are the work of Van de weg [1] and Goodman [2] for granular noise and Greenstein [3] for the slope-overload.

O'Neal [4] has obtained a simple estimate of total resultant noise power when the variance of granular and overload noise are added together. But due to the non-linearity, an exact analysis has not been presented. However, an analysis reported by Slepian [5] gives an exact relationship between SNR and optimum step size for Gaussian signals with a (non-band limited) rational power spectrum. Other notable mathematical derivations in this subject are the SNR formulae as given by Tomozaw and Kaneko [6] and Johnson [7] for sinusoidal inputs.

Adaptive delta modulation (ADM) [8] reduces the slope-overload and granular distortions encountered in linear delta modulators (LDM) to a greater extent. In each of the step-size algorithms of adaptive delta modulators (ADM), the processor detects the pattern to see if the delta modulator is operating in the quantization region, in which case it produces an alternating ......1010..... pattern, or in the slope over load region in which case it produces an all-1 or all-0 pattern. If the ADM senses a ...1010.... pattern, it decreases the step-size and if it senses .....1111.... or ....0000.... it increases the step-size. Different step-size adaptation algorithms changes the rate of change of step-size in different ways. A good amount of work has been done in this area using SONG[9] and modified ABATE[10] step-size algorithms. In the case of SONG algorithm if the output is alternatively ...1010... the step-size is minimum say $S_0$. If it is continuous 1's like 1111...11 or continuous zero's like 0000...00, the step-size adaptation increases the magnitude of step-size as $S_0$, $2S_0$, $3S_0$, etc., Modified ABATE algorithm is same as SONG but maximum step-size is limited to $8S_0$. In both SONG and modified ABATE algorithms, the rate of change of step-size in the slope- overload region is $S_0$.

A new algorithm is introduced where the rate of change of step-size in slope-overload region is made greater than $S_0$. This reduces slope-overload noise. It is shown that the performance can be further improved by pre-processing the input signal.

The proposed scheme is compared with SONG and modified ABATE algorithms taking SNR as the performance criterion. The sample speech waveform in the illustration is taken from the speech sound "i i i i i" which is shown in Fig.2.

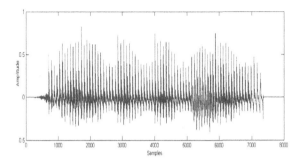

**Fig. 2.** Sample speech signal ' i i i i i '

The organization of the paper is as follows which includes the experimental results. Section 2 discusses SONG and modified ABATE step-size adaptation algorithms. The proposed new step-size adaptation algorithm is presented in section 3. A comparison with SONG, modified ABATE and the proposed algorithms are made in  section 4. In section 5, the proposed ADM with pre-processing of message signal using an integrator  is discussed.  Section 6 summarizes the conclusions.

## 2   The Existing Step-Size Adaptations

### 2.1   SONG Algorithm

Let $m(t)$ be the input signal and $\hat{m}(t)$ be its staircase approximation. Let $e(k) = m(t) - \hat{m}(t)$ at the $k^{th}$ sampling instant. $k = 0, 1, 2, 3, \ldots$ . $e(k)$ can be of positive or negative value. The $k^{th}$ transmitted symbol is '1' if $e(k) > 0$, otherwise it is '0' if $e(k) < 0$. If $e(k) = 0$, either '1' or '0' can be transmitted.

The SONG algorithm used by NASA[11] produces the step-size $S(k + 1)$ which minimizes the mean-square error between $m(t)$ and $\hat{m}(t)$. In the implementation of the SONG system ±5 V was the maximum signal level and the minimum step-size with 10 bits of arithmetic was $S_o = 10$ mV. The algorithm is illustrated in Fig 3. Here we see that as long as $e(k)$ is of the same sign as $e(k - 1)$ the magnitude of the new step-size $S(k + 1)$ will exceed the magnitude of the old step-size $S(k)$ by So, the minimum step-size. However, if $e(k)$ and $e(k - 1)$ differ in sign, the magnitude of $S(k + 1)$ will be less than the magnitude of $S(k)$ by the amount So. The equation describing the SONG algorithm is then

$$S(k + 1) = \ | \ S(k)e(k) + S_0 \ e(k - 1) \tag{1}$$

The algorithm can also be written in terms of the following equation.

$$|S(k+1)| = \begin{cases} |S(k)| + S_0 & e(k) = e(k-1) \\ |S(k)| - S_0 & e(k) \neq e(k-1) \end{cases} \tag{2}$$

Note that S(k+1) depends on S(k) and on the two past errors e(k) and e(k-1). $S_0$ is the minimum step-size.

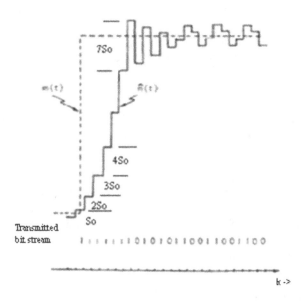

**Fig. 3.** Adaptive delta modulation showing the changing step size and bit pattern produced using SONG algorithm

## 2.2 Modified ABATE Algorithm

The modified ABATE algorithm is another step-size adaptation algorithm and is more susceptible to slope overload than the SONG algorithm. The unique feature of this algorithm is that it is designed to adaptively follow the received signal even in a channel with high error rate of approximately $10^{-1}$ [12]. The equation describing the modified ABATE algorithm is

$$S(k+1) = \begin{cases} [|\,S(k)\,| + S_0]e(k); & e(k) = e(k-1)\,\text{and}\,S(k) < 8S_0 \\ |\,S(k)\,|\,e(k); & e(k) = e(k-1)\,\text{and}\,S(k) = 8S_0 \\ S_0 e(k); & \text{otherwise} \end{cases} \tag{3}$$

When an error occurs in the received data stream the stepsize processor will produce erroneous step sizes until a correctly received data transition is detected. This feature of the proper step size recovery is illustrated in Figure 4. The average number of erroneous step sizes following a received error in the modified ABATE algorithm is less than other ADM algorithms like SONG, CVSD and Greefkes ADM [11].

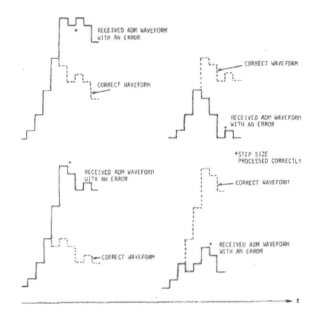

**Fig. 4.** Modified-ABATE waveforms with channel errors showing step size recovery

## 3   The Proposed Step-Size Adaptation

The new proposed technique for the step-size adaptation is described as

$$
S(k+1) = \begin{cases}
[\propto| \, S(k) \, | +S_0] \ e(k); & e(k) = e(k-1) \\
[\beta \, | \, S(k) \, | -S_0] \ e(k); & e(k) \neq e(k-1) \\
& \text{and } \beta \, | \, S(k) \, | > S_0 \\
S_0 e(k); & e(k) \neq e(k-1) \\
& \text{and } \beta \, | \, S(k) \, | < S_0
\end{cases}
\qquad (4)
$$

$\propto$ is the adaptation parameter nearly equal to 1 but, greater than 1. $\beta = {}^1\!/_{\propto}$.

In this algorithm the rate of change of step-size in the slope-overload regioncan be $S_0$ or $\propto S_0$ or $\propto^2 S_0$ etc., By proper choice of $\propto > 1$, the rate of change of step-size can be made greater than $S_0$. Hence the slope-overload noise is reduced compared to SONG and modified ABATE algorithms. Thus choice of $\propto$ gives a better performance to slope overload and the parameter $\beta$ takes care of the granular noise as a result of which a better performance is obtained as compared to SONG and modified ABATE algorithms. This can be observed in the performance comparison described in section 4.

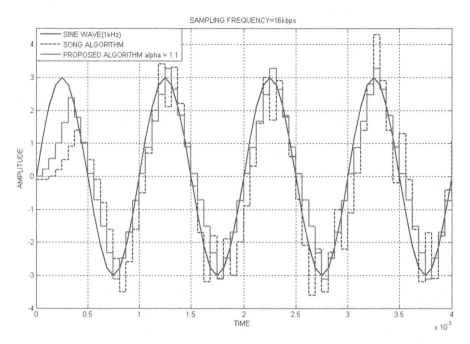

**Fig. 5.** Performance comparison of SONG algorithm with Proposed Algorithm

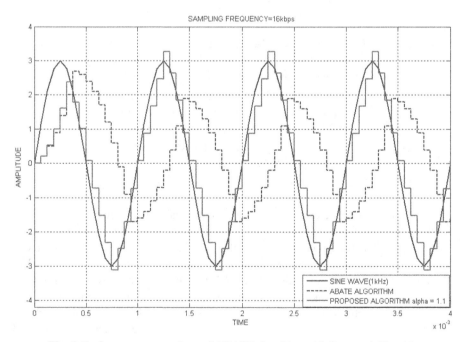

**Fig. 6.** Performance comparison of ABATE algorithm with Proposed Algorithm

## 4  Performance Comparison

In this section, the computer simulation results for comparing the performance of the proposed step-size adaptation algorithm with SONG and the modified ABATE algorithms are presented. $\propto$ is taken as 1.1 and $S_o$=0.1.

Figures 5 and 6 show the performance comparison of proposed algorithm with SONG algorithm and proposed algorithm with modified ABATE algorithm respectively with sine wave of 1kHz, amplitude 3V peak with sampling frequency of 16kHz. It is seen that in both cases the proposed step-size algorithm gives a better stair case approximation compared to SONG and modified ABATE algorithms.

### 4.1  SNR Calculation

The signal-to-quantization noise ratio (SNR) of the ADM will be employed as the performance criterion for comparison [12] - [15]. The sample speech waveform in the illustration is the speech sound "i i i i i" is used as input as shown in Fig.2. The positive peak is 0.8 V and maximum frequency is 3.8kHz  with sampling frequency of 16kHz. The SNR was calculated using standard formula

$$SNR = 10 \log_{10} \frac{\sum_{n=1}^{N}(x_n)^2}{\sum_{n=1}^{N}(x_n - \hat{x}_n)^2} \tag{5}$$

$\{x_n\} \rightarrow$        Samples of original signal (speech signal)

$\{\hat{x}_n\} \rightarrow$        Samples of final reconstructed signal

$(x_n - \hat{x}_n) \rightarrow$    Error signal

$(x_n - \hat{x}_n)^2 \rightarrow$    Squared Error signal

Where N is the total sample number of the input male speech equal to 16000 samples.

In fig. 7(a), the performance comparison of the proposed step-size adaptation algorithm with the SONG and the modified ABATE algorithms in a noiseless channel for 8Kbps is described and in fig. 7(b) the same plot of fig.7(a) is shown but the input strength is displayed for -7dB to -1dB. It is seen that the proposed step-size algorithm gives performance improvement compared to the existing algorithms, when the input strength is in the range -7dB to -1dB.

## 5  Pre-processing

In this section we show that the proposed ADM has better performance than the conventional ADM [12] – [15]. Integrator and differentiator circuits are employed for pre-processing and post-processing the signals respectively. The purpose of

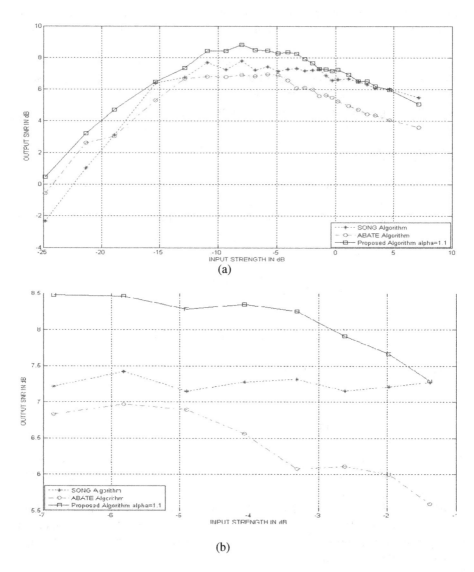

**Fig. 7.** (a) Performance Comparison of the proposed step-size adaptation algorithm with the SONG and the modified ABATE algorithms. 7(b) the same plot of figure.7(a) is shown but the input strength is displayed for -7dB to -1dB.

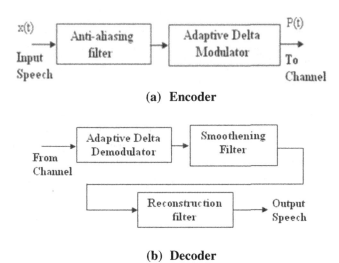

**(a)  Encoder**

**(b)  Decoder**

**Fig. 8.** The block diagram of Conventional ADM

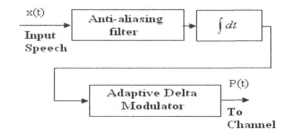

**a)   Encoder**

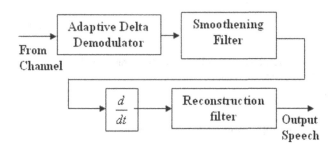

**b)   Decoder**

**Fig. 9.** The block diagram of proposed ADM

pre-filtering is to prevent or minimize aliasing effects which can be perceptually very objectionable in speech and image coding. The band limited speech signal is integrated by employing a low pass filter. A high pass filter is used in the decoder section for the purpose of differentiation. Conventional ADM and proposed ADM block diagrams are represented in figures 8 and 9.

In this section, a methodology for further improving the ADM performance by pre-processing the speech signal prior to the adaptation is presented. The large variations in the speech are removed/smoothened by a suitable pre-processing method, one of which is using an integrator which can smoothen the rapid changes. The frequency response of the integrator at the transmitting end is shown in fig. 10(a). and the differentiator at the receiver side in fig.10(b). At the receiver, the differentiator is followed by a low pass filter (LPF).

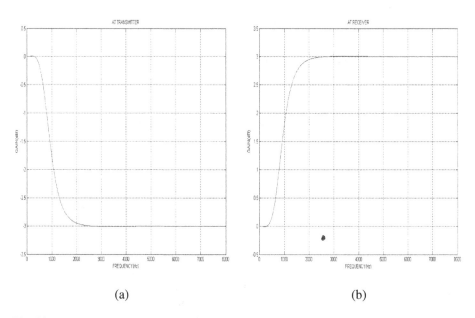

(a)                                        (b)

**Fig. 10.** (a). Frequency response of Pre-Processor (Integrator) at the transmitter. (b). Frequency response of the Differentiator at the receiver.

### 5.1 Performance Comparison with Pre-processor

The SNR performance of the proposed (with pre-processor) and the conventional ADM systems [12] - [14] in a noiseless channel for 8Kbps is shown in figure 11(a) and figure 11(b). We observe that the proposed ADM with pre-processing gives performance improvement compared to the schemes discussed in section 4.

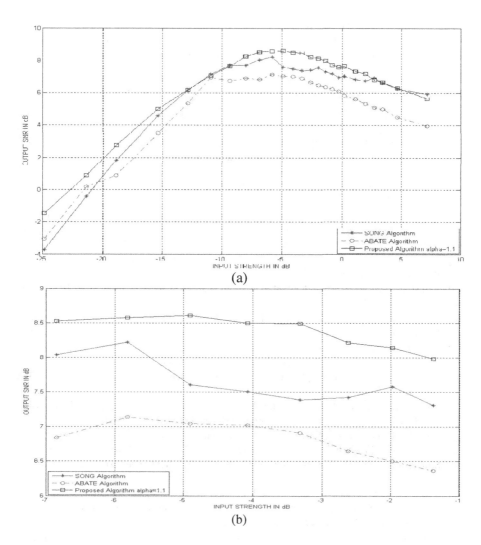

**Fig. 11.** (a)Performance Comparison of the proposed ADM with the SONG, modified ABATE and the proposed algorithms. 11(b) the same plot of figure 11(a) is shown but the input strength is displayed for -7dB to -1dB.

## 6   Conclusion

Simulations are carried out for all the schemes. $S_0$ is taken as 0.1 and $\propto = 1.1$. Simulations have also confirmed that with the input strength for -5dB to -3dB on an average a 1.1dB performance gain in the SNR  is got for the  new step-size adaptation algorithm compared to the SONG and a 1.5dB performance gain compared to the modified ABATE algorithm. Next, with the proposed methodology(pre-processing) and with the same input strength, on an average there is a 1.4dB performance improvement in the SNR for the new step-size adaptation algorithm as compared to the SONG and a 1.7dB improvement compared to the modified ABATE algorithm.

# References

[1] Van De Weg, H.: Quantization Noise of Single Integration Delta Modulation System With a N-Digit Code. Philips Res. Rept., 367–385 (October 1953)

[2] Goodman, D.J.: Delta Modulation Granular Quantizing Noise. Bell Syst. Tech. J. 52, 387–422 (1973)

[3] Greenstein, L.J.: Slope-Overload Noise In Linear Delta Modulation With Gaussian Inputs. Bell Syst. Tech. J. 52, 387–422 (1973)

[4] O'Neal, J.B.: Delta Modulation Quantizing Noise: Analytical and Computer Simulation Results for guassian and Television Input Signals. Bell Syst. Tech. J. 45, 117–142 (1966)

[5] Slepian, D.: On Delta Modulation. Bell Syst. Tech. J. 51, 2101–2137 (1980)

[6] Tomozawa, A., Kaneko, H.: Companded Delta Modulation for Telephone Transmission. IEEE Trans. Commun. Tech. 16, 149–157 (1968)

[7] Jhonson, F.B.: Adaptive Quantization with a One-Word Memory. Bell Syst. Tech. J. 52, 1119–1144 (1973)

[8] Jayanth, N.S.: Adaptive Delta Modulation with a 1-bit memory. Bell System Technical Journal 49(3), 321–342 (1970)

[9] Song, C.L., Schilling, D.L., Garodnick, J.: A Variable Step-Size Robust Delta Modulator. IEEE Trans. Comm. Tech. COM-19, 1033–1044 (1971)

[10] Abate, J.E.: Linear and adaptive delta modulation. Proceedings of the IEEE 55, 298–308 (1967)

[11] Schilling, D.L., Gorodnick, J., Vang, H.A.: Voice encoding for the space shuttle using ADM. IEEE Trans. on Communications COM-26(11) (November 1982)

[12] Yao, K., Paliwal, K.K., Nakamura, S.: Noise adaptive speech recognition with acoustic models trained from noisy speech evaluated on Aurora-2 database. In: Proc. Intern. Conf. Spoken Language Processing, Denver, Colorado, USA, September 2002, pp. 2437–2440 (2002)

[13] Yang, M.: Low bit rate speech coding. Potentials, IEEE 23(4), 32–36 (2004)

[14] Gibson, J.D.: Speech coding methods, standards and applications. Circuits and Systems Magazine, IEEE 5(4), 30–49 (fourth Quarter 2005)

[15] Dong, H., Gibson, J.D.: Structures for SNR scalable speech coding. IEEE Transactions on Audio, Speech and Language Processing 14(2), 545–557 (2006)

# Clustering Web Transactions Using Fuzzy Rough−$k$ Means

Rui Wu[1] and Peilin Shi[2]

[1] School of Mathematics and Computer Science, Shanxi Normal University
Linfen, Shanxi 041004, China
wurui_0905@163.com
[2] Department of Mathematics, Taiyuan University of Technology,
Taiyuan, Shanxi 030024, China
donglingzhen@eyou.com

**Abstract.** Whether a web page is visited or not and its time duration reveal web user's interest. In this paper, web access pattern disclosing user unique interest is transformed as a fuzzy vector with the same length, in which each element is a fuzzy linguistic variable or 0 denoting the visited web page and its fuzzy time duration. Then we proposed a modified rough $k$-means clustering algorithm based on properties of rough variable to group the gained fuzzy web access patterns. Finally, an example is provided to illustrate the clustering process. Using this approach, web transactions with the same or similar behavior can be grouped into one class.

**Keywords:** clustering, web mining, fuzzy variable, rough variable, web access patterns.

## 1 Introduction

Three important aspects of web mining, namely clustering, association, and sequential analysis are often used to study important characteristics of web users. Web clustering involves finding natural groupings of web resources or web users. However, there exists some important differences between clustering in conventional applications and clustering in web mining. The patterns from web data are non-numerical, thus Runkler and Beadek [13] proposed relational clustering method to group non-numerical web data. Furthermore, due to a variety of reasons inherent in web browsing and web logging, the likelihood of bad or incomplete data is higher than conventional applications. The clusters tend to have vague or imprecise boundaries [5]. An pattern may belong to more than one candidate clusters by different degrees of the memberships. Therefore, the role of soft computing technique such as fuzzy theory and rough theory is highlighted. Krishnapuram and Hathaway [2,3] proposed to use fuzzy set theory to group web users into several disjoint clusters. Some other researchers tried to explore clustering method by another soft computing technique, rough theory. The upper and lower approximations of rough sets are used to model the clusters [1,4,5,9].

T.-h. Kim et al. (Eds.): ASEA 2008, CCIS 30, pp. 231–240, 2009.

De [1] tries to use rough approximation to cluster web transactions. Lingras [4] applied the unsupervised rough set clustering based on genetic algorithms to group web visitors. Later, Lingras [5] proposed a modified rough $K$-means method to cluster web visitors. Mitra [9] proposed a clustering algorithm based on rough c-means and genetic algorithm.

This paper uses a rough $k$-means clustering method in fuzzy environment to group web access patterns from web logs. A web access pattern represents a unique surfing behavior of a web user, which can be denoted by a set $s_i = \{(Url_{i_1}, t_{i_1}), (Url_{i_2}, t_{i_2}), \cdots, (Url_{i_l}, t_{i_l})\}(1 \leq i \leq m)$, where $Url_{i_k}$ denotes $k$th visited web page and $t_{i_k}$ denotes the time duration on $Url_{i_k}$, $l$ is the number of visited web pages during a surfing, $m$ is the number of web access patterns extracted from web logs. If a web page appears in several web access patterns, this implies that these web users show common interests on this web page. However, the difference of time durations on this web page indicates that they show different degrees of interests on this web page during their surfing. If a web user takes more time browsing a web page, we say that he show more interests on it. According to the above consideration, whether a web page is visited or not and the time duration on it, should be considered as two important factors when web access patterns are grouped into several disjoint classes. Because the subtle difference between two time durations can be disregarded, time duration on a web page is depicted by a fuzzy linguistic variable. Then web access patterns can be transformed as fuzzy vectors with the same length. Each element in fuzzy vector represents visited web page and time duration on this web page. Thus we cluster these gained fuzzy web access patterns into several groups. Because these clusters tend to have ambiguous boundaries, a cluster is depicted by a rough variable. A rough $k$-means method based on the properties of rough variable is adopted to cluster fuzzy web access patterns. The clustering process is illustrated by an example and an experiment shows the clustering result.

The rest of the paper is organized as follows. Section 2 describes the basic notion of fuzzy variable. Rough variable theory is presented in section 3. The algorithm of clustering web access patterns is proposed using rough $k$-means method. An example and experimental results are presented in section 4 and section 5 respectively. Finally we conclude in section 6.

## 2    Review of Fuzzy Variable and Rough Variable

### 2.1    Fuzzy Variable

The concept of a fuzzy set was first introduced by Zadeh [15] in 1965. And then many researchers such as Nahmias [10] and Liu [7] enriches the fuzzy theory. In this section, some basic concepts and results of fuzzy variable are reviewed.

**Definition 1.** *(Nahmias [10] and Liu [7]) A fuzzy variable $\xi$ is defined as a function from a possibility space $(\Theta, \mathcal{P}(\Theta), \text{Pos})$ to the set of real numbers, where $\Theta$ is a universe, $\mathcal{P}(\Theta)$ is the power set of $\Theta$, and $\text{Pos}$ is a possibility measure defined on $\mathcal{P}(\Theta)$.*

**Definition 2.** *(Liu and Liu [8]) The expected value of a fuzzy variable $\xi$ is defined as*

$$E[\xi] = \int_0^\infty \mathrm{Cr}\{\xi \geq r\}\mathrm{d}r - \int_{-\infty}^0 \mathrm{Cr}\{\xi \leq r\}\mathrm{d}r \tag{1}$$

*provided that at least one of two integrals is finite.*

**Example 1**(Liu and Liu [8]). The expected value of a trapezoid fuzzy variable $\xi(r_1, r_2, r_3, r_4)$ is defined as follow

$$E[\xi] = \frac{1}{4}(r_1 + r_2 + r_3 + r_4). \tag{2}$$

The expected value of a fuzzy variable can characterize this fuzzy variable by numerical value.

## 2.2 Rough Variable

The notion of rough set theory was introduced by Zdzislaw Pawlak [11] in the early 1980s for dealing with the classification analysis of data tables. It has been proved to be an excellent mathematical tool dealing with vague description of objects. Trust theory is the branch of mathematics that studies the behavior of rough events. Liu [6] gave the definition of the rough variable and basic rough variable theory based on this trust theory.

**Definition 3.** *([6]) Let $\Lambda$ be a nonempty set, $\mathcal{A}$ a $\sigma$-algebra of subsets of $\Lambda$, $\Delta$ an element in $\mathcal{A}$, and $\pi$ a set function satisfying the four axioms. Then $(\Lambda, \Delta, \mathcal{A}, \pi)$ is called a rough space.*

**Definition 4.** *([6]) A rough variable $\xi$ is a measurable function from the rough space $(\Lambda, \Delta, \mathcal{A}, \pi)$ to the set of real numbers. That is, for every Borel set $B$ of $\Re$, we have*

$$\{\lambda \in \Lambda | \xi(\lambda) \in B\} \in \mathcal{A} \tag{3}$$

The lower and the upper approximation of the rough variable $\xi$ are then defined as follows,

$$\underline{\xi} = \{\xi(\lambda)|\lambda \in \Delta\} \tag{4}$$

$$\bar{\xi} = \{\xi(\lambda)|\lambda \in \Lambda\} \tag{5}$$

**Remark 1.** *Since $\Delta \subset \Lambda$, it is obvious that $\underline{\xi} \subset \bar{\xi}$.*

# 3   Clustering Web Access Patterns by Rough $k$-Means Method in Fuzzy Environment

In this section, a rough $k$-means method in fuzzy environment is provided to cluster web access patterns from web logs.

## 3.1    Characterizing User Access Patterns as Fuzzy User Access Patterns

Suppose there are $m$ users and user transactions $S = \{s_1, s_2, \cdots, s_m\}$, where $s_i(1 \leq i \leq m)$ discloses a unique surfing behavior of $i$th user.

Let $W = \{Url_1, Url_2, \cdots, Url_n\}$ be the union set of distinct $n$ web pages visited by users, $U = \{(Url_1, t_{1_1}), \cdots, (Url_1, t_{1_g}), \cdots, (Url_n, t_{n_1}), \cdots, (Url_n, t_{n_h})\}$ be the union set of $s_i$ $(1 \leq i \leq m)$, where $g$ is the number of all time durations on web page $Url_1$, $h$ is the number of all time durations on web page $Url_n$, $n$ is the number of all different web pages visited by users.

Each pattern $s_i \in S$ is a non-empty subset of $U$. Here, the temporal order of visited web pages has not been taken into account.

Web access pattern $s_i \in S(1 \leq i \leq m)$ can be represented as a vector

$$V_i = < v_{i1}^t, v_{i2}^t, \cdots, v_{in}^t >, \tag{6}$$

where $v_{ik}^t = \begin{cases} t_{i_k}, & (Url_k, t_{i_k}) \in s_i \\ 0, & otherwise, \end{cases}$ $(1 \leq k \leq n)$.

Thus, each pattern $s_i(1 \leq i \leq m)$ is a real numerical vector with the same length $n$. Furthermore, time duration with real value is depicted by a fuzzy linguistic variable, which makes people more understandable and can ignore subtle difference between time durations.

All time duration on web pages are clustered into $r$ different fuzzy region according to the method introduced in Wang [14]. Each fuzzy region is characterized as a fuzzy linguistic variable. Their membership functions can be gained by the simulation method [14]. Also the membership functions of time duration can be provided by experienced experts. Assume the membership functions of time duration are shown in Figure 1.

Assume the first fuzzy region is characterized as a trapezoid fuzzy variable $\xi_1(a_1, a_1, b_1, b_2)$, the last fuzzy region is characterized as $\xi_n$. From Figure 1, we can get the relation between real numerical $v_{ik}^t$ and fuzzy linguistic variable $\lambda_{ik}$ $(1 \leq i \leq m)(1 \leq k \leq n)$, which is as follows

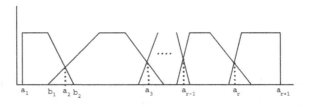

**Fig. 1.** The membership functions of time duration

$$\lambda_{ik} = \begin{cases} 0, & v_{ik}^t = 0 \\ \xi_1, & a_1 \leq v_{ik}^t \leq a_2 \\ \xi_2, & a_2 < v_{ik}^t \leq a_3 \\ \vdots & \\ \xi_r, & a_r < v_{ik}^t \leq a_{r+1}, \end{cases} \tag{7}$$

where $\xi_j (1 \leq j \leq r)$ is the corresponding fuzzy linguistic variable.

Each numerical $v_{ik}^t$ in a numerical vector $V_i$ is transformed as the corresponding fuzzy linguistic variable or 0 according to (8). Thus a fuzzy web access pattern can be denoted as follows

$$f_{vi} = < \lambda_{i1}, \lambda_{i2}, \cdots, \lambda_{in} >, \tag{8}$$

where $\lambda_{ik} \in \{0, \xi_1, \xi_2, \cdots, \xi_r\}$ $(1 \leq k \leq n)$.

## 3.2   Algorithm for Clustering Fuzzy Web Access Patterns Based on Rough k-Means

Assume there exists $m$ web access patterns in user transactions $S$, $S = \{s_1, s_2, \cdots, s_m\}$. Given any two web access patterns $s_i$ $(1 \leq i \leq m)$ and $s_j$ $(1 \leq j \leq m)$, according to the section 3.1 they can be denoted as follows

$$f_{vi} = < \lambda_{i1}, \lambda_{i2}, \cdots, \lambda_{in} >$$

and

$$f_{vj} = < \lambda_{j1}, \lambda_{j2}, \cdots, \lambda_{jn} >,$$

where $\lambda_{ik} \in \{0, \xi_1, \xi_2, \cdots, \xi_r\}$, and $\lambda_{jk} \in \{0, \xi_1, \xi_2, \cdots, \xi_r\}$, $(1 \leq k \leq n)$.

Their sum can be defined as

$$sum(s_i, s_j) \simeq sum(f_{vi}, f_{vj}) = < \lambda_{i1} + \lambda_{j1}, \lambda_{i2} + \lambda_{j2}, \cdots, \lambda_{in} + \lambda_{jn} > . \tag{9}$$

The distance between $s_i$ and $s_j$ can be defined as

$$d(s_i, s_j) \simeq d(f_{vi}, f_{vj}) \simeq \sqrt{\frac{\sum\limits_{k=1}^{n} (E[\lambda_{ik}] - E[\lambda_{jk}])^2}{n}}. \tag{10}$$

This paper adopts a rough $k$-means algorithm for clustering web access patterns. Each web access patterns is transformed as corresponding fuzzy web access pattern. Lingras and West [5] considered each cluster as an interval or rough set. Here, $i$th cluster is characterized as a rough variable $\eta_i$ $(1 \leq i \leq k)$ defined on a measurable rough space $(S, S_i, \mathcal{A}_i, \pi_i)$, where $S_i \subset S$. Then the centroid $\mathbf{m}_i$ of $i$th cluster is computed as

$$\mathbf{m}_i = \begin{cases} w_{low} \dfrac{\sum_{f_{vj} \in \underline{\eta_i}} f_{vj}}{|\underline{\eta_i}|} + w_{up} \dfrac{\sum_{f_{vj} \in (\overline{\eta_i} - \underline{\eta_i})} f_{vj}}{|\overline{\eta_i} - \underline{\eta_i}|} & \overline{\eta_i} - \underline{\eta_i} \neq Null; \\ w_{low} \dfrac{\sum_{f_{vj} \in \underline{\eta_i}} f_{vj}}{|\underline{\eta_i}|} & otherwise, \end{cases} \tag{11}$$

where the parameter $w_{low}/w_{up}$ controls the importance of the patterns lying within the lower/up approximation of a cluster in determining its centroid. $0.5 < w_{low} < 1$ and $w_{up} = 1 - w_{low}$. $|\underline{\eta_i}|$ indicates the number of patterns in the lower approximation of $i$th cluster, while $|\overline{\eta_i} - \underline{\eta_i}|$ is the number of patterns in the rough boundary lying between the two approximations $\overline{\eta_i}$ $\underline{\eta_i}$. Thus, the centroid $\mathbf{m}_i$ of $i$th cluster is a real-valued vector denoted by $\mathbf{m}_i =< c_{i1}, c_{i2}, \cdots, c_{in} >$.

The distance between pattern $s_l$ $(1 \le l \le m)$ and the centroid $\mathbf{m}_i$ is defined as follows

$$d(s_l, \mathbf{m}_i) \simeq d(f_{vl}, \mathbf{m}_i) \simeq \sqrt{\frac{\sum\limits_{k=1}^{n} (E[\lambda_{lk}] - c_{ik})^2}{n}} \qquad (12)$$

If the distance between $d(s_l, \mathbf{m}_i)$ and $d(s_l, \mathbf{m}_j)$ $(1 \le l \le m)$ is less than a given threshold, this implies that pattern $s_l$ doesn't crisply belong to a cluster. It may belongs to the upper approximations of $i$th cluster and $j$th cluster. If there doesn't exist $d(s_l, \mathbf{m}_i) - d(s_l, \mathbf{m}_j)$ less than given threshold and $d(s_l, \mathbf{m}_i)$ is minimum over the $k$ clusters, pattern $s_l$ must belong to the lower approximation of $i$th cluster. Its membership to $i$th cluster is crisp. Evidently, there exists overlaps between clusters. A web access pattern $s_l$ can be part of at most one lower approximation. If $s_l \in \underline{\eta_i}$ of $i$th cluster, then simultaneously $s_l \in \overline{\eta_i}$. If $s_l$ is not a part of any lower approximation, then it belongs to two or more upper approximations. Assume these patterns $\{s_1, s_2, \cdots, s_m\}$ are grouped into $k$ clusters, cluster scheme C=$\{C_1, C_2, \cdots, C_k\}$, where $C_i = \{\underline{\eta_i}, \overline{\eta_i}\}$ $(1 \le i \le k)$.

### Algorithm

Input: User transactions $S$ composed of $m$ different web access patterns $\{s_1, s_2, \cdots, s_m\}$, membership functions of time duration, threshold $\delta \in [0, 1]$, parameters $w_{low}$, $w_{up}$

Output: Cluster scheme $C$

step1: start.

step2: For each $s_i \in$S, denote $s_i$ by a corresponding fuzzy vector $f_{vi}$ according to the method introduced in section 3.1. Each element in fuzzy vector $f_{vi}$ is a fuzzy linguistic variable or 0.

step3: Assign initial means $\mathbf{m}_i$ for the $k$ clusters. Here, choose randomly $k$ web access patterns as the initial means.

step4: For each fuzzy web access pattern $f_{vl}$ $(1 \le l \le m)$ do
    For i=1 to k do
    Compute $d(f_{vl}, \mathbf{m}_i)$ according to Eq.(14).

step5: For each pattern $s_l$ $(1 \le l \le m)$ do
    If $d(f_{vl}, \mathbf{m}_i) - d(f_{vl}, \mathbf{m}_j)$ $(i \ne j)$ is less than some threshold $\delta$ then
    $s_l \in \overline{\eta_i}$ and $s_l \in \overline{\eta_j}$,
    else if the distance $d(f_{vl}, \mathbf{m}_i)$ is minimum over the $k$ clusters, then
    $s_l \in \underline{\eta_i}$.

step6: $C_1 = \{\underline{\eta_1}, \overline{\eta_1}\}, \cdots, C_k = \{\underline{\eta_k}, \overline{\eta_k}\}$.

step7: Compute new mean for each cluster using Eq.(13).

step8: Repeat steps 4-7 until convergence.
step9: output C.
step10: stop.

## 4   An Example

An example is provided to illustrate this clustering process using rough $k$-means method in fuzzy environment. All user browsing information is stored in web logs. There are several preprocessing tasks that must be performed prior to applying clustering algorithms to the data collected from web logs. As for our algorithm, we just need data cleaning and simple session identification. Data cleaning refers that all data irrelevant to the algorithm, such as the files with the suffixes of gif, jpeg, jpg, map, swf, cgi, ect., are deleted because only the HTML files are involved in our research. Session identification refers that a session is end if time duration on a web page is above a certain threshold. The preprocessed web access data is shown in Table 1. Each element $(Url_{ik}, t_{ik})$ in a web record represents the visited web page and time duration on this web page during the surfing by $i$th user.

Assume the membership functions of time duration on web pages by experts systems are shown in Figure 2.

Time durations are grouped into three fuzzy regions, one of which is characterized as a fuzzy linguistic variable. From Figure 2, we can get three fuzzy linguistic variables $short(0, 0, 30, 60)$, $middle(30, 60, 90, 120)$ and $long(90, 120, 150, 150)$. Their expected values can be gained by Eq. (2). The following relations

**Table 1.** User access patterns from the log data

| Client Id | Browsing sequences |
|-----------|--------------------|
| 1 | (A,30), (B,42), (D,118), (E,91) |
| 2 | (A,92), (B,89), (F,120) |
| 3 | (A,50), (B,61), (D,42), (G,98), (H,115) |
| 4 | (A,70), (C,92), (G,85), (H,102) |
| 5 | (A,40), (B,35), (D,112) |
| 6 | (A,52), (B,89), (G,92), (H,108) |

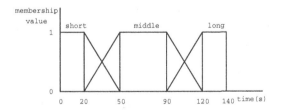

**Fig. 2.** The membership functions of the time duration

between real numeric time duration $v_{ik}^t$ with fuzzy linguistic variable $\lambda_{ik}$ can also be gained from Figure 2.

$$
\lambda_{ik} = \begin{cases}
0, & v_{ik}^t = 0 \\
short, & 0 \le v_{ik}^t \le 45 \\
middle, & 45 < v_{ik}^t \le 105 \\
long, & 105 < v_{ik}^t \le 150.
\end{cases}
\tag{13}
$$

Let $S = \{s_1, s_2, s_3, s_4, s_5, s_6\}$ be the set of user transactions, $U$ be the union set of distinct items accessed from user transactions $S$ and $W = \{A,B,C,D,E,F,G,H\}$ be the union set of distinct web pages visited by all users.

The web access pattern $s_i \in S$ $(i = 1, 2, \cdots, 6)$ can be represented as a fuzzy vector according to the method introduced in section 3.1. Each element in fuzzy vector is a fuzzy linguistic variable among $\{short, middle, long\}$ or 0.

Similarly, the six web access patterns from Table 1 can be denoted by as follows:

$$
\begin{array}{llllllllll}
s_1 =< & short, & short, & 0 & , long & , middle, & 0 & , 0 & , 0 & > \\
s_2 =< & middle, & middle, & 0 & , 0 & , 0 & , long & , 0 & , 0 & > \\
s_3 =< & middle, & middle, & 0 & , short & , 0 & , 0 & , middle, & long & > \\
s_4 =< & middle, & 0 & , middle, & 0 & , 0 & , 0 & , middle, & middle & > \\
s_5 =< & short, & short, & 0 & , long & , 0 & , 0 & , 0 & , 0 & > \\
s_6 =< & middle, & middle, & 0 & , 0 & , 0 & , 0 & , middle, & long & >
\end{array}
$$

Assume the six web access patterns are grouped into 3 clusters. Each cluster is characterized as a rough variable $\zeta_k$ $(1 \le k \le 3)$. $w_{up} = 0.3, w_{low} = 0.7, \delta = 0.1$.

Firstly we randomly choose $s_1$, $s_3$ and $s_5$ as the centroids of the three clusters, thus we can get follow equations.

$\mathbf{m}_1 = s_1$
$=< \lambda_{11}, \lambda_{12}, \cdots, \lambda_{18} >$
$\simeq< E[short], E[short], 0, E[long], E[middle], 0, 0, 0 >$.

Similarly,
$\mathbf{m}_2 = s_3$
$\simeq< E[middle], E[middle], 0, E[short], 0, 0, E[middle], E[long] >$.
$\mathbf{m}_3 = s_5$
$\simeq< E[short], E[short], 0, E[long], 0, 0, 0, 0 >$.

Here, $E[short], E[middle], E[long]$ can be gained by Eq.(3).

For each pattern $s_l$ $(1 \le l \le 6)$, compute $d(s_l, m_i)(1 \le k \le 6, 1 \le i \le 3)$. If $d(s_l, m_i) - d(s_l, m_j) \le \delta$ then $s_l \in \overline{\zeta_i}$, $s_l \in \overline{\zeta_j}$, and $s_l$ can not be a member of any lower approximation of rough variables. Else if $d(s_l, m_i)$ is minimum over the 3 clusters, we can get $s_l \in \underline{\zeta_i}$.

After one cycle, we can get the following results shown in Figure 3.

After the algorithm stops, the clustering result is shown in Figure 4. $s_1$ and $s_5$ are clustered into one group. Their surfing behaviors are similar. Similarly, $s_3$, $s_4$ and $s_6$ are partitioned into one cluster. $s_2$ has little similarity with the patterns in other clusters.

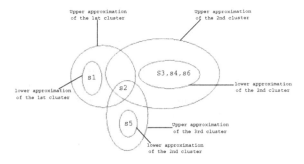

**Fig. 3.** The first clustering result

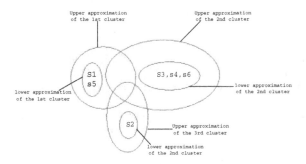

**Fig. 4.** The last clustering result

From Figure 4, we can see that the three clusters have no overlaps. Their boundaries are crisp.

## 5 Conclusion

Soft computing techniques, such as fuzzy theory and rough set theory, are suitable for handling the issues related to understandability of patterns, incomplete/noisey data, and can provide approximate solutions faster.

In this paper, a novel approach based on rough k-means in fuzzy environments is proposed to cluster the web transactions. This approach is useful to find interesting user access patterns in web log. These user access patterns will aid the web site designer and be helpful in building up adaptive web server according to the users individual behavior.

## Acknowledgments

This work was supported by National Natural Science Foundation of China Grant No.70802043 and Shanxi Provincial Natural Science Foundation of China Grant No.2008011029-2.

# References

1. De, S., Krishna, P.: Clustering web transactions using rough approximation. Fuzzy Sets and Systems 148, 131–138 (2004)
2. Krishnapram, R., Joshi, A.: Low compexity fuzzy relational clustering algorithms for web mining. IEEE Transactions on Fuzzy Systems 9, 595–607 (2001)
3. Hathaway, R., Beadek, J.: Switching regression models and fuzzy clustering. IEEE Transactions on Fuzzy Systems 1(3), 195–204 (1993)
4. Lingras, P.: Rough set clustering for web mining. In: Proceedings of the 2002 IEEE International Conference on Fuzzy Systems (FUZZ-IEEE 2002), vol. 2, pp. 1039–1044 (2002)
5. Lingras, P., West, C.: Interval set clustering of web users with rough k-means. Journal of Intelligent Information Systems 23(1), 5–16 (2004)
6. Liu, B.: Fuzzy random dependent-chance programming. IEEE Transactions on Fuzzy Systems 9(5), 721–726 (2001)
7. Liu, B.: Theory and Practice of Uncertain Programming. Physica-Verlag, Heidelberg (2002)
8. Liu, B., Liu, Y.: Expected value of fuzzy variable and fuzzy expected value models. IEEE Transactions on Fuzzy Systems 10, 445–450 (2002)
9. Mitra, S.: An evolutionary rough partitive clustering. Pattern Recognition Letters 25, 1439–1449 (2004)
10. Nahmias, S.: Fuzzy variable. Fuzzy Sets and Systems 1, 97–101 (1978)
11. Pawlak, Z.: Rough sets. International Journal of Comput. Inform. Sci. 11, 341–356 (1982)
12. Pawlak, Z.: Rough sets-Theoretical aspects of reasoning about data. Kluwar Academic Pulishers, Dordrecht (1991)
13. Runkler, T., Beadek, J.: Web mining with relational clustering. International Journal of Approximate Reasoning 32, 217–236 (2003)
14. Wang, X., Ha, M.: Note On maxmin u/E estimation. Fuzzy Sets and Systems 94, 71–75 (1998)
15. Zadeh, L.: Fuzzy sets. Information and Control 8, 338–353 (1965)

# Author Index